PETER THE GREAT:

HIS LAW ON THE IMPERIAL SUCCESSION

THE OFFICIAL COMMENTARY

HEADSTART HISTORY
OXFORD

By the same editor:

Enlightened Absolutism (1760-1790).
A Documentary Sourcebook
(Newcastle-upon-Tyne: Avero Eighteenth-Century Publications, 1985).

Frederick the Great. Letters and Documents
(Milton Keynes: The Open University Press, 1979. Reprinted 1983).

Voltaire and Catherine the Great:
Selected Correspondence
(Cambridge: Oriental Research Partners, 1974).

Prince M. M. Shcherbatov:
On the Corruption of Morals in Russia
(Cambridge: Cambridge University Press, 1969).

Russia in the Eighteenth Century;
From Peter the Great to Catherine the Great (1696-1796)
(London: Heineman Educational Books, 1973).

with M. Bartholomew and D. Hall:

The Enlightenment. Studies I-II
(Milton Keynes: The Open University Press, 1992).

PETER THE GREAT:

HIS LAW ON THE IMPERIAL SUCCESSION IN

RUSSIA, 1722

THE OFFICIAL COMMENTARY

PRAVDA VOLI MONARSHEI

VO OPREDELENII NASLEDNIKA DERZHAVY SVOEI

(THE JUSTICE OF THE MONARCH'S RIGHT TO APPOINT THE HEIR TO HIS THRONE)

Edited and Translated
With an Introduction and Notes
by
A. Lentin, M.A., Ph.D. (Cantab.) F.R.Hist.S.,
Barrister-at-Law
Reader in History, The Open University

Published by   Headstart History
                 PO Box 628
                 Oxford OX1 2NL
                 Great Britain

Printed by   Wace Specialist Print-Journals
                 Abingdon
                 Oxfordshire OX14 3LE
                 (a division of Wace UK Ltd)

ISBN 1 85943 001 5

Acknowledgements

The Publisher wishes to acknowledge with thanks the technical advice of Robert Wilton and Simon Lentin.

In Memoriam

Bernard Michael Simons
23.3.41 - 29.5.93

lawyer, judge, director of the Royal National Theatre:

a man of integrity, intellect, humour, humanity;

my oldest friend

Multis ille bonis flebilis occidit

ABBREVIATIONS

LATKIN: V. N. Latkin, *Uchebnik istorii russkogo prava perioda imperii (XVIII i XIX st.)*, 2nd edition, (St Petersburg: tipografiia Montvida, 1909).

PEKARSKII: P. P. Pekarskii, *Nauka i Literatura v Rossii pri Petre Velikom*,(vol. 2), (St Petersburg: tipografiia t-va `Obshchestvennaia Pol'za', 1862).

P. S. Z.: *Polnoe Sobranie Zakonov Rossiiskoi Imperii. Sobranie pervoe s 1649g po 12 dekabria 1825g.*, (St Petersburg: tipografiia II-go otdela ego imperatorskogo velichestva kantseliarii, 1830).

SBORNIK: *Sbornik imperatorskogo russkogo-istoricheskogo obshchestva*, (St Petersburg: russkoe istoricheskoe obshchestvo, 1867-1916).

SOLOV'EV: S. M. Solov'ev, *Istoriia Rossii s drevneishikh vremen*, (books 9-10), (Moscow: izdatel'stvo sotsial'no-ekonomicheskoi literary, 1963).

USTRIALOV: N. Ustrialov, *Istoriia tsarstvovaniia Petra Velikogo*, (vol. 6), (St Petersburg: tipografiia II-go otdela ego imperatorskogo velichestva kantseliarii, 1863).

VOSKRESENSKII: N. A. Voskresenskii, *Zakonodatel'nye Akty Petra I*, (ed.) B.I. Syromiatnikov, (Moscow/Leningrad: Akademiia Nauk SSSR, 1945).

CONTENTS

PREFACE

Pravda Voli Monarshei or, to give it its full title, *Pravda Voli Monarshei vo opredelenii naslednika derzhavy svoei - The Justice of the Monarch's Right to appoint the heir to his throne,* commissioned by Peter the Great and first published in 1722,[1] has long been recognized as one of the outstanding primary sources of early eighteenth-century Russia, a key document of state. In the words of Marc Raeff, it is "the great *pièce justicative* of Peter the Great's reforms," while Richard Wortman calls it "the chief ideological manifesto of Petrine absolutism," and Cynthia Whittaker quite simply - "the best exposition of Peter's views."[2] Its avowed function was as a weapon in Peter's policy to counter and rebut opposition to his reforms.

"This remarkable book" (as it was called by the legal historian A. D. Gradovskii)[3] was written as an extended commentary or "treatise" (*rassuditel'noe slovo*)[4] on the new and controversial Statute (*ustav*) on the succession to the imperial throne, laid down by Peter on 5 February 1722.[5] It vindicated Peter's insistence in the statute on the monarch's right to appoint his successor on his own authority, in the interests of the state and purely on grounds of merit, irrespective of primogeniture or other traditional dynastic considerations. The statute thus represented one of Peter's most extraordinary attempts to break with the past and to dictate Russia's future: in the words of M. S. Anderson, it was "an exercize of uncontrolled personal power unparalleled in any other monarch of the period."[6] By clear implication, *Pravda voli monarshei* was also intended to defend Peter's treatment of his eldest son, Aleksei, whom he had barred from the succession in February 1718 and who died in suspicious circumstances four months later, after being convicted of treason. It was written at Peter's command to accompany

1

and explain the statute of 1722, which was reproduced in the body of the work. Peter ordered an exceptionally large print-run (and it was republished under Catherine I in 1726 with an even larger print-run). In 1731 it was cited as if it were itself a piece of legislation rather than a commentary, albeit highly authoritative, on a statute,[7] a convention followed a century later with its inclusion in the *Complete Collection of Laws of the Russian Empire.*[8]

For the student of the introduction of western political ideas in Russia, *Pravda voli monarshei* is of considerable importance for its adaptation of natural law concepts in the context of European divine-right and absolutist theory in the seventeenth and early eighteenth century.[9] P. N. Berkov saw it as expressing "the Russian conception of 'enlightened absolutism'."[10] As the official Russian interpretation of imperial prerogative, of what it calls "the inherent but lawful power of monarchy," [11] it is comparable in significance to such documents as James I's *The True Law of Free Monarchies* (1598), The *Mémoires* of Louis XIV (c.1667) or Bossuet's *La Politique tirée des propres paroles de l'Ecriture Sainte* (1709). In the longer perspective it constitutes a milestone in the evolution of absolutism as the characteristic institution of government in imperial Russia, and one of the first examples of how, in the words of Gary Marker, "Russia's rulers aggressively attempted to use the printing press to convey their own absolutist vision of politics and society to the entire populace." [12]

Described by Thomas Consett, Anglican chaplain to the Russia Company (or "British factory") at St Petersburg, as "that special book" and even "the famous book," [13] *Pravda Voli Monarshei* is probably better known by its title than for its contents. It is a short work of just over 20,000 words (running to some 60 pages in the first edition, and some 40 pages of double columns in the version published in 1830). The author refers to it several times as a "booklet" (*knizhitsa*).[14] Copies, however, are difficult to obtain. The editions of 1722 and 1726 (and a third edition published

in 1788 as an item of historical interest) are a bibliographical rarity in the west and hardly less so in Russia.[15] The most recent version is that incorporated in the *Complete Collection of Laws of the Russian Empire* in 1830, the text of which, though commonly cited in the scholarly literature,[16] is extremely corrupt.

The present edition has been carefully prepared in the belief that the study of leading primary sources can be as valuable for students of history as it is essential for practitioners. Based on the 1726 text published at Moscow in the "church" type, it offers a reliable version of the Russian original for scholarly consultation; while the English translation facing the text, the first to have been attempted places the work at the disposal of a wider readership.[17] Text and translation are followed by brief explanatory notes, and by four appendices providing information on the sources of the work: Appendix 1 lists the sources cited in the text; appendices 2 and 3 provide the Latin originals of an extended passage from Justinian and Cicero respectively, quoted in the text. Appendix 4 contains the text and translation of the manifesto of 3 February 1718, in which Peter announced the exclusion of Aleksei from the succession.

My interest in *Pravda voli monarshei* was first aroused over thirty years ago. I read it mainly through the aristocratic and disdainful eyes of the late eighteenth-century critic Prince M. M. Shcherbatov (1733-1790). Writing c.1787, Shcherbatov roundly dismissed it as "a monument of flattery and monkish fawning before the monarch's whim."[18] One can see what he meant. In some ways it is a repulsive book, and demands considerable imaginative empathy. As a constitutionalist and a determined critic of absolutism, Shcherbatov had a clear sense, unusual in the Russia of his time, of what it meant to be (and not to be) a free citizen. At the same time, as a pioneering historian, charged with sorting and publishing documents from the archives of Peter the Great, he also showed a sensitive and discriminating understanding of the

tsar and his significance. Any student of petrine Russia must of course attempt to understand *Pravda voli monarshei* and its historical significance against the particular pressures and beliefs of its own time, as indeed Shcherbatov himself did;[19] and such too is the aim of the Introduction to this edition.

Professor Richard Pipes has complained that "in studying the history of Russian political thought between the fifteenth and the eighteenth centuries one is struck by the intellectual poverty of the whole autocratic tradition. Russia had neither Hobbeses nor Bossuets, nor even Filmers."[20] As far as petrine Russia is concerned, this edition may at least assist readers to decide this for themselves, and at any rate to encourage the further study of Russian intellectual history in one of its most formative epochs.

ACKNOWLEDGMENTS

For advice, information and encouragement, particularly during the Fifth International Conference of the Study Group on Eighteenth-Century Russia at Gargnano in September 1994, my thanks are due to Professor Anthony Cross, Professor Isabel de Madariaga, Dr Lindsey Hughes, Professor L. R. Lewitter, Professeur Michel Mervaud, Professor Max Okenfuss, Dr Oleg Omel'chenko, Dr Jyrki Paaskoski, Dr Victor Zhivov and Professor Cynthia Whittacker. Thanks are also due to the late Ven. David Walser, Archdeacon of Ely; to my wife for suggested amendments in the translation, and to Irene Hatt, Wendy Clarke and Mandy Topham, for processing successive drafts of the translation. The work was facilitated by a generous grant from the Canada Council, enabling me to consult unpublished diplomatic reports in archives outside Russia (to supplement those published in the *Sborniki* of the Imperial Russian Historical Society), excerpts from which

appear in the Notes to the Introduction and translation. Acknowledgements are also due to the Twenty-Seven Foundation and the Open University for grants in aid; and to the British Library and the Public Record Office, Chancery Lane, the Archives du Ministère des Affaires Etrangères, Paris, the Gemeentelijke Archiefdienst, Amsterdam, the Algemeen Rijksarchief, The Hague, and the Rigsarkivet, Copenhagen. I also wish to thank the President and Fellows of Wolfson College, Cambridge, for a second agreeable year as a Visiting Fellow, during which the work was completed; and Mrs Judith Loades, of Headstart History, for her enthusiasm and professionalism. Above all, my thanks are due to my son for his unstinting patience and assistance with word-processing.

Cambridge, October 1995

1.   *Pravda Voli Monarshei vo opredelenii naslednika derzhavy svoei. Ustavom derzhavneishego gosudaria nashego, Petra Velikogo, otsa otechestva, imperatora i samoderzhtsa vserossiiskogo, i prochaia, i prochaia, i prochaia, sego 1722 godu, fevralia v 11 den', publikovannym utverzhdena, i vsenarodnoiu prisiagoiu svidetel'stvovana, zde prostrannee, prostoserdechnykh radi, no malo vedushchikh chelovek, pokazuetsia. V Moskovskoi tipografii, avgusta v 7 den'* [The Justice of the Monarch's Right to appoint the heir to his throne. Under the statute of our most mighty sovereign, Peter the Great, Father of his Country, Emperor and Sovereign of all the Russias, etc., etc., etc., published this year, 1722, on 11th day of February, having been confirmed and witnessed on oath by the whole nation, is here demonstrated at greater length, for the benefit of honest but ignorant persons. At the Moscow press, 7th day of August]. The title of the work presents difficulties of translation. That "pravda" means "justice" in the present context is clear from the Foreword

and introductory portion of *Pravda voli monarshei* (see pp. 125 and 137). In English the work is usually and correctly, if awkwardly, referred to as *The Justice of the Monarch's "Will"* (rather than *"Right"*). Thomas Consett, writing in 1727, translates the title as *The Right of the Sovereign's Will to appoint the successor to his throne* (*For God and Peter the Great. The Works of Thomas Consett, 1723-1729,* (ed.) James Cracraft, East European Monographs No. xcvi, Boulton: Columbia University Press, (1982), p. lii). In the summary in the *Acta Eruditorum,* Leipzig, August 1723, the work is entitled *Justitia voluntatis monarchicae de successore constituendo,* and in its German translation *-Das Recht der Monarchen in willkühriger Bestellung der Reichsfolge.* One French translation of the title is *Le Droit de la Volonté du Monarque* (Archives du Ministère des Affaires Etrangères, Correspondance Politique, Russie, vol. 20/193 (1727)); another variant is "le droit du souverain à la nomination de son successeur," *La Première Catherine. Seconde femme de Pierre le Grand. Notes et anecdotes sur Catherine Iʳᵉ de Russie d'après un manuscrit inédit du 18ᵉ siècle,* (ed.) C. Ziegler, (Paris: Institut des Sciences Historiques, 1958), p. 79.

2.   *Canadian-American Slavic Studies,* 8, No. 2 (Summer 1974), p. 327; Richard S. Wortman, *The Development of a Russian Legal Consciousness,* (Chicago: University of Chicago Press, 1976), p. 9; Cynthia H. Whittaker, "The Reforming Tsar: The Redefinition of Autocratic Duty in Eighteenth-Century Russia," *Slavic Review,* 51, No. 1 (Spring 1992), pp. 84-85. T. Anderson describes *Pravda voli monarshei* as "the best general statement of... [Peter's] political ideas." (*Russian Political Thought. An Introduction,* (Cornell University Press, 1967), p. 130). Cf. B. I. Syromiatnikov, *"Reguliarnoe" Gosudarstvo Petra Pervogo i ego ideologiia* [Peter the First's "Regulated" state and its ideology], (Moscow/Leningrad: Akademiia Nauk SSSR, 1943), p. 153.

3.   A. D. Gradovskii, "Nachala russkogo gosudarst-vennogo prava" [Principles of Russian Constitutional Law],

Sobranie Sochinenii [Collected Works], 2nd edition, vol. 7 (St Petersburg: tipografiia M. M. Stasiulevicha, 1907), p. 156.

4.   p. 139. Catherine I's decree of 21 April 1726 describes it as an "explanation" (*iz'iasnenie*). P.S.Z., vol. VII, No. 4870, p. 603. V. O. Kliuchevskii called it "a short encyclopedia of constitutional law," (*Sochineniia* [Works], vol. IV, (Moscow: izd. sotial'no-ekonomicheskoi literatury, 1958), p. 269), F. V. Taranovskii as "a general treatise on public law" and "a politico-legal tract" (in G. Gurvich, "*Pravda Voli Monarshei*" *Feofana Prokopovicha i ee zapadnoevropeiskie istochniki*[Feofan Prokopovich's 'Pravda Voli Monarshei' and its western European sources], (Iur'ev: Uchenye zapiski imperatorskogo iur'evskogo universiteta, 1915), p. vii.

5.   pp. 128-33. Law (*zakon*) is a generic term covering all forms of legislation. A statute (*ustav*) denotes a law regulating a particular aspect of government (e.g. *Voinskii Ustav* (the Military Statute, 1716). A decree (*ukaz*) signifies a law issued directly by the tsar relating to any subject (e.g. the Decree on the Assemblies, 1718). A manifesto (*manifest*) or declaration (*ob'iavlenie*) was a proclamation issued by the tsar on some exceptionally important occasion (e.g. the Manifesto on tsarevich Aleksei's exclusion from the succession, 1718 (see Appendix 4, pp. 296-315); the Declaration on the trial of the tsarevich, 1718). A rescript (*reskript*) was an announcement issued by the tsar to particular governmental organs (e.g. to his envoys abroad concerning the Declaration on the trial of the tsarevich). (A. D. Gradovskii, pp. 41-3).

6.   M. S. Anderson, *Europe in the Eighteenth Century 1713-1783,* 3rd edition, (London: Longman, 1987), p. 168. Cf. G. Stökl, "Das Problem der Thronfolgeordnung in Russland," in *Der dynastische Fürstenstaat. Zur Bedeutung von Sukzessionsordnungen für die Entstehung des frümodernen Staates,* (ed.) H. Neuhaus and J. Kunisch, (Berlin: Duncker & Humblot, 1982), p. 283.

7

7. P.S.Z., Vol. VII, No. 5131; vol. VIII, No. 5909.
8. P.S.Z., Vol. VII, No. 4780, pp. 604-643.
9. The only monograph on *Pravda voli monarshei* is G. Gurvich, *"Pravda voli monarshei" Feofana Prokopovicha i ee zapadnoevropeiskie istochniki* [Feofan Prokopovich's "Pravda Voli Monarshei" and its western European sources], Iur'ev, 1915.
10. P. N. Berkov, in A. Bykova and M. M. Gurevich, *Opisanie izdanii napechatannykh pri Petre I.Svodnyi katalog. Opisanie izdanii grazhdanskoi pechati (1708-ianvar' 1725g.)* [Inventory of editions published under Peter I. Union catalogue. Inventory of editions of the civil press (1708-January 1725)],(Moscow/Leningrad: Akademiia Nauk SSSR, 1955), p. 26. Cf. E. Winter, *Halle als Auspunkt der deutschen Russlandskunde im 18 Jahrhundert,* (Berlin, Akademie Verlag, 1953), p. 132.
11. p. 127;
12. Cynthia H. Whittaker, pp. 77-86; Gary Marker, *Publishing, Printing, and the Origins of Intellectual Life in Russia, 1700-1800,* (Princeton New Jersey: Princeton University Press, 1985), p. 10.
13. Cracraft, *For God and Peter the Great. The Works of Thomas Consett, 1723-1729,* pp. lii,9.
14. The *Acta eruditorum,* August 1723, describes *Pravda voli monarshei* as a *"libellus." Pravda voli monarshei* runs to 65 pages in the first edition, some 90 pages in the 1726 edition, and around 110 in the 1788 edition.
15. Copies of the first two editions are particularly rare, because they were called in and destroyed by order of the Supreme Privy Council in 1727. Consett recorded that "probably several copies are preserved abroad, one of which I have also by me." (Cracraft, *For God and Peter the Great. The Works of Thomas Consett,* p. 9). This refers to a copy of the first edition, given to him by Feofan Prokopovich (Consett to Lord Townshend, 17 July, 1725, Public Record Office, Chancery Lane, State Papers 91/9/407). There is a copy of the first edition in the New

York Public Library and of the 1726 Moscow edition in the British Library.

16.   e.g. G. Gurvich relies on the 1830 text.

17.   The authorized German translation, also unfortunately a bibliographical rarity, is: *Das Recht der Monarchen, in willkühriger Bestellung der Reichsfolge... aus der Rußischen Sprache getreulich ins Teutsche übersetzt,* (Berlin: Ambrosius Haude, 1724). There is a copy in the British Library.

18.   Prince M. M. Shcherbatov, *On the Corruption of Morals in Russia,*(ed.) A. Lentin, (Cambridge: Cambridge University Press, 1969), p. 153.

19.   *ibid.,* pp. 66-72, 154-155; "Rassmotrenie o porokakh i samovlastii Petra Velikogo" [A consideration of the vices and despotism of Peter the Great], *Sochineniia Kniazia M. M. Shcherbatova* [Works of Prince M. M. Shcherbatov], (ed.) I. P. Khrushchov and A. G. Voronov, vol. II, (St Petersburg: izd. kniazia B. S. Shcherbatova, 1898), pp. 23-50. Summing up the basic paradox underlying all interpretations of Peter the Great and his significance in Russian history, Shcherbatov pointed out that it was from Peter's "despotism" that his critics "received the very enlightenment wherewith to censure that despotism" (*ibid.,*p. 46).

20.   R. Pipes, *Karamzin's Memoir on Ancient and Modern Russia. A Translation and Analysis,* (New York: Atheneum, 1966), pp. 12-13.

INTRODUCTION

1. The problem of the succession

On 22 October 1721, to mark the signing of the treaty of Nystad at the victorious conclusion of the war which he had waged with Sweden since 1700, Tsar Peter I, in his new capital of St Petersburg, assumed the title of Emperor, or, to give the full accolade, "Peter the Great, Emperor of All the Russias and Father of His Country."[1] The accompanying religious services were conducted by Peter's leading churchman and propagandist, Feofan Prokopovich, Archbishop of Pskov, who almost certainly devised and stage-managed the entire sequence of ceremonies, parades and firework displays.[2]

These were of unique symbolic importance. They were meant to emphasize the striking success of Peter's foreign policy, which secured Russia's access to the Baltic, made her the dominant state in northern and eastern Europe, and achieved for her the prestige of Great Power status across the continent. They also reflected recognition within Russia of Peter's startling personal charisma and the dynamic zeal with which he had sought for twenty-one years, by a continuous, unremitting effort of ruthless compulsion, to transform the face of society, and to emulate in Russia what western contemporaries called a "well regulated state" - a *wohlgeordneter Polizeistaat* or *état bien policé*.[3]

In December Peter proceeded to Moscow, to celebrate the victory and the new year with a triumphal entry into the old capital and a further succession of public spectacles, entertainments and thanksgiving services. Two months later, in the words of Peter Henry Bruce, a British army officer in the Russian service, "a new and sudden affair put a stop to this merriment, which was this: on the 22nd of February, 1722, a proclamation was made by the sound of

trumpet [*sic*], requiring every natural-born subject of the Russian empire and all foreigners residing there to swear and sign an oath."[4] Bruce was referring to the compulsory oath of allegiance to Peter's new Statute on the succession, which in turn gave rise to the writing of *Pravda voli monarshei.*

Like other monarchs before and since, Peter found the problem of the succession peculiarly intractable.[5] In his case he felt that what was at stake was the very survival of the new Russia as a modern state. The character of his heir was of constant concern to him as a ruler who violently forced the pace of reform, imposing and intensifying change in many aspects of national life, and who became increasingly aware of the widespread unpopularity of many of those changes. Peter, as one of his admirers expressed it, "pulls uphill with the strength of a dozen, while millions pull downhill."[6] Peter's physical constitution was robust, but he taxed it to the utmost and abused it with gross and frequent drinking-bouts. Conscious of his mortality, he feared for the future of his reforms without the continued pressure of vigilant enforcement. They would depend on a successor who was at least in sympathy with them. He knew his own son and heir, the Tsarevich Aleksei (1690-1718) to be not only half-hearted and critical towards them, but, in his mild and devout yet obstinate and ambitious character, a figurehead for those, probably the vast majority, who resented Peter's iron regimentation of society and the unrelenting demands of his wars, geared as they were to policies of westernization which they found deeply uncongenial. Such people looked forward to a respite and to more traditional ways under his successor.

Aleksei was the son of Peter's first wife, Evdokiia Lopukhin, whom he had married in an arranged match when he was was only 16. In 1698 he cast her off and confined her to a convent at Suzdal'. Brought up by foreign tutors, the Tsarevich Aleksei was neither unintelligent nor unreceptive to western ideas; but his bookish passivity contrasted sharply with Peter's restless drive and

boisterous enthusiasm for constant change. Likewise his religious piety contrasted with Peter's brusque impatience at Russia's material and cultural backwardness and his open contempt for the mass of the Orthodox clergy, the "longbeards," as he called them. The same utilitarian principle of individual worth, measured against practical usefulness to the state, which informed Peter's attitudes towards individuals generally (and to which he later gave institutional expression in the *Table of Ranks,* 1722), also dominated his relationship with his son. He tried repeatedly but unsuccessfully to instill in Aleksei his own military prowess and zeal for western technology. Relations between father and son deteriorated during years of confrontation and growing tension. Peter's complaints of idleness and demands for proof of amendment, accompanied by physical chastisement, resulted only in making the far weaker Aleksei increasingly devious and temporizing. Peter warned, earnestly and characteristically, that "he would rather give his dominions to a worthy stranger than be succeeded by so worthless a son."[7]

In 1715, on the birth of Piotr Petrovich, his son by his second wife, Catherine (whom he had married in 1712 despite the doubtful canonicity of his divorce from Evdokiia), Peter, seeking a clear-cut solution, proposed that Aleksei renounce his claim to the throne and retire permanently to a monastery. Aleksei longed for peace and quiet, but he also looked forward to his own accession. He intimated that he would comply with his father's demands, but only with strong mental reservations. For his part, Peter, who had presented his ultimatum in the hope, as he saw it, of bringing Aleksei to a sense of his responsibilities, was frustrated by his apparent acceptance. The situation was as strained and ambiguous as ever.[8]

In the autumn of 1716, during Peter's absence on an important diplomatic embassy in the west, Aleksei suddenly disappeared. He had fled incognito to Vienna, to the court of his brother-in-law, the Habsburg emperor

Charles VI, to whom he appealed for asylum. Charles gave him refuge, first in the Tyrol, later in the castle of St Elmo at Naples. He was tracked down by Peter's sleuth, P. A. Tolstoi, who by a mixture of assurances and threats persuaded him to return to Russia under Peter's solemn promise of forgiveness. Having failed to mould his son's very different character according to his own wishes, and concluding, with good reason, that his worst fears for Russia were likely to be realised under Aleksei, Peter now took steps to remove him from the succession. On Aleksei's return in February 1718, Peter made him renounce his rights of succession in favour of his infant step-brother, Piotr Petrovich, who replaced him as heir to the throne, and to whom a general oath of allegiance was sworn.[9]

Peter doubted, however, whether such a renunciation by Aleksei was enough.[10] He ordered an investigation into the circumstances of his flight and the identity of his supporters, setting up a special agency for the purpose under Tolstoi - the Secret Chancellery. A simultaneous enquiry began into the activities at Suzdal' of ex-tsarina Evdokiia, who was transferred to Schlüsselburg, near St Petersburg. Among the many who were taken for questioning was Bishop Dosifei, Metropolitan of Rostov, who was found to have expressed sympathy for Evdokiia and Aleksei. He was unfrocked and broken alive on the wheel.

As for Aleksei, evidence began to emerge of the extent of his opposition to Peter. It appeared that he had frequently voiced his aversion to his father's policies and his intention of setting them them aside on his accession. According to the evidence of his mistress, a serf-girl who accompanied him on his flight, he had spoken not merely of dismissing Peter's upstart coadjutors, notably the all-powerful Prince Menshikov, but of disbanding Peter's pride and joy, the newly founded Russian navy, and abandoning Peter's Baltic conquests and what the tsar called his "paradise" - St Petersburg. He would return the court and capital to Moscow, would retain an an army purely for defence, and would content himself "with our old domains,"

giving up the Great Power status so hardly won and so highly prized by Peter.[11]

After interrogation, sometimes by Peter himself, Aleksei confessed to having countenanced rebellion, and revealed the names of many associates and sympathizers. A reign of terror ensued at Moscow and St Petersburg. Those named by Aleksei were rounded up, investigated by the Secret Chancellery and summarily executed. Aleksei himself, despite Peter's promise to spare him, was taken to the Peter and Paul fortress at St Petersburg, where he made further confessions under torture. He admitted that he would have availed himself of armed assistance against Peter from Austria, had it been offered to him, in the event of a rumoured mutiny among Russian troops stationed in Mecklenburg. Such conditional intent was enough to secure his conviction for treason.[12]

Aleksei was arraigned before a special court of 130 high officials - Peter not only wishing to associate his governing elite with the invidious task in hand, but being willing to publicize his motives - and was unanimously condemned to death under the *Ulozhenie* of 1649 and the *Military Statute* of 1716 for conspiring to bring about his father's overthrow. The clergy, asked for advice, furnished a list of scriptural examples for Peter to draw on, whether his decision should be for clemency or for execution. The manner of Aleksei's death remains unknown, but it followed further sessions of interrogation under torture. It was commonly rumoured that he died at Peter's own hands, though Peter took care to announce, at home and abroad, that death was due to natural causes.[13]

The problem of the succession did not end with the death of Aleksei. Piotr Petrovich was a sickly child, and nine months later in April 1719 he died at the age of three. The loss plunged Peter into great distress and perplexity and reopened the whole question. "The death of this Prince is so much the more sensible to these people," reported Jefferyes, British Minister at St Petersburg, "because many

are of opinion that the Czarin[a] (who is grown pretty corpulent) will not be able to repair the loss by bringing forth another Prince."[14] In the eyes of traditionalists, the succession devolved incontestably upon the three-year-old Piotr Alekseevich, son of the late Tsarevich, and Peter's last surviving direct male descendant. Peter himself now showed a closer interest in his grandson's upbringing, had him schooled, even at such a tender age, in the rudiments of soldiery, and according to Peter Bruce, appeared "vastly pleased with his sprighliness and attention."[15] Others, however, complained that he he did not have him brought up as his heir. Certainly he took no step to appoint him as his successor. The young Piotr, Jefferyes commented nonetheless, "hath many in this kingdom who upon such an emergency [i.e. Peter's death] will espouse his claim to the government."[16]

It was precisely this prospect which troubled Peter. In the case of Aleksei himself, Peter had anticipated that even had Aleksei been sincere in renouncing the throne, he would have been overborne by his supporters.[17] How much greater was the danger in an "emergency" now of a regency during his grandson's minority, inevitably including former supporters of Aleksei, loyal to his memory and hostile to Peter's achievements, his associates and his widow, Catherine. The Tsar therefore kept his options open and his subjects guessing. The oath of allegiance which he exacted further to the *General Regulation* (*General'nyi Reglament*) of February 1720 (which laid down the principles of his reorganized administration) referred, after Peter himself, to "the high lawful successors who have been appointed and will in future be appointed at the volition and by virtue of the sovereign power of His Tsarist Majesty."[18] This was an obvious indication that he claimed the right to choose his successor.

Two years later he made his position explicit. By the statute of 5 February 1722, Peter reserved to himself and his successors the right to appoint as heir to the throne "whomsoever they wish" at their own absolute discretion.

16

Clearly he took this extraordinary step in order to counter the "legitimist" claims of Piotr Alekseevich and to establish that he himself retained complete freedom of choice.[19] The new enactment was received with shock as not the least revolutionary of his innovations. The associated oath of allegiance, requiring all subjects to acknowledge the statute and to "submit in everything to his designated successor," was rigorously enforced, and in the words of Peter Bruce, was "complied with by many with a heavy heart."[20]

The new law was of enormous significance. *Pravda voli monarshei* describes it as a "*glavnyi ustav.*" In the German translation this is rendered as *Hauptverordnung.* It has the sense of a "basic" or "fundamental" law.[21] Paradoxically, however, Peter himself did not make use of it, and the question of the succession remained in doubt throughout the last three years of his reign. Presumably he himself was in a quandary.[22] His conferment on Catherine of the title of empress in December 1721 and her solemn coronation at Moscow in May 1724 as empress in her own right - a unique proceeding - may have been intended by him to indicate the direction of his thoughts.[23] He kept his own counsel, however, and died in January 1725 at the age of 52, without naming a successor.

2. Peter the Great and Feofan Prokopovich

Feofan Prokopovich (c.1681-1736), ecclesiastic, polymath and prolific man of letters, was Peter's principal ideologist and close associate in the second half of the reign, and it was to him that Peter entrusted overall responsibility for the writing of *Pravda voli monarshei.*[24] One of the self-made men whose outstanding abilities won him Peter's particular favour, Prokopovich was the most learned, articulate and energetic of Peter's spokesmen in his espousal of the Tsar's ideas on state, church and society, his indiscriminate enthusiasm for the policies of

westernization, and his zeal to explain and amplify the new ideas in numerous sermons and other publications. A Malorussian, born in Kiev, he was educated there at the Theological Academy, and studied under the Jesuits in Poland before proceeding to Rome. Here he entered the College of St Athanasius, a Jesuit institution founded for the education of Greek and Slav Uniates, where he pursued further studies in classical humanism as well as in scholastic theology. Returning to Kiev in 1701, he took holy orders, and became a teacher and eventually Rector of the Kiev Academy.[25]

An erudite scholar and rhetorician, confident, eloquent and ambitious, Prokopovich attracted Peter's notice with a sermon of welcome on the tsar's first visit to Kiev in 1706; and unlike most of the clergy in the Ukraine, he supported Peter at the time of Mazepa's revolt in 1708. His first important work of propaganda was a sermon in celebration of Peter's victory over the Swedes at Poltava in 1709. In 1711 he accompanied Peter on his unsuccessful Pruth campaign against the Turks, after which he became, in the words of James Cracraft, "an ecclesiastical politician of the first rank, an All-Russian imperialist, and... the first authentic voice in Russia of the Early Enlightenment."[26] In 1716 Peter appointed him Bishop of Pskov and summoned him to St Petersburg, where, as his most favoured churchman, he intensified his personal identification with the tsar and his reforms, delivering and publishing a succession of sermons characterized less by Orthodox piety than by unbridled hero-worship of Peter.

Both men took a utilitarian view of the clergy, stressing its moral and educational function in society rather than its sacramental role. Both tended to reduce Christianity to a set of moral and social precepts enjoining obedience to the secular authorities.[27] They called on the priesthood to act as agents of the state by assuming the combined duties of schoolmaster, registrar, constable and town-crier, with the obligation to report to the authorities on young nobles evading state service, renegade serfs and recusant Old

Believers, as well as to recite official pronouncements from the pulpit and to administer oaths of allegiance (such as the oath to the Statute on the succession). Peter, while making no change to Russian Orthodox dogma, was bitterly hostile to elaborate ritual and the contemplative life, seeing them as antipathetic to the the creative endeavour and active service to state and society which he himself exemplified and which he sought to enforce throughout the community. Both men castigated sloth, ignorance and superstition and above all the indiscriminate hostility to western innovations which was a constant thorn in Peter's side. Both admired the simplicity of Protestant rites and the evangelical, particularly the Pietistic, work ethic, with its insistence on obedience to the civil authorities.[28] Prokopovich indeed was constantly suspected by his fellow prelates of leanings towards Lutheranism.

For above all, Prokopovich inculcated the duty of obedience, with a ready wealth of arguments both as to its benefits to society and the sinfulness of disobedience; and it was this, together with his fluent eloquence and knowledge of western languages, philosophy and culture, unique in the Russia of his time, which made him such a valuable spokesman of the regime.[29] At Peter's behest, he published numerous works of a didactic and propagandistic nature, notably a *Children's Catechism* or *Primer* (*Pervoe Uchenie Otrokam*) in 1720, aimed at imbuing the young with the duty of obedience.[30] With Peter's formal abolition of the patriarchate in 1721, Prokopovich, now Archbishop of Pskov, became virtual primate of the Orthodox Church in Russia. As such he master-minded the *Spiritual Regulation* (*Dukhovnyi Reglament*), the body of rules which prescribed the new role and function of the Church as an adjunct of the state and detailed the duties of the clergy, not least the obligation to preach and practise submission to the secular power.[31] In 1722, Peter appointed him Vice-President of the Church's new ruling body, the so-called Most Holy Governing Synod, which, on the model of the Lutheran synods in the west, placed the Church in Russia under

complete state control and was staffed by Peter's nominees. In 1724 Peter crowned his career by appointing him Bishop of the senior diocese of Novgorod.

As a propagandist, Prokopovich played an important part in the question of the succession. In contrast to some highly-placed churchmen, he followed Peter's lead unswervingly, taking a line hostile to the Tsarevich Aleksei, delivering and publishing sermons and official pronouncements to justify his exclusion from the succession and to celebrate the nomination of Piotr Petrovich.[32] At the same time he worked tirelessly in his sermons and writings to support the continuity of the reforms and to counter opposition to them.[33] At Peter's particular instigation, the *Spiritual Regulation* included an obligation on the priesthood not only to take an oath of allegiance to the sovereign, akin to the oath incumbent on state officials,[34] but even to violate the seal of confession by reporting to the civil authorities any evidence of dissent or opposition.[35] This obligation represented perhaps the culmination of Peter's insistence on the complete subjection of Church to state, turning the clergy into official police informers. In a wider sense it reflected his desire to eliminate, as symptomatic of what Prokopovich called the "papist spirit," any appeal by the priesthood to Christian values as a source of moral authority or inspiration independent of the state. Aleksei had revealed under interrogation that he had in confession wished his father dead, to which his confessor, who promised him God's forgiveness, replied: "we all wish him dead, for there is much suffering among the people."[36] The synodal Church fashioned by Peter and Prokopovich taught that there was no salvation outside the state, and threatened with anathema any who ventured to question the dispensations of the supreme secular ruler, who was at the same time titular head (or "supreme judge") of the Church.

3. The function of *Pravda voli monarshei*

The writing of *Pravda voli monarshei* was already in Peter's mind when he enacted the Statute on the succession. After citing two precedents for his new law (one scriptural, the other historical), the statute adds that "there are many similar examples, which for lack of time we do not mention here: but they will be published separately at a future date."[37] It was presumably at this time that Peter gave orders for the writing of a short commentary on the Statute.

Peter himself, though a remarkably quick learner, with an exceptionally penetrating, retentive and logical mind, was pre-eminently a man of action, and a practical rather than an abstract thinker. To his regret, he had little formal education, and although, as his legislation shows, he could express himself with striking clarity and verve, he lacked the linguistic, literary and dialectical skills, the knowledge of Latin, Greek, apparently even Hebrew, the close familiarity with biblical exegesis, European history, law and political theory, which emerge from *Pravda voli monarshei* and show the influence of scholarship and theology. He also lacked leisure for the research necessary for such a work. In May 1722, three months after promulgating the Statute on the succession, he left Moscow in order to oversee the war against Persia. His instructions for the publication of the commentary, which were formally addressed to the Synod, were forwarded to Feofan Prokopovich. In August 1722, six months after the promulgation of the Statute, Prokopovich wrote to inform him that *Pravda voli monarshei* was ready in print for his inspection. At the end of December, Peter ordered its publication.[38]

The title-page of *Pravda voli monarshei* succinctly states both its content and purpose: "the justice of the monarch's right to appoint the heir to his throne... is here demonstrated at greater length."[39] The book's rapid composition and publication, the tenor of the Foreword and

21

Afterword, and the argumentation throughout, indicate Peter's perception of the unpopularity of his succession-law and his determination to counter opposition to it with an exhaustive review of precedents and an authoritative restatement of his own all-embracing authority as Emperor of all the Russias.

For certainly the Statute was received by traditionalists, and probably by most Russians, with dismay and disapproval. It was considered manifestly unjust to Piotr Alekseevich, whose rights to the succession after the death of Piotr Petrovich in 1719 seemed incontrovertible. It seemed utterly wrong in principle, contrary to accepted ideas of hereditary succession.[40] In the west too it seemed no less arbitrary and tyrannical. In order to secure his achievements and the modernization of Russia, to prevent harm "to the public good and to the whole country,"[41] and in the name of rationalism and progress, Peter arrogated to himself a prerogative claimed by no other contemporary monarch.

Pravda voli monarshei opens with the bold claim that the Statute was "lovingly received, gratefully acclaimed and acknowledged as just... by all ranks of the... nation."[42] This was true only in the sense that the oath of allegiance to the Statute had been universally enforced. Peter Bruce noted that, on the contrary, the oath-taking was received with hostility. He described his own involvement, as an officer charged with administering the oath in Moscow, as "the most disagreeable service I ever performed in Russia," because of his sense of loyalty to Piotr Alekseevich, "to whose prejudice this oath was certainly administered."[43] Bruce's reaction typified much of Russian opinion. Hence *Pravda voli monarshei* stresses that the work was published "to demonstrate to all" that the Statute "admits of no suspicion of injustice."[44] Peter well may have questioned, as others did, whether the oath alone would prove effective after his death, in view of the strength of opposition to the Statute.[45] He commissioned *Pravda voli*

monarshei in a characteristic effort to persuade and convince as well as to dictate and compel.

The main point to be elaborated, then, was the "justice" of his claim, asserted in the Statute, to be entitled to override the customary right of hereditary succession to the throne. In Russia as in the west, succession by primogeniture, usually in the male line, was normally assumed to be the natural, God-given, legitimate and indefeasible order of things in a hereditary monarchy. No contemporary monarch contemplated appointing a successor outside the accepted order of descent unless, as in 1700 with Charles II, last of the Spanish Habsburgs, the reigning line had come to an end; or when its extinction was anticipated, as under the Act of Settlement in England in 1701. Louis XIV had legitimized his bastard sons to add fresh blood to the diminishing stock of lawful successors; but this had horrified his subjects, and was repealed after his death. In the 47 "examples" of personal selection or deselection of heirs recounted in *Pravda voli monarshei,* there is no more recent western example than that of Philip II of Spain in the late sixteenth century; while Russian history offered no precedent later than Ivan III at the end of the fifteenth century.[46] Aleksei himself had plainly considered hereditary succession by divine right to be the unquestioned norm. On his arrival as a fugitive at Vienna, he appealed to the Emperor to protect his right and that of his children to the throne of Russia from Peter's attempts to override it. God alone, the Tsarevich insisted, designates successors.[47]

In the 1722 statute, by contrast, Peter refers disparagingly to Aleksei's reliance on "the old custom of granting the succession to the eldest son," and while admitting that it was "deeply rooted," describes it as an "evil custom."[48] The theme is taken up throughout *Pravda voli monarshei,* which meets the traditionalist principle head-on, describing its supporters at best as "honest but ignorant."[49] It defends the appointment of successors "not according to natural birthright - a bad rule - but in

accordance with moral excellence (*po usmotrenii dobrodetel'nogo prevoskhodstva*)."[50] It also insists on the primacy of patriarchal power. The tsar, both as a father to his son and as "Father of his Country," has indefeasible and absolute rights over his sons as over "all other true sons of the Russian fatherland,"[51] rights derived from Scripture and natural law and exemplified in history, positive law and custom.

Pravda voli monarshei was by clear implication a defence of Peter's policy towards Aleksei. In the Statute on the succession, Peter compares Aleksei to King David's rebel son, Absalom, to emphasize that a ruler is entitled both to determine the order of the succession and to punish his offending offspring.[52] The book contains numerous references, especially in the "examples," to the disinheriting of unworthy heirs, clearly intended to parallel the case of Aleksei. The Statute reiterates a central point both of Peter's 1714 *Statute on unigeniture in succession*[53] and of the manifesto of June 1718 on the trial of Aleksei, (to both of which it refers), namely that patriarchal authority empowers every father, royal or commoner, to choose his successor on grounds of merit (*godnost'*).[54] The meritocratic principle was central to Peter's thinking. In the Table of Ranks in January 1722, he declared personal merit to be the sole criterion for advancement in the army and civil service, and hence for the award of noble status. He himself had worked his way up from the ranks in the army and navy. He was to crown Catherine as empress in her own right in 1724, expressly in recognition of her services to the state.[55] Conversely, for his lack of commitment to state-service, he had threatened in 1715 to cut off Aleksei from the succession "like a gangrenous poison," and had carried out that threat.[56]

The aim of *Pravda voli monarshei* was to convince his subjects that Peter's radical new enactment was rational and normative, solidly grounded in religious and historical precedent, and a necessary and desirable safeguard of

Russia's welfare, so "that if he [Peter] had not manifestly consolidated all this [his reforms] for the future, he has providently done so by this most useful statute."[57] Readers were invited to study the book "for a clearer understanding of the truth." By contrast critics of the statute are marginalized as "foolish" and "ignorant", or, more menacingly, as "malicious": they are either "utter fools or enemies of their country."[58] Either way they stand in need of instruction and indeed are subjected, particularly in the Foreword and Afterword, to admonition and rebuke.

The book's tone is earnest, didactic, dogmatic, polemical, sometimes impatient, passionate, even contemptuous. Its declared purpose is "to remove the least trace of doubt from the minds of the ignorant, and to leave no room for misunderstanding." Intended as Peter's last word on the subject, it is presented to "the honest reader," "every right-minded and impartial man" - "if you are sensible and wise," as "an opportunity to increase your wisdom."[59] The Afterword claims that "if our harshest critic sought to contradict us, he would find no grounds on which to do so."[60]

Dissent from the arguments of *Pravda voli monarshei* was not merely discouraged, however: it was formally prohibited. Criticism of the Statute, as the oath attaching to it made clear, was a treasonable and capital offence, additionally punishable by excommunication. To oppose the tsar's dispensation, as was repeated in *Pravda voli monarshei*, was to become an outlaw in this world and to be deprived of hope of salvation in the next. The Foreword makes disparaging reference to "restless minds" and "hearts seething with the passion to contradict," attributes of those who "sow seeds of rebellion in our country," "evildoers, who stir up rebellion."[61] Only one school of thought was permitted - that laid down by the authorities.

The very possibility of political debate, of the open expression or at least dissemination of alternative views in Peter's Russia was in any case extremely limited. The state

alone controlled the printing-presses and the right to publish.[62] Any form of writing, secular or religious, not specifically authorized was regarded with grave suspicion.[63] A series of laws was directed at so-called *podmiotnye pis'ma*, i.e. anonymous letters or pamphlets left in public places. At the end of the seventeenth century these were a common means of bringing popular grievances to official notice. Under Peter, they were criminalised. An edict of 25 January 1715 directs anyone finding such a document to burn it on the spot in front of witnesses without further examination.[64] There was no facility in Russia for any published response to *Pravda voli monarshei,* though there may have been written criticism of it in the form of anonymous letters. Such letters were certainly directed against the 1722 Statute soon after Peter's death.[65] The government offered large rewards to informants: 2,000 roubles (approximately £500) and hereditary possession of part or all of the property of the guilty party, a measure of the seriousness with which it regarded such criticism.[66]

Pravda voli monarshei also reflects Peter's mounting concern with opposition to his reforms generally, of which be became increasingly aware after the affair of the Tsarevich. He commissioned the book at a time when he was engaged in his vigorous campaign to harness an often reluctant and hostile clergy to the service of the state. He was also pursuing draconian measures against the schizmatic Old Believers in an effort to bring them under the control of the official Church. The Old Believers, with their apocalyptic belief that Peter was the Anti-Christ, however, were only the extreme example of the antipathy which his policies provoked among the population at large. The Afterword to *Pravda voli monarshei* includes a passionate and contemptuous diatribe against critics of foreign innovation, whom Peter, in his reformist zeal, found so banefully obstructive throughout his reign.[67]

While the overriding aim of *Pravda voli monarshei* was to win over his domestic critics, it is clear from the Foreword that Peter also sought to influence western opinion. He was anxious to rebut foreign impressions of Russians as a people "of barbarous manners, who feign allegiance to their sovereigns."[68] Such prejudices, both as to Russia's backwardness and to her political instability, were more or less latent in the west. They had been revived by Peter's massacre of the *Strel'tsy* in 1699, and more recently by the affair of the Tsarevich Aleksei and its hardly less brutal repression.[69] Peter aimed in the book, as in other publications, "to disabuse foreigners of their false opinion of our people, and to give them reason to think better of us."[70] It was particularly important to him to consolidate the growing international prestige which Russia had gained by her victory over Sweden and to rebut any suggestion of political instability at a time when he was forming dynastic compacts in the west and pursuing offers of alliance with France. He wished to convince the west that Russia, having proved a force to be reckoned with under his rule, would remain so under a disposition which guaranteed the succession.

There is evidence of interest in the book in the west. In 1723 an approving synopsis in Latin of *Pravda voli monarshei* appeared at Leipzig in the *Acta eruditorum*,[71] and an authorized German translation of the book came out at Berlin the following year entitled *Das Recht der Monarchen in willkühriger Bestellung der Reichsfolge*.[72] In 1723, Thomas Consett received a copy of *Pravda voli monarshei* from Prokopovich himself "immediately after publication," and sent a Latin "epitome" of it to the Bishop of London. Consett considered the book sufficiently important to draw it to the attention of Lord Townshend, Secretary of State for Foreign Affairs.[73]

4. Peter's ideological frame of reference and *Pravda voli monarshei*

While historians have traditionally argued that much of Peter's legislation was *ad hoc,* dictated by the immediate pressures of war, it is also plain that from the moment of his return in 1699 from his first, epoch-making visit to the west, he was not only committed to catching up materially with the west, but was also captivated by a clear and consistent long-term vision of the direction in which he intended Russia to develop, and that he remained faithful to this vision throughout his reign. This programmatic vision was encapsulated in much of his legislation. Many of his most important laws, especially in his last years, after the war with Sweden, were accompanied by a kind of internal exegesis and commentary, the purpose of which was didactic: to explain and to impress on his subjects the general goals of his reforming absolutism and to acquaint them with the motives behind particular legislative acts (as well as to deprive them of the excuse to plead ignorance of the law).[74]

Peter paid close attention to the drafting of his laws, and to ensuring that they were known and understood. In 1714, he ordered that laws of public importance should henceforth be published. As his legislation poured forth in an ever-increasing volume - there were almost as many enactments in the last five years of the reign as in the previous decade - so, at his urgent prompting they appeared in print at a rate exceeding one a week by the end of the reign: from 1708 to 1725 official pronouncements constituted three-fifths of all published titles.[75] Many of these laws were edited or drafted, in whole or in part, by Peter himself, who personally saw them through the press and energetically encouraged their dissemination.[76] He had them printed in large numbers, heavily subsidised and sold at low prices or distributed free of charge for public information and enlightenment. He ordered them to be posted up in public places and read aloud by parish clergy

and local officials. Thus in 1718, 2,341 copies of the manifesto depriving Aleksei of the succession were published at St Petersburg, and 11,000 at Moscow. 7,800 copies of the oath to Piotr Petrovich were published at St Petersburg, and 27,770 at Moscow.[77]

In contrast to his Muscovite predecessors, who issued commands by simple *fiat,* Peter was at great pains to explain himself to his subjects. The words "since," "because" (*ponezhe*) and "therefore, for this reason" (*togo radi*) characterize much of his legislation, including the Statute on the succession. He was in that sense a believer in "didactic government," a disciple of the Early Enlightenment, who sought to inform, and to communicate his own goals and enthusiasms. He wanted his numerous miscellaneous enactments, apparently random and arbitrary, to be understood as integral parts of a single coherent vision: even when issued for immediate practical purposes, they were also directed at long-term goals - "the common good" (*dobro obshchee*), "the public good" (*pol'za narodnaia*), "the common good of the people" (*vsenarodnaia pol'za*) and "the general welfare" (*obshchaia pol'za*). These expressions appear in Russian legislation for the first time under Peter. All four appear in *Pravda voli monarshei.*[78]

These concepts, borrowed from western political theory, became common in Peter's legislation from 1702 onward, after his return from his first embassy to the west, and increasingly again after his second, in the 1720s. They appear in relation to foreign policy and the recovery of territories from Sweden, the division of Russia into administrative provinces (*gubernii*), military reform, the restructuring of the governmental machinery (in the preamble to the *General Regulation* of 1720 and in the decree introducing the *Table of Ranks*, 1722), the construction of canals, the promotion of trade and industry, tax-collection, the reorganization of the judicial system and the spread of education and enlightenment.[79] They relate on the one hand to the new-found prestige, the

"increase in Russia's glory" as a Great Power resulting from Peter's foreign policy; and on the other hand to the transformation of society by the introduction of western norms of "good order" associated with the concepts of the *Polizeistaat.*[80]

Throughout his reign Peter laid stress on the necessity of universal state-service, from the tsar downwards. In 1718, in the manifesto depriving Aleksei of the succession, he reminded his subjects of the pains he himself had taken for "the benefit of the state" (*pol'za gosudarstvennaia*).[81] He demanded equally strenuous commitment from them. All were required to set to with a will and give of their best for the common good, regardless of personal hardship. What he demanded, to use the terminology of a later age, was from each according to his ability. What he complained of in Aleksei, even before his treasonable intentions came to light, was his lack of commitment: he had proved a shirker and malingerer, who failed to assist Peter in his "unbearable griefs and labours," and put his own convenience and preferences before the needs of the state.[82] Unwilling to serve, he had shown himself unfit to rule.

Peter himself, in the execution of his foreign and domestic policy, conceived of his role, to borrow the expression of his contemporary, Frederick-William I of Prussia, as that of "first servant of the state." *Pravda voli monarshei* describes Peter as "a true Father of his Country, who, in his great zeal for the country, has thought little of his own great pains and efforts."[83] The book in a sense remythologizes the tsar, reordering traditional exp-ectations of his role by emphasizing the qualities of leadership and service to be looked for in a successor, which at the same time and *a fortiori* illustrate, confirm and legitimate his own moral right to rule, and to change the face of Russia.[84]

To what specifically was the tsar's "zeal" directed? Apart from winning international prestige, or "glory" for Russia, Peter saw it as his task to realise the country's potential, to

expand Russia territorially, to bring about the military and civil reforms necessary for this, to ensure internal security and to create a "well-ordered *Polizeistaat*"; in the words of *Pravda voli monarshei,* "not only to preserve it [Russia] but also to expand it greatly; and to strengthen it with civil and military reforms, and with the bastions of reform, namely, with most excellent statutes and laws."[85] These were the unwavering goals of Peter's policy and his legislative propaganda. They exemplify his faith in the formative effects of "good laws." They were intended to realign popular attachment away from the isolationist traditions of Muscovy towards the material, social and cultural betterment of society in accordance with western notions of rational planning.

After having stressed Peter's western orientation, it is equally important to point out the preponderant weight which *Pravda voli monarshei* lends to scriptural authority. The crucial impact of religion on Peter's political outlook is often seriously underestimated. Not only do the Foreword, Afterword and 13 of the 16 sections contain biblical references, but the work includes more quotations from the Bible than from any other source. Nearly all the books of the Old Testament are cited, and most of those in the New.[86]

Several biblical passages, moreover, are accompanied by extensive patristic exegesis, with quotations, particularly from Chrysostom, but also from Jerome, Ambrose, Theophylact and others.[87] Six Old Testament examples follow the 41 "examples from secular history," conclude the main body of the work and culminate the central argument. Not only are these Old Testament precedents, set by "holy patriarchs and devout kings," discussed at greater length than the secular examples, but they are pointedly described as "the best known and most cogent," "sounder than all the previous examples," "of undoubted veracity" and "incontrovertible." They are said indeed to be able to "set the seal on this treatise and will leave no room for contradiction." Thus David's appointment of Solomon as his

successor is described as "alone sufficient to confirm our proposition."[88]

Absolute monarchy in *Pravda voli monarshei,* then, is defended first and foremost in terms of divine right, drawn from a body of Christian belief and dogma equally hallowed in Russia as in the west. *Romans* 13, the *locus classicus* of Christian apologists of absolutism, with its central dogma that "the powers that be are ordained of God," is repeatedly invoked. The reader is informed that "the people have a certain innate fear and reverence for their sovereign, and he is respected, not as a man, but as one distinct from mortal men." In an allusion to Psalm 82, it is stated that in a hereditary monarchy, the ruler personally partakes of the numinous, that "monarchs are indeed gods."[89]

Reliance on Scripture should come as no surprise in a work entrusted to the Synod and to Russia's leading churchman, and published in "church" script as well as "civil." The tsar of Muscovy had always been conceived of in divine right terms as God's viceregent on earth,[90] and Peter adhered unhesitatingly to a tradition which sanctified his own prerogatives. For Russians, as for the rest of Europe, religion remained a paramount authority, and Scripture was understood, in the words of *Pravda voli monarshei,* as "the infallible word of God."[91] The passages from Scripture cited in the book had long been familiar constituents of divine-right tradition in the west, and feature in James I's *The True Law of Free Monarchies* (1598), over a century earlier, as well as in Bossuet's apologias of the absolutism of Louis XIV. Peter subscribed fervently to that tradition. A convinced, if unconventional Christian, who saw the hand of God in all things, including his own transcendent sense of mission, he was steeped in the Bible, which he quoted readily, and was said to know by heart the Epistles of Saint Paul.[92]

The oath of allegiance to the Statute, sworn according to Russian custom, on the Gospels and the cross, was deemed binding on the conscience, and was broken, as it warned, on peril of the soul.[93] The fact that Peter enforced such

collective oath-taking on several occasions between 1718 and 1722 suggests its perceived efficacy as a means of compelling at least passive obedience, and attests to the power of religious sanction over his mind and the minds of his subjects.

Precisely because, in Russia as elsewhere, succession by primogeniture was understood as an integral part of divine-right monarchy, it was essential for Peter to demonstrate that the two were separable.[94] Hence the detailed attention given to this task throughout the work, including, in Section 16, a careful exegesis of a passage in *Judges, 8* which appears to support the traditional interpretation.[95] *Pravda voli monarshei* fought Peter's Orthodox critics with their own weapons, and turned biblical citation and exegesis against them in order to demonstrate that the the new Statute was wholly consonant with Scripture. In this respect it is hardly an exaggeration to describe the work as in large part a religious or at least a politico-religious tract: in Peter's Russia, notwithstanding his efforts to secularize Russian culture, the distinction between secular and religious was by no means as clear-cut as in later times. As Gary Marker has pointed out, the number of books with a religious content published under Peter was unprecedented in absolute terms and constituted some two fifths of all titles published in his reign.[96]

At the same time, while argument was thus firmly grounded on scriptural precept, *Pravda voli monarshei* also introduces a frame of reference almost entirely new to Russia, against which to project the Statute in a favourable light. This frame of reference came directly from western Europe: from a Renaissance background of classical and civic humanism and neo-stoicism, from a view of world history, ancient and modern, as a well-spring of philosophy and a school of virtue; from the study of Roman law and the development of natural law concepts. In adopting wholesale these western traditions - in itself another form of cultural revolution - *Pravda voli monarshei* took up a more modern weapon against Peter's critics. Implicitly the book

represents Russia as belonging to a common western cultural and philosophical heritage and sharing the values on which the book draws.[97] Adducing 41 examples of disinheritance from the history of "the Persians, the Egyptians, the Greeks, the Romans, the Parthians, the Spaniards, the Germans, and others... and the Christians of the Eastern and Western Empire," *Pravda voli monarshei* claims that "the whole civilised world is our witness."[98]

This western frame of reference, with its new language of political discourse, was thus a further means of binding subject to state in Russia in a new conceptual nexus of loyalties and duties. The tsar who now styled himself *Petrus Magnus, Pater Patriae, Imperator Russiarum,* and whose public emblems and official imagery featured Greek and Roman symbolism, could now invoke the loyalty of his subjects in the language of civic humanism, as "true sons of the Russian fatherland" and "staunch supporters of the common good."[99] Against this neo-classical background, it was also natural to introduce ideas of *patria potestas,* in order to complement an analogous Russian tradition of patriarchal authority; and to cite *exempla* from Roman history to illustrate the attitudes adopted *pro bono publico* by stoic patricians towards unworthy or treacherous sons.[100]

Classical and natural law traditions in *Pravda voli monarshei* contained yet another powerful new element: that of rationalism. Reliance on Scriptural authority is complemented by arguments drawn from natural law, with appeals to "man's common sense" (*zdravyi razum chelovecheskii*) and "natural reason" (*estestvennyi razum*); and there is frequent reference to "natural law" (*estestvennyi zakon*) itself.[101] Natural law in *Pravda voli monarshei* presented a set of universal moral principles which paralleled scriptural law but differed from it by deriving their authority not from divine revelation through the "Holy Spirit" (as, for example in the Decalogue), but from conscience, right reason and instinct. Though God-given, natural law is inborn in each individual: it is "the

law that is written in men's hearts" by "the Creator of Nature." Arguments based on natural law are "self-evident: for man's common sense can reach no other conclusion."[102]

In almost every section of the book, the central issue is analysed from two and sometimes three or more separate but mutually supportive standpoints: from Scripture (including patristic exegesis), from natural law, and from positive or "civil laws"[103] and customary law. "Civil laws" and customary law include reference to "the writings of jurists" and to Roman law, especially *patria potestas*, with citations from Justinian and other Roman legislators, chiefly imperial.[104] But the main sources of authority are divine law and natural law. Thus the book's stated purpose is to show that the Statute on the succession "accords both with natural common sense and with the infallible word of God himself." Section 8 states that "both political theorists and theologians agree" on the duty of filial gratitude; while section 11 refers to the duty of fathers to educate their sons as "a duty, placed on them by God and nature." In section 11 again, a hypothetical proposition regarding paternal obligation is rejected as untenable because "there is no mention of it in natural, divine or civil law; but rather they show the very opposite."[105]

Much of Peter's political philosophy was drawn from the rationalist and natural law concepts of western cameralist writers. His models were seventeenth-century Sweden, Prussia and other German states. His legislation adopts the cameralist notion of the "well-ordered *Polizeistaat*" or "regulated state," in which the welfare of society is identified with the interests of the state. State and society are regarded as interdependent, and there is assumed to be no conflict between them: every state, whatever its political form, "has one ultimate reason for its establishment, namely, the common good of the people" (*vsenarodnaia pol'za*).[106] The common interests of state and people are best promoted under the paternal aegis of a monarch with juridically unlimited powers. As the ultimate source of

law, he legislates dispassionately for "the common good," but is not himself bound by his own laws or any others, because his duty to state and people derives from God and is not enforceable by his subjects.[107]

The virtually synonymous concepts of "state" (*gosudarstvo*) and "country" or "fatherland" (*otechestvo*), expressions rare in Muscovite legislation, were constantly invoked by Peter as an autonomous object of allegiance distinct from the person of the tsar.[108] The petrine state was conceived of as more than the tsar's private patrimony (*votchina*), as had been the case in Muscovy. It represented the sum of the common interests of society and the focus of national loyalty and duty, with its own imperatives of order, security and prosperity, and a transcendant, self-justifying goal of "glory" (*slava*), akin to the *gloire* invoked by Louis XIV, but associated by Peter with the state rather than with himself. To the service of the state and its interests as he perceived them, Peter subjected himself as rigorously and selflessly as he did his subjects, and as the book emphasizes, "has thought little of his own great pains and efforts."[109]

At the same time, *Pravda voli monarshei* invests the tsar's authority with greater importance than ever before in the history of Russian political thought. In accordance with Peter's policy of publicizing his political goals, the necessity of absolute power and the comprehensive nature of monarchical prerogative, more or less taken for granted in Muscovite tradition, are here expounded and justified in depth, both on scriptural grounds and by reference to rational and utilitarian criteria. Absolute monarchy is presented as an institution divinely ordained, as the instrument most effective to bring about the "common good" of state and society, and also as a power vested in the monarch by the "will of the people" (*narodnaia volia*).[110]

The argument from divine right thus receives important fresh support from the appeal to common sense and on consensual grounds. One result of this is to raise the issue of the personal competence of the individual monarch (and

his successors). Personal capacity now assumes far greater significance than in conventional divine-right philosophy, since "the condition of the whole country (*otechestvo*), for better or for worse, depends on the supreme power."[111] For the first time in Russian political thought, the question of the tsar's fitness to rule is overtly raised as a condition of his right to rule, even though the choice of a successor rests firmly with the reigning monarch. The potentially revolutionary implications of this line of argument, however, are not drawn out: the concept of the absolute monarch, ruling for "the common good" remains firmly within a framework of "enlightened absolutism," of the tsar as "first servant of the state," but accountable only to God and his conscience.

In reformulating the role of Russia's rulers in rational and utilitarian terms, *Pravda voli monarshei* also redefines and expands that role. It is now presented in dynamic and proactive terms. Their duty is not merely "to keep, and protect their subjects, to maintain them in all safety" in traditional fashion, but also "to instruct and improve them,"[112] that is, to re-educate them and change their attitudes, to make them receptive to the challenge of the modern world, able to master the hitherto unfamiliar concepts and technologies of contemporary western civilisation essential to Russia's transformation - "printing, architecture and the other liberal arts."[113] The tsar is conceived of as reformer, modernizer and *Kulturträger*, who directs Russia's progress from backwardness to civilisation.

The 1721 regulations for the "chief magistracy" (*glavnyi magistrat*) or town council of St Petersburg present a blueprint of organized society as Peter envisaged it: a "welfare state," based on rationality and modernity. The concept of "*Polizei*" in the seventeenth and eighteenth century signified far more than the maintenance of law and order. It embraced a wide-ranging complex of social responsibilities, including the administration of justice, the elimination of vagrancy and the provision of

employment and poor relief, the imposition of price controls, the promotion of trade and industry, measures relating to town-planning, road maintenance and street cleaning, medical care and sanitation, the provision of education and the inculcation of morality and good conduct, including "humble allegiance" to the tsar.[114] The *Polizei,* in the words of the legislation, "represents the spirit of good citizenship (*dusha grazhdanstva*) and all good order and is the fundamental basis of security and convenience."[115]

Such detailed regulation of daily life, typical of the *Polizeiordnungen* of cameralist legislation, was a concept which Peter found continually inspiring in his policies of modernization. The statutory prohibition on the wearing of beards, the introduction of western dress by decree and the official establishment of social gatherings conducted according to formal regulations, are well known examples of his fondness for imposing and accelerating europeanization through legislation. The ideal of the "well-ordered *Polizeistaat*" found classic expression in his new capital. Designed at his command to mark a clean break with the inward-looking conservatism of Moscow, St Petersburg was built *ex nihilo*, not only to secure permanent maritime contact with the west, but also to exemplify western European norms of civil society. The regularity of its architectural layout reflected the rational and mathematical order with which Peter endeavoured to inspire the governance of Russia in general.[116]

As a serving officer, who, like Frederick-William I of Prussia, habitually wore army uniform, Peter attributed Russia's Great Power status to her schooling in western military discipline in the war with Sweden. He revelled in the sight and symbol of serried ranks of uniformed troops performing complex manoeuvres according to fixed rules. As ruler of a modernizing state, he aspired to lend to the reorganisation and operation of his administration a similar sense of regimented precision, co-ordinated routine and purposeful efficiency. On the advice of Leibniz, he

systematically reapportioned the business of government among twelve boards or "colleges" at St Petersburg in 1719, and the same rationalist and mechanistic spirit inspired the procedural rules of the administration under the *General Regulation* of 1720, which postulated collective decision-making by well-drilled bureaucrats.[117]

There were two basic corollaries to Peter's vision of Russia as a 'well-ordered *Polizeistaat*": absolute power for the tsar and unquestioning obedience by his subjects. The tsar, like the Leibnizian "Creator of Nature," saw himself as prescribing the necessary laws and setting in motion the institutional and administrative machinery of reform. For this he required unrestricted political authority. The *Military Statute* of 1716 made this clear in its trenchant definition of the tsar's power: "His Majesty is a sovereign (*samovlastnyi*) monarch who need not account for his actions to anyone on earth, but, as a Christian sovereign, has the power and authority to govern his realms and territories according to his own will and at his discretion."[118] This concept was re-emphasized in the *Spiritual Regulation* of 1721, which introduced the element of obedience with an allusion to *Romans* 13: "the Emperor of Russia is a sovereign and absolute monarch (*monarkh samoderzhavnyi i neogranichennyi*). To obey his supreme power not only from fear, but also for conscience sake, God himself commands."[119]

In *Pravda voli monarshei,* the meaning of absolutism is elaborated more precisely. In a citation from Hugo Grotius, sovereign power, or *majestas,* is defined as "that [power] whose actions are not subject to the power of anyone so as to be annulled at the will of another."[120] It is "the supreme legislative, judicial and executive power, that power which is itself not subject to any laws whatsoever."[121] As *princeps legibus solutus,* "a sovereign monarch (*monarkh gosudar'*) can lawfully command of the people not only whatever is necessary for the obvious good of his country, but indeed whatever he pleases (*vse, chto emu ni ponravitsia*), provided that it is not harmful to the people

and not contrary to the will of God."[122] This echoes the *quicquid principi placuit, legis habet vigorem* of imperial Roman legislation.[123] Indeed the unqualified assertion is made that "every sovereign... is absolutely free to act as he chooses." The ruler is not accountable for his actions: "the king's power (*vlast' tsarskaia*) to command and to act is absolute (*ves'ma svobodna*), and is not subject to anyone's scrutiny... so great is the power which God grants to kings, that no one has the power to question a king about his deeds and to ask him, *what doest thou?*"[124] The monarch is superior to any man-made law, canon law or civil law, including his own enactments; even in respect of divine law, however grave his sin, his subjects may not judge him. Even if he proves a tyrant, they must submit, in accordance with Saint Peter's injunction, *not only to the good and gentle, but also to the froward.*[125]

There is no suggestion, however, in *Pravda voli monarshei,* of the tsar's traditional attributes as head of a confessional state, son of the one true Church, defender of Orthodox Christianity from heresy, or as personally guided by a specifically Christ-like ethic. There is scant reference to the faith and piety traditionally expected of a tsar, little admonition to rule mercifully, no reminder of the people's sufferings or warning of God's judgment, (as there is, for example in analogous writings of Bossuet).[126] The purpose of scriptural citation in *Pravda voli monarshei* is to emphasize and indeed to expand the scope of the tsar's God-given authority, not to limit it within the confines of Muscovite tradition. Obedience is enjoined from the Pauline premiss that *there is no power but of God.* "He [God] subjects everyone... to their [monarchs'] complete and absolute authority."[127] That authority includes the right to punish: *"he is the minister of God, a revenger to execute wrath upon him that doeth evil,"* no doubt a reminder of the fate of the tsarevich Aleksei and his supporters. There is also a reminder from I *Peter* that *"For so is the will of God, that with well doing ye may put to silence the ignorance of foolish men"* - one of the declared aims of *Pravda voli*

40

monarshei.[128] While part of his duty is said to be to furnish his subjects with the means to lead "a way of life both devout and honourable,"[129] there is no definition of "devout" and no suggestion of Orthodox particularism.

It is clear why there is no appeal to the Orthodox attributes as traditionally understood - conservative, hieratic and static - of the Muscovite tsars. Manifestly, with his forceful and enthusiastic programme of westernization, Peter rejected the gradualist pattern of his predecessors, including his own father and grandfather, just as he declined to adopt their formal title of "most meek and orthodox" (*tishaishii i blagovernyi*). The ruler described in *Pravda voli monarshei,* though "a Christian sovereign" (in the words of the *Military statute*) is universalized and non-denominational, acceptable to Peter's new non-Orthodox Christian subjects and coadjutors, whose freedom of worship he guaranteed. The former included the Lutheran communities, mainly German, in the newly annexed Baltic provinces. The latter included those many western experts, especially Protestants, whom he had welcomed into Russia since 1702 and who included some of his closest associates.[130] The needs of the new Russia ruled out Orthodox sectarianism. Besides, not only was Peter himself impressed by the practices and institutions of the Protestant churches and thought that his subjects had much to learn from them; unlike most of his co-religionists, unthinkingly suspicious of the west, he also believed faith and reason, religion and science, to be compatible and complementary.[131]

Pravda voli monarshei makes particular use of arguments drawn from the school of natural law, notably from Grotius, *On the law of war and peace* (1625), and possibly from Samuel von Pufendorf, *On the duty of man and citizen according to natural law* (1673). These and other books on natural law entered Russia in Peter's reign and were translated at his order.[132] Tribute is paid in *Pravda voli monarshei* to Grotius as "the eminent jurist, in his

sagacious treatise on the law of war and peace."[133] Natural law arguments are used to justify absolute rule with reference to social contract theory. In the discussion of the origin of monarchical government, the monarch is said to receive his sovereign power not only from God, but also from "the people" through its implied consent in the original exercize of its "general will" (*vsenarodnaia volia*): "every form of government... derives its origin from an initial agreement among this or that people."[134] Sovereignty originally resided with the people, but was transferred by the people to its first monarch by an act of "voluntary submission."[135] The tenor of the original transfer is expressed as follows: "*We all unanimously desire,* says the people to its first monarch, *that you rule over us for our common good* (k obshchei pol'ze nashei) *for as long as you shall live; and we all renounce our freedom and submit to you, without leaving ourselves any freedom to decide the common weal.*"[136] In an elective monarchy, the surrender of popular sovereignty is coterminous with the monarch's life; in a hereditary monarchy, the people renounces its freedom to the monarch and his successors in perpetuity or as long as the reigning dynasty lasts, or indeed for as long as there exists a nominated successor.[137]

Pravda voli monarshei also outlines the duties of the absolute monarch. As with his sovereignty, these duties are imposed on him by natural law as well as by God, since monarchy exists for "the common good of the people." The overall duty of monarchs is defined in the spirit of the *Polizeistaat* as being "to maintain their subjects in safety, and to provide them with the best instruction of every kind for a way of life both devout and honourable."[138] Specifically, as has been seen, their duties relate to the provision of justice, the armed forces and education. But the monarch is also entitled to regulate by decree the details of his subjects' private lives. Explicit reference is made to those elements of Peter's reform which marked some of the clearest and most controversial breaks with the past: changes in social and cultural mores associated with

the creation of St Petersburg and the transformation of Russian culture into a culture europeanized by the tsar's *Polizeiordnungen* - "changes in customs and dress, house-building, procedures and ceremonies at feasts, weddings, funerals, etc."[139]

Pravda voli monarshei concedes that the monarch is bound by the moral law, divine and natural - "the laws of God, both those which he has written in men's hearts and those which he has handed down in the Decalogue."[140] But this could be of little practical comfort to the people, since the book immediately goes on to emphasize that the monarch is "accountable for his stewardship" only to God: "in the exercize of his care... he is answerable not to the people, but to God alone." He is not bound by his own laws: "no sovereign monarch is obliged to observe man-made law." If he chooses to adhere to them, he does so at his sovereign will and from considerations of expediency; and if he breaks them, he cannot be judged by his subjects. Absolute power "is subject to God's law only in the sense that it is answerable for transgressing it to God's judgment alone, and not to man's."[141] To all intents and purposes, the obligation is a personal and a moral one, not susceptible of legal enforcement.

5. *Pravda voli monarshei*, absolutism and limited monarchy

Partly no doubt because of the criminalisation of unauthorized writings, written examples are lacking of contemporary ideological opposition to *Pravda voli monarshei* in Russia.[142] There was, as has been seen, no question of a published reply to the book. The existence of some kind of opposition, however, whether published or not, can be inferred from the work itself. The very fact that Peter deemed it necessary for it to be written suggests his perception of the existence of opposition to his succession law. But the book is at the same time much more than a

defence of that law. It is an apologia of Peter's absolutist rule in general, supported by a detailed excursus into political theory and a discussion of alternative forms of government. There would be no need for such a discussion, were it not that, as the book significantly admits, "there is a debate among political theorists as to which monarchy, elective or hereditary, is the better and more advantageous."[143]

Moreover *Pravda voli monarshei* is significant both in what it says and in what it omits to say about alternative forms of government. Its argument is frequently tendentious. It allows for the existence of democracy, aristocracy, elective monarchy and even "a mixed form of government" in addition to absolute hereditary monarchy;[144] but having raised basic issues of political theory and briefly discussed them, it dismisses further argument, often quite peremptorily, and closes down the debate. While the "general will" is agreed to be at the basis of all government,[145] the concept of the social contract is interpreted extremely narrowly. There is no suggestion that it might be invoked to justify resistence to absolute power, or that a breach of divine or natural law by the monarch might serve to release the people from its promise of submission. Such contentions are indeed explicitly denied.

Discussion of alternative forms of government, though laboured, is often fleeting and superficial. There is no discussion of "a mixed form of government." English parliamentarianism is cursorily touched on. Reference to Charles I is made in order to denounce out of hand the "most heinous deed" of the regicides in presuming to judge their king.[146] There is no mention of the 1688 Revolution, no reference to John Locke, though Peter himself was in England in 1698, met William III and was familiar with the principles of parliamentary government.[147]

He was still better acquainted with the workings of elective monarchy in neighbouring Poland, with which Russia had been familiar since at least the "Time of

Troubles" in the early sixteenth century. Peter was directly involved in Polish affairs throughout the war with Sweden. By 1720, as a result of Russia's military predominance, his influence over electoral politics and king-making at Warsaw was paramount. Stanislas-Augustus II was his nominee and client-king of what was virtually a Russian protectorate. Elective monarchy on the Polish model could not therefore be wholly ignored in a discussion of forms of government. So though Poland itself is summarily dismissed as an example of the evils associated with elective monarchy, a significant part of the discussion nonetheless takes up the general theme of elective monarchy as the main and obvious alternative to absolutism.

Section 16, the second longest in the work, is thus ostensibly devoted to a comparison of hereditary and elective monarchy.[148] But the discussion is tendentious and dismissive, beginning with the assertion that the question is "easily demonstrated by the supporters of hereditary monarchy, who confirm the superiority of hereditary monarchy over elective with many most powerful arguments"[149] Though calling itself a "treatise," *Pravda voli monarshei* was no academic disquisition; it was not, nor did it claim to be, an original work of scholarship addressed to western *savants*, but was in this respect a political tract, written for a political purpose.

Whatever its novelty for Russia, there was little that was new in the propositions laid down in *Pravda voli monarshei* in terms of western political theory. It repeated the biblical nostrums of the defenders of patriarchal authority and divine-right monarchy, familiar before and after James I's *True Law of Free Monarchy*; and its arguments on the social contract were drawn from well-known tenets of the seventeenth-century school of natural law. Its *exempla* came from well-known biblical and patristic literature, from classical and ecclesiastical historians, and from sixteenth-century compendiums of world history. It took

little account of more recent political thought. Grotius' book was after all almost a century old.

There did exist, however, native Russian critics of absolutism whose views were influenced by contemporary western political thought. No doubt in order to address their concerns, *Pravda voli monarshei* mentions some obvious contemporary examples of republican government or limited monarchy, namely Venice, Holland, Poland and the Holy Roman Empire.[150] But no more is said of Venice and Holland; and Poland and the Holy Roman Empire are singled out only as examples of the supposedly disastrous effects of elective monarchy. No mention is made of France under the Regency, or of Sweden, where the absolutist system established in 1680 was replaced in 1720 by a limited monarchy advised by a *Riksrad* or council of state and accountable to a representative *Riksdag*. This was a significant omission.[151]

Still more remarkable is the lack of any reference to Russian precedents for the election of a tsar by a representative assembly. In 1598 the *Zemskii Sobor* elected tsar Boris Godunov on the extinction of the Riurikovid dynasty, and in 1613 it elected Peter's own grandfather, Mikhail Romanov. Neither of these precedents is mentioned in *Pravda voli monarshei,* though the situation arising at the extinction of the ruling house, when "the freedom conferred on the previous monarchs reverts to the people," is referred to, possibly as a vague allusion to the election of the Romanovs in 1613, or, more probably, as a remote and hypothetical possibility in the future.[152]

Yet paradoxically, within 8 years of *Pravda voli monarshei*, came the celebrated though short-lived attempt to introduce legal restraints on Russian absolutism. On the death of Peter's 14-year-old grandson and last direct male descendant, Piotr Alekseevich, who reigned for two years as tsar Peter II (1727-1730), the question of Russia's political system was suddenly thrown open. The terminology of the debate which ensued among those who fought out the issue

was already foreshadowed in *Pravda voli monarshei*. The protagonists of elective monarchy were politically aware and articulate representatives of two aristocratic families, the Golitsyns and the Dolgorukies; the defenders of absolutism were Feofan Prokopovich himself and the historian V. N. Tatishchev (1686-1750), members, together with A. D. Kantemir, of an elite scholarly circle devoted to defending the petrine legacy.[153]

A Supreme Privy Council (*Verkhovnyi Tainyi Sovet*) had been established in February 1726 to assist Peter's widow and immediate successor, empress Catherine I, under whom it exercized *de jure* legislative power and *de facto* executive power. As regents acting in the name of Peter II, the Council exercized absolute power in all matters, with the single exception of the nomination of a successor.[154] This last prerogative soon fell into their hands. In a succession of cabals, the Golitsyns and Dolgorukies had ousted their rivals and increased their own membership of the Council, and by January 1730 they monopolized it.[155] With the death of Peter II, the prospect now offered itself of radical constitutional change.

The *Verkhovniki*, as they were called, entertained hopes not only of choosing a new monarch (since Peter II had named no successor), but of revolutionizing the basis of government in Russia and of institutionalising some form of limited monarchy on the British, Polish or Swedish model.[156] Their choice of candidate fell on Peter's niece, Anna Ivanovna, the widowed Duchess of Courland, who they supposed would prove tractable to their designs, having otherwise no claim to the throne. Anna accepted the crown, on signing an undertaking whereby, except by consent of the Supreme Privy Council, she would not make war or peace, levy new taxes or spend state revenues, appoint to high office, marry, name a successor or penalise members of the nobility without due trial. For breach of any of these stipulations, she would forfeit the throne.[157]

These radical limitations on absolutism appeared to burgeon spontaneously in 1730; but they grew from an

existing intellectual seedbed planted by Peter himself. Russians sent abroad by Peter on diplomatic missions or to learn western skills returned with experience of life under constitutional government. Books on political theory and constitutional history were translated into Russian at Peter's own command. The leading *verkhovnik,* Prince D. M. Golitsyn (1665-1737), who had spent some years in the republic of Venice, was Governor of Kiev when Prokopovich was teaching at the Kiev Academy. He and Prokopovich had collaborated in the translation of western classics of natural law, including Grotius, Pufendorf, and Locke's *Treatises of Civil Government* (1690). His substantial library also contained such works as Hobbes' *Philosophical Rudiments concerning Government and Society* and two of the classic French critiques of the absolutism of Louis XIV, Fénelon's *Les aventures de Télémaque* (1699) *and* Montesquieu's *Lettres persanes* (1721). Among Golitsyn's political models was Sweden's era of freedom (*Frihetstiden*) inaugurated under the 1720 constitution by the Chancellor, Count Arvid Horn. It was Golitsyn who drew up the constitutional proposals for Russia in 1730.[158]

His fellow *verkhovnik,* Prince V. L. Dolgorukii (1672-1739), who presented these proposals to Anna Ivanovna, was a veteran diplomat with wide experience as ambassador to Denmark, France, Poland and Sweden. He was well acquainted with the constitutions of these states, which left a deep impression on his political outlook.[159] Moreover, *Pravda voli monarshei* contemplates precisely such a situation as arose in 1730, when, "at the election of the... monarch, certain conditions were laid down with his consent or were confirmed by him on oath, whereby it was stipulated that if the monarch did not fulfil them, he would be deposed." Significantly, however, the book begs the whole question, dismissively asserting that "such a monarchy, however, would not be a true monarchy."[160]

Arguments from natural law could of course be applied to more than one theory of government.[161] In the century and a half since the Huguenot *Vindiciae contra Tyrannos*

(1579), natural law arguments had frequently been applied, particularly in France and England, to query the patriarchal basis of divine right monarchy, to formulate a theory of popular rights and to justify the establishment of limited monarchy. Such arguments had been conspicuously revived in Britain by John Locke to defend the Revolution of 1688. To some extent *Pravda voli monarshei* took this into account when conceding, at least in theory, that sovereignty ultimately resided in the people and that legitimate government was based, however remotely, on popular consent: "It is clear that every form of government, including hereditary monarchy itself, derives its origin from an initial agreement among this or that people."[162] However this statement, borrowed from Grotius and the seventeenth-century natural law school, was not intended in *Pravda voli monarshei* to have any revolutionary implications. There is little evidence that official political thought in Russia had kept pace with post-1688 developments. This may have been the result of a cultural time-lag: western ideas introduced under Peter tended to be those of the seventeenth rather than the eighteenth century.[163]

More probably, however, it was the result of deliberate policy. For plainly the doctrine of popular sovereignty and of government based on the consent of the governed could lead, and had already led in the west to a line of argument highly prejudicial to divine-right monarchy, which had begun to lose its former lustre; and *in Pravda voli monarshei* both doctrines are noticeably hedged around with caveats and reservations.[164] The notional transfer of popular sovereignty to the first hereditary monarch is expressed in unequivocal terms: *"we, having once renounced our freedom, will never avail ourselves of it hereafter, not even after your death; but we bind ourselves by a solemn oath to submit to you and after you to your successors, and we bind our heirs after us by the same obligation."*[165] That hereditary absolutism in Russia is based on popular consent is said to be evidenced by the

oath of allegiance, which allegedly reflects the "will of the people."[166] Now it is true that the oath of allegiance, notably to the 1722 statute, binds the people in advance to "submit in everything to his [the monarch's]... successor."[167] What is not pointed out here is that the oath was compulsory, enforced on pain of death, which puts the consensual argument somewhat into question.

The people's original act of submission to the monarch, it is argued, cannot be rescinded without inconsistency or perjury, because "having conferred on him perpetual hereditary rule over itself, it [the people] has sworn to obey his will," and because by rescinding its decision, "the people would contradict itself and violate its oath."[168] Such consent, once given, is said to be irrevocable, *inter alia* because *vox populi, vox Dei*: "the will of the people... is also that of God."[169] The social contract is said to be concluded "in every case at God's volition and under his wise and active providence."[170] The surrender of popular sovereignty to the monarch is therefore final: once vested in him, "his power is inalienable."[171] Furthermore the transaction is unilateral, not mutual: "the people, in conferring all its freedom on the monarch, did not take from him any freedom in exchange."[172] The monarch is not a party to the social contract and is not bound by it. Although the monarch is invited "to rule over us for our common good," no provision is made for regulating his conduct, still less for removing him if he fails the test of "the common good." The surrender once made, "the people cannot now depose him."[173]

Indeed, as has been seen, not only popular resistence but even popular remonstrance is rigorously excluded, since by virtue of its transfer of sovereignty the people divests itself of "any freedom to decide the common weal," and commits itself to "do all that the sovereign commands without criticism or complaint... For if the people has renounced its common freedom and has conferred it on its sovereign, then it must surely obey his commands, laws and statutes, without reservation."[174] *A fortiori,* "the people

cannot judge its sovereign's actions," but "every subject must carry out the king's orders without questioning his designs and intentions." The surrender of popular sovereignty also binds succeeding generations, this being "the foundation of monarchical succession."[175]

The basic argument is a circular one. Instead of deducing the powers of the monarch from the nature of the social contract, the nature of the contract is defined by reference to the powers of the monarch: "the will of the people can only be interpreted from the type and form of the monarchy itself; for it should be understood that, whatever the form of any monarchy, it corresponds to the will of the people, which was present at its origin."[176] Such a premise, together with the statement that monarchy exists for "the common good," might appear to suggest at least the possibility of some degree of accountability by the monarch to the "will of the people" in a monarchy instituted by popular demand.

However, God is introduced as a *deus ex machina*, in this case not to facilitate, but to foreclose such a possibility, by depriving the people of its last resort, the right to withdraw its allegiance. The monarch cannot be deposed under any circumstances, because "even if the people insisted on changing its mind... it cannot change the will of God, which inspired the will of the people and acted in concert with it in establishing the monarchy."[177] *Romans* 13 is reintroduced in order to close down the argument completely by ruling out any resistence to tyranny: "rather the people must endure any failing and vice in its sovereign (for the Holy Spirit commands us to submit *not only to the good and gentle, but also to the froward*)."[178] While ostensibly branching out into political theory and a comprehensive discussion of alternatives to absolutism, therefore, *Pravda voli monarshei* ultimately returns to its original starting-point in Saint Paul, from which, in reality, it seldom strays far.

The only occasion when the people exercizes freedom is on an interregnum following the death in intestacy of the

last monarch of the reigning house, when its original sovereignty reverts to it and "when a new monarch is elected by the people."[179] Even then, the people appears to be bound to adhere to absolute hereditary monarchy by virtue of its original covenant, and is not entirely free to consider alternative forms of government. For not even the death of the last monarch releases the people from the covenant: it is obliged to try to elucidate his likely wishes regarding his successor, and to be guided by them. Its one area of discretion - though, perhaps unwittingly, it is a revealing one - arises where the choice of a candidate apparently preferred by the last monarch might lead to "rebellion or unrest."[180] In these exceptional circumstances the people itself may exercize its sovereign judgment in accordance with its perceptions of "the common good": but only because until it does so, and transfers its sovereignty to the new incumbent, no other lawful source of authority exists.

With the single exception of an interregnum, then, the Russian people is never accorded rights, only the obligation of permanent, unqualified submission. Its juridical position remains as under the Muscovite tsars, despite the introduction of natural law arguments. These serve in fact only to lend an authoritative air of modernity to an essentially traditional ideology. Revolutionary in so much of his outlook, Peter the Great unhesitatingly retained the core institution of Russian government, while directing it towards novel ends. So far as political theory was concerned, westernization had strict limits.[181]

6. *Pravda voli monarshei* and political dissent

Peter sincerely believed that he occupied the rational and moral higher ground. He felt that he had acted rightly in the case of the tsarevich Aleksei in view of his overriding duty to the state. To him his succession law was of a piece with the rest of his reformist legislation, part of a

consistent and all-embracing ideology of religion, government and society. Absolutism, with its unique ability to enforce necessary change, was the cornerstone of this ideology. *Pravda voli monarshei* describes the Statute on the succession as "this most useful statute," the source of "all the blessings which our country needs."[182]

Peter took seriously the attitudes implicit in his title "Father of his Country." Frequently in his legislation (including the Statute on the succession), he stressed his paternal concern for his people, with the phrase "taking pity on our subjects" (*miloserduia my o nashikh poddannykh*).[183] To his mind, only the ignorant, the idle or the ill-intentioned could fail to follow his lead, once explained, published and disseminated in his legislation. Reform must be imposed on such malcontents by coercion and punishment. Such an attitude was clear from the creation of St Petersburg itself, a triumph of compulsion, built on a deserted swamp at one man's will by forced labour, regardless of the cost in lives, and populated at his edict. Absolutism, as Philip Longworth puts it, "was the *sine qua non* of St Petersburg and all it stood for."[184]

Leaving aside outbreaks of open rebellion, which, with specific political, economic and ethnic origins, punctuated the early part of the reign and were savagely repressed, there was throughout the period a continuous undercurrent of popular discontent. *Pravda voli monarshei* refers to "secret grumbling," liable to erupt into "open criticism" of the tsar.[185]

Early in his reign, Peter set up the *Preobrazhenskii Prikaz* and entrusted it with responsibility to root out dissent, by which he understood not merely active rebellion or treason, but, as successive legislation made clear, anything critical of "the high monarchical honour."[186] The *Military Statute* formally criminalised criticism of the Emperor, "his actions or intentions." What was forbidden were "abusive words" (*khulitel'nye slova*) or "unseemly remarks" (*nepristoinye rechi*), that is, any disrespectful expression of discontent with the regime; and

intent to commit an offence was treated as equivalent to its commission. A range of miscellaneous offences, collated in the *Military Statute,* now became "police" matters, applicable to the population at large, for direct referral to the *Preobrazhensky Prikaz,* which enjoyed independent and exclusive jurisdiction for political offences throughout the reign, even after the establishment of the collegiate system.[187]

The *Preobrazhenskii Prikaz* operated through a nation-wide system of informers. Peter presented delation as a public, patriotic and Christian duty, rewarded the successful informer with his victim's goods, and threatened those who failed to report a suspect with the penalties meted out to a convicted party. Torture was the statutory means of establishing proof. The defendant who denied his guilt underwent up to three or more degrees of torture. If he still maintained his innocence, his accuser was put to the same test, and so on, until one or other confessed. The ordeal itself could prove fatal, as apparently happened in the case of the Tsarevich Aleksei himself. Peter, who suspected that behind dissent lay actual resistance, passive or active, to his reforms, determined to stamp out both. Those convicted of "unseemly remarks" were subject to the death-penalty or to a variety of lesser penalties, including branding, excision of the tongue, degrees of flogging, and exile.[188]

Most victims of the *Preobrazhensky Prikaz* were ordinary peasants or townsfolk, guilty of some remark derogatory to "the sovereign's word and deed" (*slovo i delo gosudarevo*); and the commonest type of political offence dealt with by the *Preobrazhenskii Prikaz* between 1697 and 1708 was that of "unseemly remarks." Offenders included many Old Believers, who, in common with some conservative Orthodox, identified Peter with the long-predicted Antichrist and St Petersburg with the new Babylon.[189] Most expressions of discontent, without going that far, reveal widespread discontent with Peter's policies and conduct: his enthusiastic espousal of western habits hitherto taboo -

shaving, smoking, the wearing of western dress - and his radical breaks, violent and dismissive, with Muscovite custom.[190] Because he did not rule like a traditional tsar and his behaviour was often eccentric, coarse, drunken, blasphemous and brutal, because of his low-born or foreign associates, his harsh treatment of his first wife and eldest son, popular resentment at his policies and their inexorable demands was directed at Peter himself and his henchmen. Even his assumption of the imperial title was questioned as sacrilegious. It was wondered whether Peter was indeed the true tsar, or one of the impostors familiar in Russian history, a foreigner and heretic. Catherine, undeniably a foreigner and an interloper, who had ousted the rightful tsarina, was also the object of popular prejudice (though she was in fact homely and benign), and some of the most derogatory remarks reported to the *Preobrazhenskii Prikaz* related to her.[191]

Peter became particularly suspicious of opposition after 1718. The Secret Chancery, which he set up under Tolstoi as an extraordinary commission of enquiry to investigate the affair of the Tsarevich Aleksei, was later subsumed by the *Preobrazhenskii Prikaz* as the agency for the investigation and punishment of political dissent. The 1722 Statute on the succession not only reordered the principle of the succession, but prescribed a special oath of allegiance, and declared that "any who opposes it [the statute] or interprets it differently shall be deemed a traitor, and be liable to the death penalty and to excommunication."[192] A month after issuing the Statute, Peter enacted a personal decree requiring the clergy to report to the *Preobrazhenskii Prikaz* any treasonable intention, particularly "statements concerning His Imperial Majesty's high honour."[193] *Pravda voli monarshei* warned its readers not to "be false to the oath of allegiance."[194] No more dissent was allowed under Peter than under his predecessors. Peter himself took the lead in referring suspected cases of *lèse-majesté* to the Secret Chancellery, which by the end of his reign could hardly

cope with the mounting volume of charges and counter-charges.[195]

It is significant, however, to note the kind of opposition which Peter sought to suppress. Severe punishment by the Secret Chancery for complicity in the affair of the tsarevich Aleksei or generally by the *Preobrazhenskii Prikaz* for criticism of the regime, was normally restricted to lower-class offenders, peasants, townsfolk, or to those whose language or conduct was gross and manifest, like the Old Believers. Such critics, bewildered at the changes, the increasing burdens imposed on them by the state and the personal hardships in their lives brought about under Peter, found a variety of more or less fantastic and apocalyptic explanations for their misfortunes. Their ideological opposition was entirely backward-looking. They thought in terms of the Muscovite stereoptype of the "good" tsar, not of alternative forms of government, of which they knew little, borrowed from the hated west. Their objection to the Statute on the succession was that it broke with custom and displaced the righful heir, under whom they hoped for a gentler life.

The case with the nobility was different. There were aristocratic sympathizers of the Tsarevich, for example among the Golitsyns and Dolgorukies, but most of them suffered relatively lightly, with the temporary loss of their honours and a period of exile. Prince D. M. Golitsyn, though a co-signatory of the death-sentence on Aleksei, was known to sympathize with him, his mother, ex-tsarina Evdokiia, and his son, Piotr Alekseevich, and to deplore the rise of Catherine. Yet no harm befell him under Peter. He held high office and enjoyed the tsar's respect.[196]

While employing draconian methods to discourage dissent in the population at large, Peter took no steps against members of the nobility whose basic loyalty to him was not in question, whatever their private reservations. As long as he was alive, their political speculations would remain academic, since his own legitimacy as ruler was not in question. Had he resorted to their systematic suppression,

he would have deprived himself of some of the most gifted and qualified among those whose cooperation was essential to the implementation of his reforms. In such qualified supporters, therefore, he might overlook attitudes which he did not tolerate in the populace at large. To expressions of discontent from the illiterate masses he responded with savage repression. Arguments drawn from natural law, learned citations from Grotius or *exempla* from ancient history could mean little or nothing to them. Even biblical exegesis was probably beyond their grasp.[197] For more literate and articulate criticism of his ideology, emanating from a social and cultural elite with access to western political thought, a more sophisticated response was called for. Hence the elaborate if selective and tendentious argumentation of *Pravda voli monarshei* and its continual attempts to anticipate and to rebut such critics, in part at least on their own grounds.

7. The authorship of *Pravda voli monarshei*

Pravda Voli Monarshei was published anonymously. Traditionally it has always been ascribed to Feofan Prokopovich. As with his *Children's Catechism* (*Pervoe Uchenie Otrokam*) and the *Spiritual Regulation,* anonymity no doubt lent it greater authority than it could have exerted had any particular name been attached to it, especially one so controversial and unpopular with traditionalists as that of Prokopovich, mistrusted as he was for his ambition, his enthusiasm for Protestant models and his supposed heterodoxy. "Cet homme," observed Campredon, "est également hai du Clergé et du peuple."[198]

There is, however, an inherent problem of authorship. No original manuscript of *Pravda voli monarshei* is extant. The most that has been found is a manuscript copy, with corrections attributed to Prokopovich by P. V. Verkhovskoi.[199] Yet for over two and a half centuries, authorship of the work was never thought to be in doubt.

Beginning with his own claims, Prokopovich's authorship was taken for granted throughout the eighteenth century, for example by Kantemir, Novikov and Shcherbatov, and in the nineteenth by professional scholars such as P. P. Pekarskii and S. M. Solov'ev.[200]

The question of authorship was first raised by James Cracraft in 1981 in an article entitled "Did Feofan Prokopovich really write *Pravda Voli Monarshei?*" Cracraft argued that conclusive proof of Prokopovich's authorship is lacking (and indeed that similar doubt arises in respect of most of the works conventionally ascribed to him).[201] On the evidence of a letter, now in the Public Record Office, dated 17 July 1725, from Thomas Consett to Lord Townshend, Secretary of State for Foreign Affairs, Cracraft suggests that Prokopovich contributed to and took overall editorial responsibility for a work produced by more than one author, and notably by a Greek archimandrite in Russian service, Anastasios Contoeides, or Afanasii Condoidi.

Condoidi, who had studied in Italy and taught at Constantinople, came to Russia as a refugee in 1711 with the defeated hospodar of Moldavia, Dimitrii Kantemir, to whose sons (including the future poet and diplomat, Antiokh Kantemir) he taught Latin, Greek and Italian. He worked at the patriarchal press at Moscow, taught theology at the Greco-Latin-Slavonic Academy, and became archpresbyter (*protoierei*) at the cathedral of Saint Peter and Paul at St Petersburg. In 1721 he was appointed to the newly founded Synod as an "assessor," and in 1722 he became a monk and abbot of a monastery in Iaroslavl'.[202] According to Consett, who was introduced to him, not only was Condoidi "a person of distinction," "a scholar (which is here rare) and a man of good parts"; but Condoidi also claimed in conversation with Consett to have "had a principal hand in composing" *Pravda Voli Monarshei,* while alleging that Prokopovich's role "was only to peruse and dispose the matter of it."[203] On the strength of this

assertion, Cracraft concludes that the case for ascribing the book to Prokopovich "rests on sand."[204]

How far does Consett's evidence, based on the briefest acquaintance with Condoidi, affect the question of authorship? First, the "we" which features throughout the work seems authorial rather than indicative of plural authorship, though it may signify collective Synodal authorship.[205] Whatever may be the case with other works attributed to Prokopovich, there is no reason to doubt that he did take part in the preparation of *Pravda voli monarshei*. Indeed Condoidi's admission that he did may be taken as proof positive of the fact. Condoidi does not deny Prokopovich's contribution: he merely purports to marginalize it. The issue therefore boils down to the extent and nature of that contribution.

It is important to stress that we have only Condoidi's word that he, not Prokopovich, was the substantive author. Why should Condoidi be believed rather than Prokopovich? By Consett's own account, Condoidi, at the time a protegé of the influential Count P. A. Tolstoi, was (like Prokopovich himself) worldly and disingenuous: "I observe the bent of his studies directed more to politics than divinity," Consett noted, adding in a further letter written a few days later: "my Archimandrite plays the true politician, by fencing off hardest, where he would least receive a stroke."[206] Nor was Condoidi, it seems, particularly well disposed to Prokopovich. At any rate he was one of five ecclesiastics who early in 1722 endorsed Stefan Iavorskii's complaints of heresy against Prokopovich.[207] Finally, on his own admission, Condoidi spoke little Russian, so that any contribution by him to *Pravda voli monarshei* must presumably have been translated or at least checked by another.[208]

The question of the relative contributions of Prokopovich and Condoidi therefore remains open until more definite conclusions can be reached, *inter alia* from closer analysis and comparison, both textual and thematic, of *Pravda voli monarshei* with authenticated works by both writers. From

a cursory interim comparison of *Pravda voli monarshei* with several sermons published between 1718 and 1725 and undoubtedly the work of Prokopovich, there emerge several striking similarities of phrase, from which it appears reasonably certain that at the very least Prokopovich wrote the Foreword and Afterword.[209] Similarly the ideology of *Pravda voli monarshei,* its political argumentation and natural law terminology, as well as its characteristics of style, suggest that it is of a piece with analogous works by Prokopovich.[210]

Meanwhile, however, notwithstanding the relative weakness of Condoidi's evidence, it is certainly safest, in the present state of knowledge, to give him the benefit of the doubt, and to accept that *Pravda voli monarshei* may also have been the work of someone other than Prokopovich, or, in Cracraft's words, that it was "probably written by him [Prokopovich] in collaboration with one or more persons."[211] There is nothing inherently unlikely in the proposition of a shared workload, particularly given the desirability of bringing out the book as soon as possible after the appearance of the Statute on the succession and the need for research as well as for writing; so that, as Cracraft suggests, parts of it may have been written by Condoidi and edited by Prokopovich.

There is some corroborative evidence to support the case for dual or plural authorship. As Cracraft notes, the work is not stylistically homogeneous. In particular, the markedly rhetorical character of the Foreword and Afterword contrasts with the often pedestrian style of much of the remainder. Such stylistic differences within the text may indicate more than one author rather than simply more than one style - that is, as Cracraft concludes, a collaborative effort under Prokopovich's "editorial" supervision.

On the other hand, to dismiss Prokopovich's role as "only" editorial, as Condoidi does, would be to beg the question. The overall unity of theme throughout the work and the close-knit interconnections of the 16 sections, as

well as their internal consistency and coherence, suggest that such supervision was anything but superficial. Structurally, *Pravda voli monarshei* is a tightly organized work with very few loose ends.[212] As Peter's most trusted and experienced propagandist, closely attuned to the tsar's thinking in matters of state policy, as the undoubted author of sermons relating to the succession, and as the recipient of Peter's commission to publish *Pravda voli monarshei,* it is inconceivable that Prokopovich failed to take with the utmost seriousness his overriding responsibility for the preparation of a work of such supreme political importance.

It is also significant that nearly all the sources cited in *Pravda voli monarshei* were to be found in Prokopovich's own unique library of over 3,000 volumes.[213] These sources include not only standard examples of classical and patristic literature, but also such rarer items as Theodor Zwinger's *Theatrum Vitae Humanae* (1565), Johann Jacob Hofmann's *Lexicon Universale* (1674), Dionysius Goth-ofredus' *Corpus Iuris Civilis*, and Sethus Calvisius' *Chronology* (1605).[214] Even excluding, for the sake of argument, the obvious explanation that Prokopovich himself consulted his own books in the writing of *Pravda voli monarshei* - he may have permitted Condoidi to do so, as he permitted others,[215] - the presence of these books in his library strengthens the case for his association with the production of the work in the broadest sense.

Cracraft also suggests, partly on the evidence of Consett, that the Foreword to *Pravda voli monarshei* may have been written "or at least drafted" by Peter himself.[216] However, the flattering references there to Peter suggest another hand than his so that it is unlikely that Peter was the sole author of the Foreword, and his contributions, if any, remain a matter for speculation.[217] It is likely from other known examples that he gave detailed instructions as to the content of the Foreword and Afterword, as well as of the work generally. For the student of Peter's political ideology, what is important is that the book was commissioned and approved by him, and represents a

learned elaboration of his own general views. Certainly, in scrutinizing this peculiarly important work, Peter no doubt showed the characteristic attention paid by him to the smallest detail of similar works published at his behest.[218]

8. Content and Argument

The main body of *of Pravda voli monarshei* consists of 16 numbered sections of varying length, described as "reasons or arguments," in support of the 1722 statute, followed by 47 "examples" from history and scripture. The work opens with a "Foreword to the Honest Reader" and ends with a separate but unheaded concluding section in similar style to the Foreword (here called the "Afterword"). The Foreword is followed by the Statute on the succession and the associated oath of allegiance. Next comes a short introductory passage leading to the first of the sixteen sections.

The Foreword explains the book's purpose. *Pravda voli monarshei*, an official publication authorized by "the supreme authorities, spiritual and temporal," is addressed to "the honest (*prostoserdechnyi*) reader" in need of instruction.[219] It is not intended for experts in political theory, who "do not have the slightest doubt of a father's absolute right to decide the succession."[220] Nor does it purport to furnish readers with reasons for accepting the 1722 statute, which, like all legislation of an absolute monarch, enjoys divine sanction and is automatically binding "*for conscience sake.*"[221] The book's aim, as the Foreword makes clear, is to demonstrate and publicize the "justice" of the statute, to rebut criticism from dissidents and malcontents who "sow seeds of rebellion in our country," to enlighten "honest but ignorant persons" who may have been misled by the former, and to counter anti-Russian prejudice abroad and dispel the reputation of Russia as a country seething with rebellion.[222]

There then follows the text of the Statute on the succession and the accompanying oath of allegiance.

The work proper begins with an introductory section which refers to the oath of allegiance and claims that the statute has won universal approval. "That is right and proper," since obedience is enjoined on the subjects both by Scripture and by natural law. The statute, however, should command particularly loyal support because it offers the greatest benefit for Russia in authorizing succession by appointment, given that the national welfare depends "for better or for worse" on the character of the monarch.[223]

The decision to publish the book has been taken by the tsar's "chief ministers" at a joint session of Synod and Senate, "in order to remove the least trace of doubt from the minds of the ignorant, and to leave no room for misunderstanding."[224] Its purpose is to demonstrate the monarch's right to disinherit a son for cause and generally to override his birthright.

There then follows the central core of the work, consisting of sixteen sets of "arguments" in support of the statute. Arguments 1-9 define "the power of parents generally"; arguments 10-16 define "the power of parents who are monarchs."

Section 1 argues that there exists under natural and divine law an obligation on parents to maintain their children, qualified by a corresponding duty on children to obey and respect their parents: "so when children, by their wickedness, violate their duty, they release their parents from the duty to look after them" and, depending on the gravity of the offence, entitle their parents to disown them.[225] Section 2 contends that in certain circumstances a son's behaviour may leave his father with no alternative than to disown him.[226] Section 3 shows on what grounds disinheritance is justified in civil law, citing Justinian's 14 definitions of "filial ingratitude" by way of persuasive, though not exclusive authority.[227] Section 4 quotes the Old

Testament to show that inheritance by primogeniture is not an indefeasible, but a conditional right.[228] Section 5 deduces a father's right to disinherit from the practice of adoption. Since, by virtue of adoption, a father makes his adopted son his heir, thereby depriving his own son of part of his patrimony, he must *a fortiori* have the right to disinherit his son for cause.[229] Section 6 draws the same conclusion from the inherent disciplinary authority which vests in parents.[230] Section 7 argues from Roman and Mosaic law that "every father has an absolute right to disinherit a wicked son."[231] Section 8 shows from civil law and the New Testament that "a patrimony is bequeathed, even to a worthy son, out of good will, not out of duty."[232] The points made in Sections 1-8 are briefly recapitulated in Section 9, which argues that they must all hold doubly good in the case of a monarch.[233]

Sections 10-16 discuss the characteristics of monarchical power. Section 10 states on biblical authority that every monarch, whether hereditary or elective, derives his power from God, and hence that a monarch's son cannot "demand the throne from his father as of right."[234] Section 11 argues that though monarchs should "bring up their sons to be fit to rule," they are under no obligation to bequeath the succession to a son "regardless of his merit."[235] Section 12 cites the lament "against unknown heirs" in *Ecclesiastes*, 2, in order to refute the proposition "that monarchs are bound, under all circumstances and regardless of their sons' intellect and morals, to make them their successors."[236] Section 13 introduces contemporary political theory with a discussion of Grotius' definition of *majestas* or sovereign power, adding authority from the Old Testament and the Early Fathers to prove that sovereign power is inviolable and unimpeachable: "the king's power to command and to act is absolute."[237] Section 14 contends that the monarch is under a positive moral and religious obligation to appoint a successor for the good of society and the state.[238]

Sections 15 and 16 are the two longest sections in the work. Section 15 discusses the origins of hereditary and elective monarchy and the duties of people and monarch under hereditary monarchy. "The people's duty [is] to submit in everything to the king's will," especially in the matter of the succession.[239] An apparent objection in *Judges,* 8 is explained.[240] Section 15 shows how the monarch's wishes may be ascertained if he dies intestate, and concludes by enumerating the monarch's rights and duties, including the appointment of a successor.[241] Section 16 compares and contrasts hereditary and elective monarchy to the advantage of the former.[242] There follow the 47 "examples or instances, which confirm the right and power of parents to appoint their heirs." 41 are taken from secular history, from classical times to the early sixteenth century, followed by 6 examples from Old Testament history.[243]

The Afterword echoes the Foreword, recapitulates the central argument, and stresses the probative effect of the arguments individually and cumulatively. It claims that the work refutes all criticism of the 1722 statute, and, like the Foreword, it brands such critics as malicious or "people of scant intelligence."[244] It also attacks those who criticize the statute on the grounds of its novelty. So much of the modernization of Russia depended on innovation. But the Afterword concludes by pointing out that in fact the statute follows numerous precedents.[245]

9. The publication and history of *Pravda voli monarshei*

Pravda voli monarshei was ready in print in Moscow on August 7, 1722.[246] On August 24, in response to Peter's demand, Prokopovich, on behalf of the Synod, sent 10 copies from Moscow to the Tsar (then in Astrakhan, directing his war against Persia), for approval and permission to publish the work.[247] Peter returned to Moscow on 4 December.[248] On 24 December, in personal attendance at the Synod, he

authorized immediate publication. His order was formally implemented by a decree of the Synod on 28 December.[249] The book was thus ready for distribution and sale in 1723. There were two versions: one in the traditional "church", "ecclesiastical" or "cyrillic" type, the other in the new "civil" (*grazhdanskii*) type introduced by Peter in 1708.[250] The latter version ran to 1200 copies, between four and six times the normal print-run for the time and striking evidence of the importance which Peter attached to the distribution of this work.[251] By May 1726 550 copies had been sold and 50 distributed free of charge.[252]

Pravda voli monarshei also appeared in an anonymous German translation, published at Berlin in 1724 under the imprint of Ambrosius Haude, official publisher to the Prussian Academy of Sciences, as *Das Recht der Monarchen, in willkühriger Bestellung der Reichsfolge*.[253] Copies of this translation found their way to Russia in large numbers,[254] doubtless intended for the use of the German nobility of the new Baltic provinces and for that of the many Germans serving as officers in the Russian army and administration.

Important as it was during the last two years of Peter's reign, *Pravda voli monarshei* was deemed even more important as a document of state after his death. Whatever the criticism of his person, the legitimacy of his own title to the throne was not normally in question. It was otherwise with his successors. The Statute on the succession proved a *damnosa hereditas*, which condemned Russia to chronic constitutional uncertainty, sparked off a series of succession crises in 1725, 1727 and 1730, and cast its shadow across the remainder of the century.

The statute was invoked by Peter's two immediate successors as proof of their title to the throne. On his death on January 28, 1725, his widow Catherine was proclaimed empress by the Senate, Synod and *generalitet*. Her accession was secured by the assembled guards regiments, speedily summoned by Menshikov and Tolstoi (with the approval of Prokopovich) in order to forestall possible counteraction in

the cause of Piotr Alekseevich by his "legitimist" supporters among the Golitsyns and Dolgorukies. Formally, however, Catherine's accession was presented as if she had been designated as successor by Peter in accordance with the Statute of 1722.[255]

Certainly, without that sanction her legal claims were weak, and they were soon questioned in several anonymous letters found at St Petersburg and elsewhere.[256] The newly established Supreme Privy Council thought it necessary to counter these in strength; and in a personal decree (*immenoi ukaz*) of 21 April 1726, Catherine not only insisted on her right to appoint a successor under the 1722 statute, but also ordered publication of a second impression of *Pravda Voli Monarshei*.[257] This appeared at Moscow in July in "church" type,[258] and at St Petersburg in August in "civil" type.[259] together with Catherine's decree affirming Peter's law, which it described as "the permanent (*vechnyi*) statute on the succession to the Russian Empire."[260] Authors and distributors of the anonymous letters, denounced as "thieves and perjurers", were threatened with a solemn anathema, which, when they could not be identified, was duly drawn up by Prokopovich and published on 2 July, 1726. The usual rewards were offered to informers.[261]

Originally, the Synod authorized publication of 1200 copies, the same number as were printed for the first edition. The Senate, however, decided on a far larger circulation. The print-run of this second edition was enormous, fourteen times greater than the already exceptional first edition ordered by Peter. In all, 19,051 copies of *Pravda voli monarshei* were printed, 14,031 at Moscow, 5,101 at St Petersburg. Orders were given for its distribution throughout the empire and for its public recitation in all parish churches and monasteries after mass on Sundays and holy days. How far these orders were carried out may be doubted. Less than 3000 copies were distributed to the provinces.[262]

On 7 May 1727, in a manifesto issued on the accession as Peter II of the eleven-year-old Piotr Alekseevich, son of the Tsarevich Aleksei, reference was again made to the statute of 1722, Peter having been named as successor by Catherine in her will.[263] Two months later, however, a decree of the Supreme Privy Council of 26 July formally reinstated the principle of succession by primogeniture, implicitly represented Peter's accession as having taken place by right of birth, abrogated the Statute on the succession and ordered the suppression of named official publications prejudicial to the reputation of his late father and his grandmother, Evdokiia.[264] By implication these proscribed publications included *Pravda voli monarshei*. The book, in Consett's words, was "called in, and forbid to be sold or read in Russia."[265] 14,507 copies were handed in by June 1728, including 63 copies of the German translation.[266]

Peter II died suddenly of smallpox in January 1730. The last direct male descendant of Peter the Great, he had not appointed a successor. This unexpected event sparked off a fresh constitutional crisis, culminating in the abortive attempt by the *verkhovniki* to impose some form of limited monarchy on Anna Ivanovna. Notoriously, Anna, encouraged by the bulk of the gentry, who were assembled in Moscow for the coronation of Peter II, reneged on the terms which she had signed as a condition of her accession, and assumed absolute power. The succession law of 1722 was duly reinstated by a decree of 17 December 1731;[267] and it was invoked by Anna to justify her nomination of candidates which bypassed the direct descendants of Peter the Great (including his younger daughter, Elizabeth).

No direct reference to the 1722 Statute or to *Pravda voli monarshei* appears in subsequent eighteenth-century legislation, though the line of succession remained as arbitrary and unpredictable as before. The Empress Elizabeth (1741-1761), ousting the successor appointed by Anna Ivanovna, appeared to revert to the pre-1722 principle of propinquity of blood in claiming her "lawful right" to the throne as her parents' daughter.[268] In 1742

she invoked the same principle in nominating as her successor her nephew, Peter, Duke of Holstein, though she may later have contemplated replacing him as heir by his son, Paul. Acceding as tsar Peter III on her death in 1761, Peter reverted to the 1722 prerogative, reserving to himself the right to appoint his heir, (though he nominated no-one and may have considered excluding Paul),[269] before he in turn was dethroned six months later by his wife Catherine, who acceded as Catherine II (1762-1796). Catherine, though originally lacking any legal claim to the throne, came to acquire a *de facto* title. In her accession-manifesto she named Paul as her "lawful" successor.[270] In the late 1780s, however, she may have contemplated nominating her grandson, Alexander (later tsar Alexander I) in his stead. In August 1787 she approvingly read to her secretary Khrapovitskii an excerpt from *Pravda voli monarshei* and from the 1722 statute.[271]

A reprint of the second edition of *Pravda voli monarshei* was published at St Petersburg in 1788 by Fiodor Tumanskii as part of a series of collected documents on Peter the Great.[272] The same year, Paul drafted an act of succession, which he translated into law on the day of his coronation, 5 April 1797. By virtue of this *Decree* (*uchrezhdenie*) *concerning the Imperial Family*, the law of 1722 was implicitly repealed, and the succession to the throne was placed on the basis of hereditary male succession by primogeniture in the Romanov family.[273] *Pravda voli monarshei* was republished in 1830, from the second edition, in volume VI of the *Complete Collection of Laws of the Russian Empire*.[274]

10. The present text and translation

The present Russian text is reconstituted from the edition published in "church" type by the Moscow press in July 1726, (hereafter referred to as "M"). To this there are two exceptions. First, the title page is reproduced from the

description of the title of the first edition in T. A. Bykova and M. M. Gurevich, *Opisanie izdanii napechatannykh pri Petre I. Svodnyi katalog. Opisanie izdanii grazhdanskoi pechati (1708-ianvar' 1725g.)* [Inventory of editions published under Peter I. Union catalogue. Inventory of editions of the civil press (1709-January 1725)], (Moscow/Leningrad: Akademiia Nauk SSSR, 1955), p. 381. Second, Catherine I's decree of 21 April 1726, which follows the Statute on the succession in M., is here omitted. The pagination of M (93 pages, excluding the 1726 decree) is indicated in square brackets. Stress accents are omitted. Words abbreviated in M are given in full, e.g. *gosudari* for *gdri*. Arabic numerals replace Slavonic numerals.

Fidelity to the original has been the guiding editorial principle. However, spelling normally follows the orthographical conventions in use in Russia since 1918: for example, *velikogo*, not *velikago*, *edinye pomianutye obychai*, not *edinyia pomianutyia obychai*. Modern orthography has been the more readily followed where M alternates arbitrarily between two different spellings, e.g. *zdelat'/ sdelat', samoderzhtov/samoderzhtsev, detem/detiam*; and where confusion might arise between instrumental singular and dative plural, e.g. *synom/synam, roditelem/roditeliam*. Where M varies somewhat more substantially, e.g. between *delakh* and *delekh*, *vole* and *voli* (dative), the conventional case-ending is preferred. Neuter plural possessive pronouns and adjectival and participial endings in *a* or *ia* are retained where consistency requires, e.g. *v nasha vremena*; *ot kotorykh vsia prochaia rozhdenna byti skazuetsia*. Plural endings in *i* or *ii* are retained, e.g. *dolzhni, grazhdanskii, frantsuszstii, rimstii, politicheskii filosofi*. Likewise no attempt is made to "correct" such usages as *mnozi, v knize, mesiatsei, vostal, kharaktir, neschasliv, prezhdnei, nuzhdnye, rassuzhden'mi*. Tumanskii's 1788 text (hereafter referred to as "T") is followed in inserting "soft signs" where necessary (these sometimes appear, but are more often omitted in M, (e.g. *vol'no* and *volno*), and by inserting the "hard sign," e.g. *neot'emlemoi*,

iz'iavleniiu. The spelling of proper names in M is retained, e.g. *Sanktpiterburkh, v Afinekh, v Pol'shchi, Arkadia i Onoria* (and by analogy, *istoria*).

There are five substantial textual emendations. *Nekogda* (p. 164) has been amended to *Nikogda. Karolem*, an obvious error, has been amended to *Karolom* (p. 210) and likewise *Ne ravensto* to *Neravenstvo* (p. 218). *Banitom* (p. 260) has been amended to *banditom*, (nominative *bandit*), from the Italian *bandito* (originally = exiled or outlawed), which is vouched for by Max Vasmer, *Russisches Etymologisches Wörterbuch* vol. 1, (Heidelberg: Universitätsverlag, 1953), p. 51. Following the 1830 text, ia is amended to *i* in *Ty li ia postavliashi tsariami?* (p. 178)

Punctuation follows modern convention. In M, bibliographical references appear variously in the text, in the margin, or in both text and margin; in the present edition, following the German translation of 1724, all marginal references are incorporated in the text. Two explanatory headings, each relegated to a margin in M, are likewise here incorporated in the text. Paragraphing sometimes follows that of the German translation. Other paragraphs have been further subdivided.

A few minor numerical inaccuracies in bibliographical references have been amended, some in accordance with T, some in accordance with the epitome of the work published in the *Acta eruditorum* in 1723, others in accordance with the German translation of 1724.[275]

The primary importance of *Pravda voli monarshei* being that of a historical document, the first aims of the translation have been accuracy and clarity. These are not always mutually compatible or easily compatible with readability. As with the German translation, the aim has been to render the original faithfully (*getreulich*); and the German translation has been found useful in elucidating particular expressions, though it too occasionally errs. Biblical citations are from the Authorized Version, with occasional adaptations to correspond with variants in the Russian text.

71

NOTES TO INTRODUCTION

1.   Solov'ev, Book 9, p. 321; Voskresenskii, pp. 155-161. *Pravda voli monarshei* itself was an important early contribution to the petrine mythology. The title-page, Foreword, introductory section and Afterword cite Peter's new titles. For the significance of the imperial title, see Isabel de Madariaga, "Tsar' into Emperor: the title of Peter the Great," to appear in *Royal and Republican. Sovereignty in early modern Europe*, (eds.) R. Oresko, G. C. Gibbs and H. M. Scott,(Cambridge: Cambridge University Press, 1995).
2.   Martinus A. Wes, *Classics in Russia 1700-1855*, (Leiden: E. J. Brill, 1992), p. 34; Pekarskii, pp. 528-530.
3.   M. M. Bogoslovskii, *Oblastnaia reforma Petra Velikogo* [Peter the Great's Provincial Reform], (Moscow: Imperatorskoe Obshchestvo Istorii i Drevnostei Rossiiskikh pri Moskovskom Universitete, 1902), p. 18. Cf. B. I. Syromiatnikov, *"Reguliarnoe" gosudarstvo Petra Pervogo i ego ideologiia* [Peter the First's 'Regulated' state and its ideology], (Moscow: Akademiia Nauk SSSR, 1943); Marc Raeff, *The Well-Ordered Police State. Social and Institutional Change through Law in the Germanies and Russia 1600-1800*, (London: Yale University Press, 1983). The expression '*reguliarnye gosudarstva*' appears in the manifesto of 3 February 1718 (see p. 298).
4.   *Memoirs of Peter Henry Bruce, Esq. A Military Officer in the services of Prussia, Russia and Great Britain*,(Dublin: J. and R. Byrn, 1783), p. 267. The French ambassador Campredon reported the following day that the Statute was proclaimed "en présence d'une très nombreuse assemblée" in Red Square, "où l'on voit encore les têtes des principaux complices du feu czarevitz" (Archives du Ministère des Affaires Etrangères, Correspondance Politique, Russie, vol. 12/65).
5.   Campredon observed of Peter that "le plus intéressant de ses soins est d'établir solidement la

succession de sa couronne," (9 January, 1724, *Sbornik*, vol. 52, p. 145). Historical and biblical precedents for Peter's dilemma over the succession are listed in *Pravda voli monarshei* pp. 244-73.

6.   I. T. Pososhkov, quoted by V. Ulanov, "Oppozitsiia Petru Velikomu"[Opposition to Peter the Great], in *Tri Veka. Rossiia ot smuty do nashego vremeni. Istoricheskii sbornik* [Three Centuries. Russia from the Time of Troubles to Our Own Time. A Historical Collection], (ed.) V. V. Kallash, vol. III, (Moscow: izd. t-va I. D. Sytina, 1912), p. 69.

7.   Bruce, p. 231. Cf. Peter to Aleksei, 11 October, 1715 (Ustrialov, p. 348). An almost identical expression appears in *Pravda voli monarshei*, p. 243. Cf. his manifesto of 3 February 1718 (p. 313), where Peter also declared the deprivation to be irrevocable, "even if there should not remain a single person in our family after us." For a sympathetic view of Peter's predicament by one of his "fledglings," Z. D. Mishukov, see Prince M. M. Shcherbatov, *On the Corruption of Morals in Russia*, (ed.) A. Lentin, (Cambridge: Cambridge University Press: 1969), pp. 146-149.

8.   Ustrialov, pp. 346-350.

9.   Appendix 4, pp. 302-15. The British Ambassador at the Hague, on the basis of an account from De Bie, the Dutch resident in Russia, reported that "This act has been performed with all possible solemnity... The Czarewitz was brought in without his sword, fell on his knees, begged for pardon, wept bitterly, and delivered the Czar his act of renunciation, acknowledging himself unworthy of the Crown."(Whitworth to Lord Sunderland, 11 March, 1718, British Library, Whitworth Papers, Add. Mss. 37,367/194. (Cf. report of the Danish minister, Tyrholm, 10/21 February, 1718, which includes Peter's speech, Rigarkivet, Copenhagen, TKUA Speciel Del. B49. Relationes aus Rusland). The *Oprechte Haerlemse Dingsdaegse Courant*, No. 21, reporting from St Petersburg on 29 April, 1718, confirmed that the oath of allegiance was also obligatory on

foreign merchants resident in Russia, including "the English and Dutch, despite all their protests and remonstrances." The oath for German officers in the Russian service and other German residents was headed *Iuramentum, welches die sowohl in Ihre Grosz-Czarischen Majest. Diensten stehende als andere hier lebende Teutsche und auswärtige Nationen allhier in ihren Kirchen Öffentlich abgelegt. Nachdem durch ein Manifest von unsern allergnädigsten Czaaren und Herren.* 11,000 copies were printed of the manifesto on Aleksei's exclusion from the succession, 27,770 copies of the oath of allegiance to Piotr Petrovich and 1020 copies of the oath in German (Pekarskii, p. 665; T. A. Bykova and M. M. Gurevich, *Opisanie izdanii grazhdanskoi pechati* (*1708-ianvar' 1725g.*), p. 488.

10.   Even in 1716, Peter doubted whether Aleksei would abide by a promise to renounce the throne; and Aleksei himself predicted civil war between his supporters and those of Piotr Petrovich after Peter's death. (Ustrialov, pp. 51, 501).As for retiring to a monastery, one of Aleksei's advisers observed: "A cowl is not nailed to the head: it can be taken off" (Solov'ev, Book 9, p. 145). In 1718 De Bie reported rumours of a plot to place Aleksei on the throne after Peter's death notwithstanding his renunciation. (24 February 1718, The Hague, Algemeen Rijksarchief, Archief Staaten Generaal, 17a/7368. Cf. his report to the States General, 25 July, 1718, in Ustrialov, p. 553).

11.   Ustrialov, p. 500. According to Vockerodt, Secretary to the Prussian embassy at St Petersburg, Aleksei's intentions represented the hopes expressed by many Russians after Peter's death. (*Modernization of Russia under Peter I and Catherine II*, (ed.) Basil Dmytryshyn, (New York: John Wiley, 1974), pp. 42-43). Reporting Peter's words on the occasion of Aleksei's renunciation of the succession, Tyrholm quotes him as saying that the Russian people, "sous le règne de cet indigne Prince [Aleksei], en cas qu'il y fût parvenu, serait infailliblement devenu le mépris et la risée de toutes les nations voisines:

déjà la nation, contre laquelle je suis depuis 18 ans en guerre ouverte [i.e. Sweden], comptait-elle sur son règne, comme sur un temps de dieu-donné, pour rétablir ses affaires délabrées, au dépens de la Grande Russie."(10/21 February, 1718, Rigsarkivet, Copenhagen, TKUA, Speciel Del.B.49. Relationen aus Rusland). On hearing rumours of Peter's ill-health in the autumn of 1718, the British ambassador in Paris observed: "s'il [Peter] venait à mourir, la paix du Nord serait aisée." (Stair to Robethon, British Library, Stowe MSS, 321, vol. X, f. 229). In the Statute on the succession, Peter emphasizes his "concern for the preservation" of a Russia "today greatly expanded, as is evident to all." (p. 131).

12.   According to Peter's manifesto of 25 June, 1718, the death-penalty was mandatory even for "those who have conspired only in thought to rebel, or have had a bare intention against the life of the sovereign, to usurp his empire" ("Manifesto of the Criminal Process of the Czarevich Alexei Petrowitz, judged at St Petersburg by order of his Czarish Majesty, the 25th day of June, 1718," in F. C. Weber, *The Present State of Russia*, volume II, (London: W. and J. Innys, 1723), p. 200). Vockerodt takes a sceptical view of Aleksei's culpability towards Peter. The Tsarevich "hat sich... niemals das geringste Complot oder Conspiration wider seine Person oder Souveraineté geäussert. Dann hochgedachter Kronprinz hatte nie weder die Intention, noch die Courage gehabt, einen Anschlag gegen seines Vaters Regierung oder Leben zu formiren, und niemals etwas mehrers gesuchet, als sich gegen seines Vaters Hass und Verfolgung in Sicherheit zu setzen," *Russland unter Peter dem Grossen. Nach den handschriftlichen Berichten J. G. Vockerodt's*, (ed.) E. Herrmann, (Leipzig: Duncker & Humblot, 1872), pp. 29-30.

13.   The official cause of death was apoplexy. Aleksei was reported as having taken communion and begged Peter's forgiveness before he died. (Solov'ev, book 9, pp. 188-9; *Ob'iavlenie rozysknogo dela i suda, po ukazu ego Tsarskogo Velichestva, na tsarevicha Alekseia Petrovicha, v*

Sanktpiterburkhe otpravlennogo, i po ukazu ego Velichestva v pechat', dlia izvestiia vsenarodnogo, [A declaration concerning the investigation and trial of the Tsarevich Aleksei Petrovich, held by order of His Czarish Majesty at St Petersburg, and published by His Majesty's order for general information], (St Petersburg: June 25, 1718). (For an English version of Peter's rescript on Aleksei's death, see John Motley, *The History of the Life of Peter the First, Emperor of Russia,* (London: J. Read, 1739), pp. 289-290). Cf. *Oprechte Haerlemse Dingsdaegse Courant,* 1718, No. 31. Aleksei's death did not affect celebrations attended by Peter and Catherine the same day to mark the anniversary of the battle of Poltava.

14.   5 May, 1719, Public Record Office, Chancery Lane, State Papers 91/9/152. "The Czar took the loss of his only son so much at heart," Jefferyes reported, "that he run his head against the wall of the chamber and was seized with two convulsive fits" (8 May 1719, State Papers 91/9/156. Jefferyes' forecast concerning Catherine proved correct. F. C. von Bergholz, Peter's chamberlain, claimed that Catherine was delivered of a still-born son in September 1721, 5 months before the Statute on the succession. (Lindsey Hughes, "A note on the children of Peter the Great," *Study Group on Eighteenth-Century Russia Newsletter,* No. 21, 1993, pp. 10-16). The death of Piotr Petrovich was seen by some as a visitation on Peter for his treatment of the Tsarevich Aleksei.

15.   Bruce, p. 232.

16.   5 May, 1719, State Papers 91/9/153. In January 1720 there was much speculation in the British press about Peter's plans for the succession. (J. Black, "Russia and the British Press in the early eighteenth century," *Study Group on Eighteenth-Century Russia Newsletter,* No. 11, 1983, p. 20).

17.   Solov'ev, book IX, p. 145.

18.   Voskresenskii, p. 483. Even during the life of Piotr Petrovich, Peter reserved to himself the possibility of appointing other successors. (Voskresenskii, p. 454). Books

published at Moscow between 1700 and 1721 included an entry referring to the imperial family. This indicated Aleksei as heir apparent until 1717, when Piotr Petrovich and Piotr Alekseevich were also included. After Aleksei renounced the succession in February 1718, Piotr Petrovich (described as "the most noble hereditary sovereign"), headed the list, followed by Aleksei (until his death in June 1718) and Piotr Alekseevich. After the death of Piotr Petrovich in May 1719, the name of Piotr Alekseevich continued to feature until 1720, when, in the prayer recited in church for the health of the imperial family, his name appeared below that of his aunts Anna and Elizabeth, Peter's daughters by Catherine and both born out of wedlock. (Pekarskii, pp. 386-390).

19.   B. Titlinov, "Feofan Prokopovich," in *Russkii Biograficheskii Slovar'* [Russian Biographical Dictionary] (*Iablonskii-Fomin*), (St Petersburg: Imperatorskaia Akademiia Nauk, 1913), p. 446; "F. C. von Bergholz, Großfürstlichen Oberkammerherrns Tagebuch, welches er in Rußland von 1721 bis 1725 als holsteinischer Kammerjunker geführt hat," in *Magazin für die neue Historie und Geographie*, (ed.) A. F. Büsching, vol. XX, (Halle: 1785), p. 392.

20.   The Statute on the succession, wrote Bruce (pp. 267-268), "struck a damp on the spirits of everybody, when they reflected on the undoubted title of the young prince Peter, his Majesty's grandson and only remaining male heir of the imperial family, who was as promising and hopeful a young prince as any of his age could be." The oath was first sworn in the Cathedral of the Assumption in Moscow by 9 members of the Senate and 2 members of the Synod, one of whom was Prokopovich. (Voskresenskii, pp. 176-177). Bruce, who participated in the administration of the oath in Moscow, testifies to the thoroughness with which the operation was carried out: "All the officers of our division were ordered to different parishes to administer this oath and see it subscribed; one of the parishes within the city fell to my lot, which, being very numerous, took me no less

than five weeks close attendance, from daylight in the morning till late at night by candle."(Bruce, p. 268). 430 copies of the Statute on the succession and oath of allegiance (and 100 copies in German of the statute and 2200 copies of the oath) were published at St Petersburg; 1200 copies of the statute and oath were published at Moscow. Of the St Petersburg print-run, 226 of the Russian copies and all the German copies were distributed; of the Moscow print-run, 570 copies were distributed (Pekarskii, p. 665. There is a handwritten German version of the statute in the Whitworth Papers, British Library, Add. Mss. 37, 388/177, and in the Archives du Ministère des Affaires Etrangères, Correspondance Politique, Russie, vol. 12/43-45; cf. f. 67 for a French translation).

21.   p. 134; V. O. Kliuchevskii, *Sochineniia* [Works], vol. IV, p. 211; Ditiatin, "Verkhovnaia vlast' v Rossii XVIII stoletiia" [Supreme power in 18th-century Russia], *Stat'i po istorii russkogo prava* [Articles on the history of Russian law], (St Petersburg: izd. O. N. Popovoi, 1895), p. 623. The imperial historiographer, Gerhard Friedrich Müller, commented c.1760 that Peter was free to appoint or debar his successor at will, "suivant la constitution fondamentale de l'empire" (E. Shmurlo, *Vol'ter i ego kniga o Petre Velikom* [Voltaire and his book on Peter the Great], (Prague: Orbis, 1929), p. 230).

22.   Immediately after the promulgation of the 1722 Statute there was speculation that Peter would marry his elder daughter Anna to the Duke of Holstein (as indeed happened in 1724) and name the latter as his successor. (Whitworth Papers, Add.Mss. 37,388/190/206/235/248/266-7/270/276/314/346/369). (For further speculation in 1724, see report of the Prussian ambassador, Mardefeld in *Sbornik*, vol. 15, pp. 237-241, and of the Saxon resident, Lefort, 15 May, 1724, in *Sbornik*, vol. 3, pp. 374-375).

23.   *Pravda voli monarshei* declares daughters to be eligible to succeed in the absence of sons if the monarch dies intestate. (p. 221). This would have allowed for the

succession of one of Peter's daughters, Anna or Elizabeth, after his death. The book does not, however, include the monarch's widow among its examples of likely candidates. This suggests that Peter was not, in 1722, thinking of nominating Catherine to succeed him. For Catherine's coronation and speculation on its significance in 1724, see Campredon's reports of 1 and 26 May, 1724, (*Sbornik*, vol. 52, pp. 212-213, 220), and Lefort's report of 15 May, 1724, (*Sbornik*, vol. 3, pp. 374-375); cf. Richard S. Wortman, *Scenarios of Power. Myth and Ceremony in Russian Monarchy. vol. 1. From Peter the Great to the death of Nicholas I* (Princeton: Princeton University Press, 1995, pp. 69-75). In the manifesto issued on her accession in January 1725, Catherine declared that by crowning her in 1724 Peter clearly intended her to succeed him (P.S.Z., vol. VII, No. 4643, p. 410). However, her chances of nomination may in reality have been adversely affected by the disgrace and execution of her chamberlain and favourite, William Mons, in November 1724; and in a secret clause of the marriage contract concluded on the betrothal of his daughter, Anna, to the Duke of Holstein in November 1724, Peter reserved the right to nominate as heir to the throne of Russia any male offspring of the marriage. (Korsakov, *Votsarenie imperatritsy Anny Ioannovny. Istoricheskii Etiud* [The accession of the Empress Anna Ioannovna. A historical study], (Kazan: tipografiia imperatorskogo universiteta, 1880), p. 95). The historian M. M. Shcherbatov claimed that Peter never intended Catherine to succeed him (*On the Corruption of Morals in Russia*, pp. 158-9).

24.   pp. 57-61, 65.

25.   After Russia's annexation of the Ukraine from Poland in 1654, Kiev became the main centre of higher learning and culture in late seventeenth- and early eighteenth-century Russia. The Kiev Theological Academy, influenced both by Counter-Reformation Catholic thinking and by Protestant theology, served to bring Russia into contact with western philosophy generally. Prokopovich

brought to Russia a knowledge of neo-scholastic philosophy, natural law concepts and contemporary political theory.

26.   James Cracraft, *The Church Reform of Peter the Great*, (London: Macmillan, 1971), p. 54.

27.   J. Tetzner, "Theophan Prokopovic und die russische Frühaufklärung," *Zeitschrift für Slawistik*, iii, 1958, p. 359.

28.   James Cracraft, *The Church Reform of Peter the Great*, pp. 26-27; Marc Raeff, "The Enlightenment in Russia and Russian Thought in the Enlightenment," in *The Eighteenth Century in Russia*, (ed.) J. G. Garrard, (Oxford: the Clarendon Press, 1973), p. 35; Marc Raeff, "Les slaves, les allemands et les 'Lumières'," in *Canadian Slavic Studies*, 1, No. 4 (Winter, 1967), pp. 546-548.

29.   Prokopovich prided himself on his "many sermons and the publication of more than one booklet, in which I zealously and repeatedly teach, how loyal and obedient to their sovereigns subjects must be." (Solov'ev, book X, p. 103).

30.   *Pervoe uchenie otrokam. V nemzhe bukvy i slogi. Tozhe: kratkoe tolkovanie zakonnogo desiatisloviia, molitvy gospodni, simvola very, i deviati blazhenstv* [A children's primer. Containing letters and syllables. Also: a short explanation of the Ten Commandments, the Lord's Prayer, the symbols of faith and the nine beatitudes], (St Petersburg: tipografiia Aleksandro-Nevskogo monastyria, 1720]. Frequently republished, the book was translated by J. T. Philipps as *The Russian Catechism, composed and published by order of the Czar* (London: W. Meadows, 1723). The abbé Jubé (p. 105) described it as "tout Lutherien." According to the *Catechism*, the fifth commandment requires us "to honour and respect not only our natural parents, but those that are in the dignity and place of parents and have any degree of authority over us" (trans. Philipps, p. 100). Of the 16 core sections of *Pravda voli monarshei*, 9 discuss "the duties of parents and children."

31. "Preachers should preach firmly, with arguments from Holy Scripture,... on respect for the authorities, especially the supreme authority of the Tsar," *The Spiritual Regulation of Peter the Great*, (ed.) A. V. Muller, (Seattle: University of Washington Press, 1972), p. 43.

32. Pekarskii, p. 374. See *Rech', kotoruiu derzhavneishego gosudaria tsaria i velikogo kniazia, Petra Velikogo, po dolgom stranstvovanii v tsarstvuiushchii svoi Sanktpeterburg vozvrativshegosia, syn ego velichestva, blagorodneishii gosudar' tsarevich i velikii kniaz', Petr Petrovich, dvoeletnyi mladenets, aki svoimi usty privetstvuet* [A speech with which His Majesty's son, the most noble sovereign tsarevich and Grand Duke, Piotr Petrovich, a lad two years old, as it were greets with his own lips the most mighty sovereign tsar and Grand Duke, Peter the Great, on his return to his capital of St Petersburg, after his long journey], (St Petersburg: 1717); *Slovo pokhval'noe v den' rozhdeniia blagorodneishego gosudaria tsarevicha i velikago kniazia, Petra Petrovicha, nadezhda dobrykh i dolgikh let rossiiskoi monarkhii, syn Bogom dannyi ego tsarskomu presvetleishemu velichestvu, Petru Pervomu* [A sermon to celebrate the birthday of the most noble sovereign tsarevich and Grand Duke, Piotr Petrovich, the Russian monarchy's hope for many good years, the God-given son of his serene Majesty, Peter I], (St Petersburg: 1717); *Rech' k ego tsarskomu velichestvu Petru Pervomu vo vremia ob'iavleniia syna ego velichestva, gosudaria tsarevicha i velikago kniazia Petra Petrovicha, naslednikom vserossiskogo gosudarstva* [A speech to his Czarish Majesty, Peter I, on the occasion of the declaration of his Majesty's son, the sovereign tsarevich and Grand Duke Piotr Petrovich, as successor to the all-Russian state], (St Petersburg: 1718); *Slovo v nedeliu tsvetnuiu o vlasti i chesti tsarskoi* [A sermon during Holy Week on royal authority and honour], (St Petersburg: 1718), translated by H. Lunt as "Sermon on royal authority and honour," in M. Raeff, (ed.) *Russian Intellectual History. An Anthology*, (New York: Harcourt, Brace & World) 1966), pp. 14-30.

Pekarskii (vol. 1, p. 410) took the view that the Manifesto of 3 February, 1718 (Appendix 4) was written either by Prokopovich or by Peter himself.

33. e.g. *Slovo pokhval'noe o batalii poltavskoi* [A sermon in celebration of the battle of Poltava], St Petersburg, 1717; *Slovo pokhval'noe o flotom rossiiskom* [A sermon in celebration of the Russian fleet], St Petersburg, 1720; "Slovo pri nachatii sviateishego pravitel'stvuiushchego Sinoda," [A sermon at the commencement of the Most Holy Governing Synod] in *Slova i rechi Feofana Prokopovicha* [Sermons and speeches of Feofan Prokopovich], vol. II, (St Petersburg: 1761), pp. 63-70; *O voznoshenii imene patriarshego v tserkovnykh molitvakh. Chego radi onoe nyne v tserkvakh rossiiskikh ostavleno* [On the exaltation of the name of the patriarch in church prayers. Why it is now omitted in the Russian churches], St Petersburg, 1721. *Kanon molitvennyi o mnogoletnom zdravii blago- chestiveishego gosudaria nashego tsaria i velikogo kniazia vseia Rossii, Petra Alekseevicha* [A canon for the long-continued health of our most devout sovereign, tsar and grand duke of all Russia, Peter Alekseevich], (St Petersburg: 1721, 1723).

34. The clergy were also liable to take oaths such as the oath of allegiance to the Statute on the succession. Prokopovich stressed that the clergy were a *chin*, like the army and civil service (Pekarskii, vol. 1, p. 485). He justified oath-taking in his *Rassuzhdenie o prisiage ili kliatve. Podobaet li khristianam prisiagat' ili kliatisia vsemogushchim Bogom?* [Consideration on taking an oath or vow. Should Christians take an oath or swear by Almighty God?]

35. P.S.Z., vol. VI, No. 4012.

36. Ustrialov, p. 269.

37. p. 131.

38. pp. 65, 282.

39. p. 121.

40. According to Campredon, "les russes, persuadés... que la couronne appartient de droit au Grand-Duc [Piotr

Alekseevich], légitime héritier de Sa Majesté Czarienne en droite ligne, ne perdraient jamais cette idée, quelque disposition qu'il [Peter] pût faire... L'image de la succession héréditaire a été jusqu'à présent inviolablement observé de proche en proche." (30 July, 1722, *Sbornik*, vol. 49, pp. 129-131). For a more nuanced account of the history of the succession, see M. Zyzykin, *Tsarskaia vlast' i zakon o prestolonasledii v Rossii* [Royal authority and the law of the succession to the throne in Russia], (Sofia: izd. kn. A. A. Liven, 1924, pp. 23ff).

41.   p. 171.

42.   p. 135.

43.   Bruce, p. 268.

44.   p. 137.

45.   Campredon observed: "quelque grande que fût son [Peter's] autorité, c'était une prétention mal fondée de vouloir la conserver en l'autre monde et de prétendre être obéi après sa mort." (30 July, 1722, *Sbornik*, vol. 49, p. 129). Whitworth, formerly British envoy in Russia, now ambassador at Berlin, agreed: "'Tis thought his [Peter's] view now is to settle his succession and his domestic affairs; but as the foundation is like to be strangely lay'd and against all the rules of art, the whole building will be very tottering and may one day fall on the head of the projectors" (Letter to Tilson, 24 March/4 April, 1722, British Library, Whitworth Papers, 37,388/206).

46.   p. 261

47.   Ustrialov, p. 581. On learning, in the course of his flight, that Piotr Petrovich was ill, Aleksei exclaimed: "You see how God acts. My father does his will, and God His." ibid., p. 490.

48.   p. 129

49.   p. 127

50.   p. 137

51.   p. 281

52.   p. 129

53.   P.S.Z., vol. V, No. 2789.

54.   Raeffi, in *Cahiers du monde russe et soviétique*, vol. xxxiv (1-2), 1993, p. 36.

55.   Voskresenskii, p. 150. Peter presented his decision to crown Catherine as an exercize of his personal authority and as a reward for her merit (her help and support during his wars): "by virtue of our God-given sovereignty (*samovlastie*) for such labours on the part of our wife," Manifesto, 15 November, 1723. (Voskresenskii, p. 179-180).

56.   Ustrialov, p. 348.

57.   p. 137.

58.   pp. 123, 127, 137, 245.

59.   pp. 139, 123, 127, 243.

60.   p. 275.

61.   pp. 125, 191.

62.   There were 7 printing-presses in Russia by 1725: the traditional press at Moscow (the former *pechatnyi dvor*, now known as the *moskovskaia tipografiia*, which published *Pravda voli monarshei*); 3 presses at St Petersburg (one each at the Senate and the School of Navigation, for the printing of decrees and other official publications; and one at the monastery of St Alexander Nevskii, for religious publications, e.g. the *Children's Primer*, 1720); and 3 presses for religious publications under the authority of the Synod, at Moscow, Chernigov and Kiev (K. A. Papmehl, *Freedom of Expression in Eighteenth Century Russia*, (The Hague: Martinus Nijhoff, 1971, pp. 6-7).

63.   In August 1725 Ivan Pososhkov was arrested and imprisoned, almost certainly for his unauthorized writing of the *Book on Poverty and Wealth* (*Kniga o skudosti i bogatstve*). He died in prison six months later. (Ivan Pososhkov, *The Book of Poverty and Wealth*, (ed.) A. P. Vlasto and L. R. Lewitter, (London: the Athlone Press, 1987), pp. 9-10). Under the *Spiritual Regulation*, all writings of a religious nature were subject to censorship by the Synod before publication.

64.   P.S.Z., vol. V, No. 2877; cf. vol. V, No. 3479. On anonymous letters directed against Peter's church policy

and his prohibition on beards, see Jacques Jubé, *La Religion, les moeurs et les usages des Moscovites*, (ed.) M. Mervaud, (Oxford: The Voltaire Foundation, 1992), pp. 100, 115. Under Catherine I it was laid down that anonymous letters should be reported to the authorities on pain of death.

65. A manifesto of Peter II of May 1727 (P.S.Z, vol. VII, No. 5084) refers to "those fraudulent and turbulent persons who last year, 1726, in a very perverse manner questioned the legality of this oukaz or edict in a paper dropt in the street." (Cracraft, *For God and Peter the Great. The Works of Thomas Consett, 1723-1729*, p. lii).

66. The monetary reward was just under the annual salary of 2,160 roubles paid in 1723 to a foreign vice-admiral, five times the annual salary of Peter's secretary, A. V. Makarov, or ten times the salary of the artist I. Nikitin in 1721. (*200-letie Kabineta ego imperatorskogo velichestva 1704-1904* [The bicentenary of His Imperial Majesty's Cabinet], (St Petersburg: 1911), pp. 222).

67. pp. 277-81.

68. pp. 125. Cf. Philip Longworth, *The Making of Eastern Europe* (London: Macmillan, 1994), pp. 173, 179-80.

69. In August 1718 Peter complained to the States-General of the unfavourable reports of De Bie, their resident in Russia: "Il fait souvent mention dans ses lettres à la grande disposition des sujets de S[a] M[ajesté] Cz[arienne] à se révolter contre Elle." (Algemeen Rijksarchief, The Hague, Archief Staaten Generaal, 17a 7368, ff. 749-750. Peter ordered his envoys abroad to keep foreign governments informed of his motives in excluding Aleksei from the succession. Forwarding a French translation of his manifesto of 3 February, 1718 to the States-General through his ambassador at the Hague, B. I. Kurakin, on 23 March 1718, Peter stated that he did so "afin que L[eurs] H[autes] P[uissances] soient informées plus précisément des motifs importants que Sa Majesté Zarienne a eus pour établir la succession à la Couronne." He

described the manifesto as "mettant dans tout leur jour la justice et l'importance de ces motifs."(Gemeentelijke Archiefdienst van Amsterdam, Archief Burg, Lands=en Gewestelijk Bestuur, 130). Cf. *Europische Mercurius*, Amsterdam, 1718, pp. 97-98, *Oprechte Haerlemse Dingsdaegse Courant*, 1718, No. 31; *Manifeste du Procez criminel du Czarevitch Alexei Petrovitch, jugé et publié à Saint Petersbourg, le 25 jour de juin (v.st.). Traduit sur l'original russien, et imprimé par ordre de Sa Majesté Czarienne, à la Haye, chez Jean Van Duren, marchand libraire, 1718*, Gementelijke Archiefdienst van Amsterdam; *Manifeste de Sa Majesté Czaarienne, fait à Moscou le 3 février, 1718, à Paris, chez François Fournier, rue St Jacques, 1718*; *Manifeste de Sa Majesté Czarienne, traduit sur l'original en langue russienne, Paris, Relation fidèlle de ce qui s'est passé au sujet du jugement rendu contre le Prince Alexei, et des circonstances de sa mort*, Paris, 1718, Archives du Ministère des Affaires Etrangères, Correspondance Politique, Russie, volume 9/4-5,20. The *Relation fidèlle* took the form of 2 letters from Peter to Baron Schleinitz, his minister plenipotentiary in Paris. Peter advised Schleinitz: "en cas aussi que quelqu'un voulût publier cet événement [the death of Aleksei] d'une manière odieuse, vous aurez en main de quoi détruire et refuter solidement les discours injustes et mal fondés"; *Manifest welches Seine Grosz-Czaarische Majestät Peter Alexewitz etc. bey Dero hohen Anwesenheit in Moscau öffentlich ausgegeben, und zum Druck kommen lassen; so nachgehends nach der hohen Erlaubnisz ins Teutsche übersetzet gedruckt worden. Zu St Petersburg den 4 Martii 1718 in dero Hoff-Buchdruckerey durch Gustaff Enegreen; Ihrer Czaarischen Majestät Herrn Petri Alexiewiz Manifest, warum Sie dero erstgebohrnen Sohn Herrn Alexium Petrowiz der Nachfolge in der Regierung Ihres Reichs unfähig erkläret..*, Moscau, den 3/11, 1718; *Acta, betreffende die Inquisition und Gericht, welches auf Seiner Czaarischen Majest. Befehl über den Czarovicz Alexium Petrovicz in St Petersburg gehegt worden. Auf Befehl*

Hochgedachter Seiner Majestät zu Männiglicher Nachricht den 25 Juni 1718 in den Druck gegeben nachdem Sie ausz Russischer Sprache in die Hoch-Teutsche übersetzet worden. Zu St Petersburg den 25 Juni 1718, in Dero Hofbuchdruckerey durch Gustav Enegreen (Pekarskii, vol. 2, pp. 412, 427; T. A. Bykova and M. M. Gurevich, *Opisanie izdanii nepechatannykh pri Petre I. Svodnyi katalog. Opisanie izdanii grazhdanskoi pechati (1708-ianvar' 1725g.)* [Inventory of editions published under Peter I. Union catalogue. Inventory of editions of the civil press (1708-January 1725], (Moscow/Leningrad: Akademiia Nauk SSSR, 1955), pp. 488-9. Cf. K. R. Minzloff, *Pierre le Grand dans la littérature étrangère*, (St Petersburg: I. I. Glasounow, 1872, pp. 424-429, which includes Dutch and Polish versions).

70.   p. 127.

71.   *Acta Eruditorum Lipsiae*, 1723 an. mensis Aug., pp. 348-353.

72.   *Das Recht der Monarchen in willkühriger Bestellung der Reichsfolge... aus der Rußischen Sprache getreulich ins Teutsche übersetzt, Berlin, bey Ambrosius Haude, Kön. Preuß. und der Societät der Wissenschafften priviligirten Buchhändler,* 1724.

73.   Consett to Lord Townshend, 17 July, 1725, State Papers 91/9/407. Consett's "epitome" was probably that published in the *Acta Eruditorum*, Leipzig, August, 1723. In his letter, Consett assures Lord Townshend that the Bishop of London would forward the epitome to Townshend "upon the first information of your Lordship's pleasure to read it."

74.   In a decree of 1713, Peter declared the need "to explain exactly what the interests of state (*interesy gosudarstvennye*) are in order to make people understand them" (P.S.Z., vol. V, No. 2673). He ordered his manifesto of 3 February 1718 on the exclusion of the Tsarevich Aleksei from the succession to be published "for the information of all the people" (*dlia vsenarodnogo izvestiia*, p. 315). The title-page of *Pravda voli monarshei* states that the work is

intended "for the benefit of honest but ignorant persons." The second edition published at St Petersburg in 1726 included a warning that it was written "so that if anyone opposes it, he should not be able to plead ignorance to excuse his malice" (Pekarskii, p. 574).

75.   G. Maker, *Publishing, Printing, and the Origins of Intellectual Life in Russia 1700-1800*, (Princeton, New Jersey: Princeton University Press, 1985), p. 24; N. I. Pavlenko, "Petr I (k izucheniiu sotsial'no-politicheskikh vzgliadov" [Peter I (towards the study of his socio-political views], in *Rossiia v period reform Petra I* [Russia in the period of the reforms of Peter I], (ed.) N. I. Pavlenko, (Moscow: Akademiia Nauk, 1973), p. 85.

76.   On Peter's contribution to the *Military Statute* (1716), see Latkin, p. 19, and to the *Naval Statute* (1720), see N. I. Pavlenko, "Petr I" [Peter I], pp. 86-87. The *General Regulation* of 1720 underwent 12 drafts, 9 of which include Peter's amendments. (*Ocherki istorii SSSR. Period feodalizma. Rossiia v pervoi chetverti XVIIIv. Preobrazovaniia Petra I* [Outlines of the history of the USSR. The Period of Feudalism. Russia in the first quarter of the 18th century. The Reforms of Peter I], (ed.) B. B. Kafengauz and N. I. Pavlenko, (Moscow: Akademiia Nauk SSSR), 1954, p. 316). In 1721 Peter was simultaneously engaged in drafting his Admiralty regulations and editing P. P. Shafirov's *Discourse* on the war with Sweden. (N. I. Pavlenko, "Petr I" [Peter I], pp. 85, 86-87).

77.   Success in distributing these publications outside St Petersburg was variable. 1,937 copies of the manifesto on the exclusion from the succession by the Tsarevich Aleksei, printed at St Petersburg, were disposed of, but only half of the Moscow print-run; all copies of the oath to Piotr Petrovich printed at St Petersburg, but only 828 of the Moscow print-run. (Pekarskii, pp. 664-5).

78.   N. I. Pavlenko, "Idei absoliutizma v zakonodatel'stve XVIIIv" [Ideas of absolutism in 18th-century legislation], in *Absoliutizm v Rossii (XVII-XVIIIvv.). Sbornik statei*

[Absolutism in Russia (17th-18th centuries). A collection of articles], (Moscow: Nauka, 1964), pp. 61-65.

79.   A. Liutsh, "Russkii absoliutizm XVIII veka" [18th-century Russian absolutism], in *Itogi XVIII veka v Rossii* [Results of the 18th century in Russia], (ed.) A. Liutsh, V. Zommer and A. Lipovskii, (Moscow: tipografiia t-va I. D. Sytina, 1910), p. 28.

80.   See Appendix 4, pp. 299, 311.

81.   Appendix 4, p. 311. According to Tyrholm (report of 10/21 February, 1718), Peter declared that he had sought to give Aleksei "une éducation non seulement conforme à sa naissance, mais conforme à mes vues par rapport au bien de l'état et à la gloire de la nation russe." In his manifesto of 3 February, 1718, Peter cited Aleksei's unwillingness to fulfil his military and administrative duties; his association with anti-social elements (*nepotrebnye i podlye liudi*); his flight abroad, bringing disgrace on his father; and his slanderous remarks against Peter.

82.   Ustrialov, p. 350.

83.   pp. 135-7

84.   Cynthia H. Whittaker, "The Reforming Tsar: the Redefinition of Autocratic Duty in Eighteenth-Century Russia," *Slavic Review*, 51, No. 1 (Spring 1992), pp. 77-87.

85.   p. 137.

86.   See Appendix 1, p. 289. G. Gurvich goes too far in my opinion in claiming (p. 37) that "the centre of gravity of the whole thesis [of *Pravda voli monarshei*] lies in its rational arguments," as opposed to its reliance on scriptural authority.

87.   In section 13 Chrysostom, Jerome, Ambrose, Arnobius and Theodor Balsamon are quoted extensively for their glosses on Psalm 50, to support the proposition of "perfect obedience to the king" (p. 193-5; and see section 8, Chrysostom on Colossians, 1). Sumner Benson exaggerates therefore in claiming that *Pravda voli monarshei* "used scriptural references almost to the exclusion of Orthodox patristic writings in establishing the Christian obligation

of obedience," 'The role of western political thought in Petrine Russia', *Canadian-American Slavic Studies*, 8, No. 2 (Summer, 1974), p. 268.

88.   pp. 245, 149, 265, 271.

89.   p. 235. Cf. Bossuet, "La politique tirée des propres paroles de l'Ecriture sainte," in J. B. Bossuet, *Textes choisis et commentés*, (ed.) H. Bremond, (Paris: Plon, 1913), vol. II), p. 201.

90.   I. I. Ditiatin, "Verkhovnaia vlast' v Rossii XVIII stoletiia" [Supreme power in 18th-century Russia], *Stat'i po istorii russkogo prava* [Articles on the history of Russian law], (St Petersburg: izd. O. N. Popovoi, 1895), p. 592. It is not possible to agree with Cynthia Whittaker (p. 83) that Peter "had no use for theories of divine right"; cf. footnotes 55, 99, 118 and 119 for official allusions to his divine-right and sacrosanct attributes. (Cf. R. Stupperich, *Staatsgedanke und Religionspolitik Peters des Großen*, (Berlin: Osteuropäische Foschungen, neue Folge 1, vol. 21, 1936), pp. 26-27)

91.   pp. 275-7.

92.   Cracraft, *The Church Reform of Peter the Great*, pp. 22-23. The Saxon resident, Lefort, noted of Peter in 1721: "Il fait ses dévotions plus attentivement qu'à l'ordinaire avec des *mea culpa*, génuflexions et beaucoup de baisers en terre," (S. Platonov, *Petr Velikii* [Peter the Great], (Paris: izd. t-va 'N. P. Karbasnikov', 1927), p. 110). In 1723 Campredon noted Peter's regular attendance at matins, "ce qu'il pratique toutes les veilles des grandes festes et les dimanches, se donnant la peine de chanter avec les officians pour les accoutumer à l'exactitude et de marquer en même tems en sa personne la fonction du Patriarche, dont il a supprimé la dignité" (Correspondance Politique, Russie, vol. 13/283).

93.   p. 133. In 1730, when it was sought to change the oath of allegiance, removing all mention of absolute monarchy, Prokopovich, addressing the Synod and other senior clergy, pointed out (in his own words) "that an oath was a serious matter and that eternal damnation awaited

whomsoever swore to anything contrary to his conscience, or which he did not wish for or believe in," quoted in James Cracraft, "The Succession Crisis of 1730: A View from the Inside," *Canadian-American Slavic Studies*, vol. 12, No. 1, (Spring 1978), p. 65.

94.   See, e.g. *The Prerogative of Primogeniture, shewing that the Right of Succession to an Hereditary Empire depends not upon Grace, etc., but only upon Birthright... Written on occasion of the Czar of Muscovy's Reasons in his late Manifesto for the Disherison of his Eldest Son from the Succession to the Crown. To which is added the manifesto itself,* (London: W. Boreham, 1718). The book drew on arguments from divine and natural law to oppose "this fanatical doctrine of excluding a right heir from the Crown." In Moscow, Ilarion Dokukin, a sub-deacon, executed in 1718 for declining to swear allegiance to Piotr Petrovich, justified his refusal by referring to a theological work of Gregory Nazianzus. (Solov'ev, book 9, p. 178). However, for a work by a German jurist defending Aleksei's disinheritance on grounds of natural law, see G. S. Treuer, *Untersuchung nach dem Recht der Natur wie weit ein Fürst Macht habe seinen erstgebohrnen Printzen von der Nachfolge in der Regierung auszuschliessen,* (Wolffenbüttel: 1718).

95.   p. 213-17.

96.   Marker, p. 31.

97.   Marc Raeff, "La noblesse et le discours politique sous le règne de Pierre le Grand," *Cahiers du monde russe et soviétique,* vol. xxxiv (1-2), 1993, p. 40.

98.   p. 145.

99.   p. 281, For a description of Peter's acceptance of the imperial title at St Petersburg in October 1721 and of visual symbolism to mark this during his visit to Moscow in January 1722, see "F. C. von Bergholz, Großfürstlichen Oberkammerherrns Tagebuch, welches er in Rußland von 1721 bis 1725 als holsteinischer Kammerjunker geführt hat," in *Magazin für die neue Historie und Geographie,* (ed.) A. F. Büsching, (Halle: 1984) vol. XIX, pp. 142-3, vol. XX, p.

369. Cf. *Vrata triumfal'nye v tsarstvuiushchem grade Moskve na vkhod tsarskogo sviashchenneishego velichestva, imperatora vserossiskogo, otsa otechestva Petra Velikogo s torzhestvom okonchennoi voiny blagopoluchnym mirom mezhdu imperieiu rossiiskoiu i koronoiu shvedskoiu* [The triumphal gates in the capital city of Moscow, on the entry of his most sacred Czarish Majesty, the Emperor of All the Russias, Father of his Country, Peter the Great, at the celebration of the conclusion of the war with a felicitous peace between the Russian empire and the crown of Sweden], (Moscow: moskovskaia tipografiia, 1721); and Pekarskii (pp. 529-531), who also cites quotations from Virgil and Horace which featured on this occasion. Cf. Wortman, *Scenarios of power*, pp. 42-60.

100. pp. 155, 247-9.

101. pp. 141, 145. In *The Children's Catechism*, Prokopovich describes "the moral law" [i.e. in this context, natural law] as "unchangeable, universally binding on all nations... in all places and at all times." *The Russian Catechism*, trans. J. T. Philipps, p. 25 (slightly amended).

102. p. 163, 145.

103. "Civil laws" in *Pravda voli monarshei* denotes positive municipal law as opposed to divine or natural law. No formal distinction yet existed in Russia between civil and criminal law (*Ocherki istorii SSSR. Period Feodalizma. Rossiia v pervoi chetverti XVIIIv. Preobrazovaniia Petra I* [Outlines of the history of the USSR. The period of Feudalism. Russia in the first quarter of the 18th Century. The Reforms of Peter I], p. 410).

104. p. 145.

105. pp. 137, 163, 181.

106. pp. 225.

107. Reporting the disinheriting of Aleksei on 3 February, 1718, Tyrholm recorded a speech by Peter which encapsulates his view of his absolutism as divinely ordained, and the nature of his duty as monarch: "Quoiqu'il n'y aie point de contrat, ni capitulation quelconque entre moi et mon peuple, qui me puisse obliger à faire une action

et omettre une autre, il y a pourtant quelque chose qui surpasse toutes les lois du monde, à savoir, la volonté de Dieu, qui assujettit tous les souverains à un devoir dont ils ne peuvent se dispenser. Ce leur devoir est de tourner tous leurs soins et applications au bien et à la prosperité et au salut de leurs peuples." (10/21 February, 1718, Rigsarkivet, Copenhagen, TKUA Speciel Del. B.49. Relationen aus Rusland).

108.   M. Raeff, "La noblesse et le discours politique sous le règne de Pierre le Grand," *Cahiers du monde russe et soviétique*, vol. xxxiv (1-2), 1993, p. 38.

109.   p. 137.

110.   p. 207.

111.   p. 135.

112.   p. 201.

113.   p. 279.

114.   Latkin, p. 4.

115.   P.S.Z., vol. VI, No. 3708.

116.   The chief of police (*ober-politseimeister*) of St Petersburg was instructed under the *Glavnyi Magistrat* to ensure that "streets and lanes are level and regular, and that no building is built obliquely or out of line." (Latkin, p. 434). Cf. Sidney Monas, "Anton Divier and the Police of St Petersburg," in *For Roman Jakobson. Essays on the occasion of his sixtieth birthday*, (The Hague: Mouton, 1956), pp. 361-66; James Cracraft, *The Petrine revolution in Russian architecture*, (Chicago: Chicago University Press, 1988), p. 181.

117.   P.S.Z., vol. VI, No. 3890. To Mardefeld, even Peter's church reforms suggested an attempt to establish "eine geistliche regulirte Miliz," (report of 9 June, 1724, in *Sbornik*, vol. 15, p. 240).

118.   P.S.Z., vol. V, No. 3006, article 20. This formula (literally translated from a 1693 resolution of the Swedish Riksdag) was reproduced in the *Naval Statute* of 1720, P.S.Z., Vol. VI, No. 3485, p. 39. (Latkin, p. 245).

119.   P.S.Z., vol. VI, No. 5718. The death-sentence passed on Aleksei, 24 June, 1718, refers to "the absolute power

and will (*samoderzhavnaia vlast' i volia*) of his Czarish Majesty, which depends on Almighty God alone and is not restricted or limited by any laws." (Ustrialov, p. 530).

120.   p. 187.

121.   *ibid.*

122.   p. 223.

123.   In 1718, on the Tsarevich Aleksei's renunciation of the succession, the Habsburg court requested an explanation. Peter's minister reportedly replied that "the Tsar is sovereign in his own realm and can do as he likes." (*Oprechte Haerlemse Dingsdaegse Courant*, 1718, No. 15).

124.   pp. 195, 189, 191.

125.   pp. 195, 213.

126.   e.g. letter to Louis XIV, 1675, or *La Politique tirée des propres paroles de l'Ecriture sainte* (1709): Bossuet, *Textes Choisis et Commentés*, (ed). H. Bremond, (Paris: Plon, 1913), vol. II, pp. 124, 201. R. Mettram observes, "even Bossuet, often cited as the panegyrist of divine-right absolutism, tempered his enthusiasm for powerful monarchy with some severe moral strictures," (in *Absolutism in Seventeenth-Century Europe*, (ed.) J. Miller, (London: Macmillan, 1990), p. 50.

127.   pp. 171-3.

128.   p. 199.

129.   p. 197.

130.   In 1721, following the Treaty of Nystad, Peter invited former Swedish prisoners-of-war to fill vacancies in the Russian administration. He guaranteed for them and their descendants freedom of worship, "their own churches and pastors" (P.S.Z., vol. VI, No. 3778). At the same time marriage between Russian Orthodox women and Lutheran Swedish prisoners working in the Ural iron mines was authorized by a decree of the Synod. Such intermarriage (hitherto forbidden) was justified by Prokopovich in a tract *O brakakh pravovernykh lits s inovernymi. Rassuzhdenie v Sviateishem Pravitel'stvuiushchem Sinode sochinennoe* [On marriages between Orthodox persons and those of other faiths. A treatise written in the Most Holy Governing

Synod], (St Petersburg: 1721). In his manifesto of 1702, inviting westerners to bring their skills to Russia, Peter referred to himself as a "Christian monarch." D. Zharinov argues that the word "Christian" in Peter's legislation normally signified "European." ("Petr Velikii kak zakonodatel' i 'Pravda voli monarshei'" [Peter the Great as legislator and "Pravda voli monarshei"], pp. 187, 189.

131.   Alexander Vucinich, *Science in Russian Culture. A History to 1860*, (London: Peter Owen, 1965), p. 70.

132.   Gurvich, pp. 30-31; Pekarskii, vol. 1, p. 212. In 1703 P. P. Shafirov recommended as an introduction to international law Grotius or Pufendorf, "in which one can study the basis of all law." The only eighteenth-century Russian translation of Grotius (1712) remains unpublished (W. E. Butler, "Grotius' influence in Russia," in *Hugo Grotius and International Relations*, (eds.) H. Bull, B. Kingsbury, A. Roberts, (Oxford: Oxford University Press, 1990), p. 258-9). In 1721 Peter ordered the Synod (through G. Buzhinskii) to translate Pufendorf's *De Officio Hominis et Civis iuxta legem naturalem* (a digest of his *De Lege Naturae et Gentium*). The translation, by I. Krechetovskii, was approved by Peter in 1721 and appeared as *O dolzhnostiakh cheloveka i grazhdanina po zakonu estestvennomu*, (St Petersburg: sankt-peterburgskaia tipografiia, 1726. Cf Correspondance Politique, Russie, vol. 15/121 (1724)). The unpublished introduction to a Russian version of Locke's *Treatises of Civil Government* describes Grotius and Pufendorf as the "founders" of political theory: "they have explained and established the principles of morality and civil life" (Lappo-Danilevskii, *loc. cit.*, p. 373).

133.   p. 153.

134.   p. 205.

135.   p. 207.

136.   *ibid.*

137.   *ibid.*

138.   p. 197.

139. p. 223. The effect of such changes is well put by M. Bogoslovskii: A subject of Peter, he says, "was not only bound to carry out state-service as laid down by statute, he must live only in a building constructed according to an 'official' plan, wear 'official' clothing and footwear, devote himself to 'official' entertainments in accordance with 'official' procedure, be cured in 'official' places, be buried in 'official' coffins, etc. etc." (quoted in *Itogi XVIII veka v Rossii* [Results of the 18th century in Russia], (ed.) A. Liutsh, V. Zommer and A. Lipovskii, pp. 40-41). *Pravda voli monarshei* itself was a vehicle of linguistic as well as ideological innovation, serving to introduce and explain such neologisms as: *prezervativa ili predokhranitel'noe vrachestvo; na konferentsii ili sobesedovanii; rezony ili dovody; po proportsii ili po razmeru; maestet ili velichestvo; konkurrenty, to est' ishchushchii korony soperniki; eksempli ili primery; suktsessora ili preemnika korony; personal'noe ili samolichnoe.* (For an analogous introduction for Russian readers to the terminology of international diplomacy, see W. E. Butler, introduction to P. P. Shafirov, *A Discourse concerning the Just Causes of the War between Sweden and Russia: 1700-1721*, Oceana Publications, (Dobbs Ferry, New York: Oceana Publications, 1973), p. 17).

140. p. 187.

141. pp. 203, 225, 187.

142. p. 26.

143. p. 227.

144. pp. 203-5.

145. p. 205.

146. p. 209.

147. Peter rejected "English liberty" as unsuitable for Russia. (V. O. Kliuchevskii, "Petr Velikii sredi svoikh sotrudnikov" [Peter the Great among his associates], *Sochineniia* [Works], vol. VIII, p. 345; cf. Papmehl, p. 2).

148. The comparison of hereditary and elective monarchy in section 16 is described in the *Acta Eruditorum* (August, 1723, p. 352) as having been treated "satis verbose."

149.   p. 229.

150.   pp. 203-5.

151.   It is also likely that in such a public document as *Pravda voli monarshei*, intended for western as well as Russian readers, the need was felt for tactful handling of the constitutions of neighbouring, friendly or client states. Thus Poland is mentioned as a victim of "misfortune" (p. 239); and criticism of Habsburg domination of the Holy Roman Empire is couched obliquely (p. 237).

152.   p. 223.

153.   Prokopovich, Tatishchev and A. D. Kantemir formed a so-called "Learned Guard" (*uchenaia druzhina*). For Prokopovich's account of the events of 1730, see James Cracraft, "The Succession Crisis of 1730: A View from the Inside," *Canadian-American Slavic Studies*, vol. 12, No. 1 (Spring 1978), pp. 60-85. For Tatishchev's defence of absolutism in 1730, see his discourse "The Voluntary and Agreed Dissertation of the Assembled Russian Nobility about the State Government," in Paul Dukes, *Russia under Catherine the Great*, vol. 1, *Select Documents on Government and Society*, (Newtonville, Massachusetts: Oriental Research Partners, 1978), pp. 15-27. For the later development of his political theory, see Tatishchev, *Istoriia rossiiskaia* [A History of Russia], vol. I, (Moscow/Leningrad: Akademiia Nauk SSSR, 1962), pp. 359-370.

154.   Ditiatin, p. 598. The French chargé d'affaires, Magnan, observed that while some members of the Supreme Privy Council were for preserving "le pouvoir despotique conformément aux anciennes constitutions de Russie," others intended "d'établir au contraire une nouvelle forme de gouvernement aristocratique" (31 May, 1727, Correspondance Politique, Russie, vol. 20/185).

155.   Of the 8 members of the Supreme Privy Council, there were 4 Dolgorukies and 2 Golitsyns by January 1730. (David. J. Ransel, "The Government Crisis of 1730," in *Reform in Russia and the USSR*, (ed.) Robert O. Crummey, (Chicago: University of Illinois Press, 1989), p. 47.

156.   According to the Duke de Liria, the Spanish ambassador, and Magnan, the alternatives canvassed were English parliamentarianism, limited monarchy on the Swedish pattern, elective monarchy as in Poland or a republican oligarchy. (De Liria, report, 31 January, 1730, in *Osmnadtsatyi Vek. Istoricheskii sbornik*, (ed.) P. Bartenev, Book 3, (Moscow: 1869), p. 30; Magnan, 3 February, 1730, (*Sbornik*, vol. 75, p. 466). Cf. *Plans for Political Reform in Imperial Russia*, (ed.) Marc Raeff, (Englewood Cliffs, New Jersey: Prentice-Hall, 1966), pp. 44-52). Campredon had anticipated a move towards Swedish-style control over royal power at the time of the creation of the Supreme Privy Council in 1726 (*Sbornik*, vol. 64, p. 187); and I. I. Ditiatin (p. 598) points out that some limitation was contemplated at the time of the accession of Catherine I. On the constitutional crisis of 1730, see D. A. Korsakov, *Votsarenie Imperatritsy Anny Ioannovny* [The Accession of the Empress Anna Ioannovna]; D. L. Ransel, "The Government Crisis of 1730," pp. 45-71.
157.   Korsakov, pp. 17-18.
158.   Korsakov, pp. 280-286; Pekarskii, vol. 1, p. 261. D. M. Golitsyn's library included over 6000 items of historical and political interest. (Korsakov, pp. 34-38; H. Hjärne, "Ryske Konstitutionsprojekt år 1730 efter Svenske förebilder," *Historisk Tidskrift*, No. 4 (1884), pp. 189-272; P. N. Miliukov, *Verkhovniki i Shliakhetsvo*, (Rostov-on-Don, 1905); A. Lappo-Danilevskij, "L'idée de l'état et son évolution en Russie depuis les troubles du XVIIe siècle jusqu'au réformes du XVIIIe," in *Essays in Legal History*, (ed.) P. Vinogradoff, (Oxford: Oxford University Press, 1913), pp. 372, 377-9; V. Iu. Poresh, "Kniaz' D. M. Golitsyn (Verkhovnik) i franzuszkie knigi ego biblioteki" [Prince D. M. Golitsyn (the Verkhovnik) and the French books in his library], in *Knigopechatanie i knizhnye sobraniia v Rossii do serediny XIXv.* [Book-publishing and book collections in Russia to the mid-19th century], (ed.) A. I. Kopanev et al., (Leningrad: Akademiia Nauk SSSR, 1979), p. 108; Isabel de Madariaga, "Portrait of an Eighteenth-

Century Russian Statesman: Prince Dmitry Mikhaylovich Golitsyn," *The Slavonic and East European Review*, vol. 62, No. 1, (January 1984), pp. 36-60. Those who doubt the Swedish prototype include W. Recke, "Die Verfassungspläne der russischen Oligarchen im Jahre 1730," *Zeitschrift für Geschichte Osteuropas*, 1911, vol. 2; G. A. Protasov, "Konditsii 1730g. i ikh prodolzhenie" [The Conditions of 1730 and their continuation], *Uchenye zapiski tambovskogo pedagog-icheskogo instituta* [Learned papers of the Tambov Pedagogical Institute], 1957, vol. 9.

159.   Korsakov, pp. 25-29. As ambassador at Stockholm, V. L. Dolgorukii possessed a copy of the 1720 Swedish constitution (G. A. Nekrasov, *Russko-shvedskie otnosheniia i politika velikikh derzhav v 1721-1726gg* [Russo-Swedish relations and the politics of the Great Powers 1721-1726], (Moscow: Nauka, 1964), p. 110). He was identified by James Keith as "chief projector" of the constitutional proposals of 1730. (Paul Dukes and Brenda Meehan-Waters, "A neglected account of the succession crisis of 1730: James Keith's Memoir," *Canadian-American Slavic Studies*, vol. 12, No. 1, (Spring 1978), p. 172.

160.   p. 213.

161.   Campredon described the supporters of Piotr Alekseevich as persuaded of his rights of succession "par les lois de la raison et de la nature." (30 July, 1722, *Sbornik*, vol. 49, p. 129). Mardefeld agreed: "man den von Gott und der Natur eingesetzten rechtmäßigen Erben excludiren wolte," (*Sbornik*, vol. 15, p. 238).

162.   p. 205.

163.   Marc Raeff, "Transfiguration and Modernization. The Paradoxes of Social Disciplining, Paedogogical Leadership and the Enlightenment in 18th Century Russia," *Political Ideas and Institutions in Imperial Russia*, (Boulder, Colorado: Westview Press, 1994), p. 342.

164.   As Sumner Benson suggests (p. 272), Peter and the author of *Pravda voli monarshei* "made a conscious selection among competing European political models, and the significance of their decision can only be appreciated

by comparison with the alternatives proposed by contemporaries." The introduction to the Russian translation (in manuscript) from Locke's *Treatises of Civil Government* revealingly explains the differences of opinion among political theorists on the origins of the social contract: while some hold that the people agreed "to submit to the strongest and to live under the laws which he might deign to give them," others argue that the ruler was chosen "as a guardian of the laws," to which he was himself subject, having no arbitrary power over "the citizens' liberty, property and life." Others contend that the people entrusted political power "not to one man alone, but to several, for one man alone is more prone to error than several." (Lappo-Danilevskii, *loc. cit.*, p. 373).

165. p. 207.
166. pp. 207-9.
167. p. 133.
168. p. 221, 213.
169. p. 209.
170. p. 205.
171. p. 235.
172. p. 225.
173. pp. 207, 211.
174. pp. 207, 209.
175. pp. 209, 191, 221.
176. p. 207.
177. pp. 211-13.
178. p. 213.
179. p. 205.
180. p. 219.
181. A. Lappo-Danilevskii in "l'idée de l'état et son évolution en Russie depuis les troubles du XVIIe siècle jusqu'aux réformes du XVIIIe," (*Essays in Legal History*, (ed.) P. Vinogradoff, Oxford, 1913, pp. 356-83) and G. Gurvich, in *'Pravda Voli Monarshei' Feofana Prokopovicha i ego zapadnoevropeiskie istochniki* [Feofan Prokopovich's 'Pravda voli monarshei' and its western european sources], Iur'ev, 1915, argue that much of the political ideology of

Pravda voli monarshei is borrowed from Grotius, Pufendorf, Thomasius, Buddeus and Wolff. Apart from Grotius, who alone of these is actually quoted in *Pravda voli monarshei*, a work rich in bibliographical references, the evidence for the others, with the possible exception of Pufendorf, seems tenuous. Lappo-Danilevskii's claim for Hobbes' influence has often been reiterated. Most of the political theory in *Pravda voli monarshei* was commonplace in natural law writing, e.g. Pufendorf, and such general borrowings from this common body of doctrine as appear in the work are not in my opinion striking enough to justify the inference of the direct influence of particular passages from the authors named in the secondary sources. Gurvich argues exhaustively, and in my view convincingly, against the view of Hobbes as a conscious influence on the book, despite some general similarities. F. Taranovskii, in a Foreword to Gurvich's book, argues the contrary. Assuming Prokopovich to have been the principal author of *Pravda voli monarshei* (see pp. 57-62), it is noteworthy that Hobbes was not among the titles listed in his library.

182.   pp. 137, 135.

183.   p. 131. Cf. manifesto of 3 February, 1718, p. 311.

184.   Philip Longworth, *The Making of Eastern Europe*, (London: Macmillan, 1994), p. 175.

185.   p. 197.

186.   James Cracraft, "Opposition to Peter the Great," in *Imperial Russia 1700-1917. State. Society. Opposition. Essays in honour of Marc Raeff*, (ed.) E. Mendelsohn and M. S. Schatz, (DeKalb, Illinois: Northern Illinois University Press, 1988), p. 22; N. B. Golikova, *Politicheskie protsessy pri Petre I. Po materialam Preobrazhenskogo prikaza* [Political trials under Peter the Great. From the records of the Preobrazhenskii Prikaz], (Moscow: izd. Moskovskogo Universiteta, 1957), p. 16

187.   Cracraft, "Opposition to Peter the Great," p. 23.

188.   Golikova, p. 25.

189.   After 1718, reversing a policy of relative toleration, Peter took measures aimed at suppressing the

Old Believers and reintegrating them into the Orthodox church (Robert O. Crummey, *The Old Believers and the World of Antichrist. The Vyg Community and the Russian State, 1694-1855,* (University of Wisconsin Press, 1970), pp. 79-85.

190.   Peter commissioned Prokopovich to write a tract on false martyrdom (*Ob'iavlenie s uveshchaniem ot sviatogo Sinoda narodu o proderzateliakh, nerassudno na muchenie derzaiushchikh* [Manifesto together with an admonition from the Holy Synod to the people on the impudent persons who attempt martyrdom for no reason], St Petersburg, 1722) against what Prokopovich called "fanatics," who lambasted the tsar "on account of the change in dress, wigs, shaving the beard and similar trifles" (Pekarskii, pp. 559-60).

191.   The tsarevich Aleksei pinpointed some of the main objections to Peter's attitude towards Muscovite custom and belief. Excerpts which he made from Baronius' *Ecclesiastical Annals* (Baronius is also cited in *Pravda voli monarshei,* pp. 257 and 259), condemn emperors for heresy, adultery, forcing their children to take monastic orders and enforcing the wearing of short robes. (*Chteniia v imper-atorskom obshchestve istorii i drevnostei rossiiskikh* [Lectures at the Imperial Society of Russian History and Antiquities], 1861, No. 3, part 2, pp. 140). As for Peter's brutality, on his flight to Vienna, the tsarevich told the Austrian Chancellor, Count Schönborn, that his father was "very cruel, has no respect for human life, and thinks that, like God, he has the right of life and death" (Ustrialov, p. 583).

By assuming the title "Father of His Country" (*Otets Otechestva*) it was objected that Peter usurped the attribute of the patriarch; by calling himself Peter the First, he was said to usurp the attributes of Christ as "alpha and omega, the first and the last" (*Rev.,* I, 11). The slavonic numerals represented by the letters in his title of Emperor (*Imperator*) added up to 666, the number of the Beast of the Apocalypse (Ulanov, pp. 82-83; Isabel de Madariaga, "Tsar into Emperor: the title of Peter the Great," *loc. cit.*)

One complainant alleged that Peter was a Swede, on the grounds of his banishment of Evdokiia and his marriage to Catherine, also said to be a Swede. He was said to have murdered the Tsarevich Aleksei "so that he, the Tsarevich, should not be tsar." For lack of children by Catherine, he had issued a decree commanding that allegiance be sworn to the next monarch, also a Swede, a brother or relative of Catherine. (V. Ulanov, pp. 69-100. D. A. Schafly, jr., "The popular image of the west in Russia at the time of Peter the Great," in *Russia and the World of the Eighteenth Century*, (ed.) R. P. Bartlett, A. G. Cross, Karen Rasmussen, (Columbus, Ohio: Slavica, 1988), pp. 10-11; Cracraft (1988), p. 28; Papmehl, p. 5). As for the legitimacy of Peter's marriage to Catherine, Bishop Dosifei testified that he had been asked: "Why do you Bishops not protest at the Sovereign's marrying a second wife while his first wife still lives?" (Ustrialov, pp. 212-13). Opposition to Catherine as a foreigner is also alluded to in *Pravda voli monarshei*: "many who are ignorant of history... suppose that marriages with foreigners were not customary among our monarchs: but we know that the opposite is true." (p. 279).

192.   p. 133.

193.   P.S.Z., vol. VI, No. 3984.

194.   p. 189.

195.   Cracraft, "Opposition to Peter the Great," p. 28. Campredon reported from Moscow on 21 August 1722: "on execute tous les jours ici des prêtres et autres personnes qui ont eu l'audace de soutenir que le Czar étoit un tiran qui avoit renversé toutes leurs loix ecclésiastiques et civiles. Il seroit étonnant dans un autre pays après les supplices qu'ont soufferts plus de quarante mil personnes pour cause de sédition qu'il s'en trouvât encore qui osassent tenir des discours aussi offensant à un Prince dont le pouvoir est le plus absolu qu'il y ait au monde" (Correspondance Politique, Russie, vol. 12/176).

196.   Korsakov, pp. 34-39. The British resident, Rondeau, described Golitsyn's "active mind of deep foresight and penetration with a solid judgment... and surpassing all men

in the knowledge of the Russian laws," ("Characters of some Russian noblemen," 26 February, 1730, Public Record Office, State Papers 91/107). Peter held Prince Ia. F. Dolgorukiĭ (1659-1720), a forthright critic of the tsar, in still greater respect, (V. O. Kliuchevskii, "Petr Velikii sredi svoikh sotrudnikov" [Peter the Great among his associates], *Sochineniia* [Works], vol. 8, pp. 338-339).

197.　According to Just Juel, Danish envoy in 1710, most Russians knew nothing of their religion and only one in five could read the Lord's Prayer (L. R. Lewitter, in Ivan Pososhkov, *The Book of Poverty and Wealth*, p. 88). To judge from complaints in the *Spiritual Regulation*, not even the clergy were likely to be qualified to participate in biblical exegesis. The only complete printed Bible available in petrine Russia was the sixteenth-century Ostrog Bible or the seventeenth-century *pervopechatnaia Bibliia.*

198.　12 May, 1725, Correspondance Politique, Russie, vol. 17/370.

199.　Gosudarstvennyi Arkhiv (Kabinet 1, No. 32, ff. 377-437); P. V. Verkhovskoi, vol. 1 p. 124.

200.　Prokopovich refers to his part in the writing of *Pravda voli monarshei* in a letter to Peter of 24 August, 1722, (Voskresenskii, pp. 113-114). Cracraft, however, argues that Prokopovich did not in terms state that he was the author or sole author of the work. He points out that in the eighteenth century the verb *sochiniat'*, used by Prokopovich in his letter (*knizhitsa, mnoiu sochinennaia*), usually meant to compile, compose or edit rather than to write, be the author of a work ("Did Feofan Prokopovich really write *Pravda voli monarshei?*," *Slavic Review*, vol. 40, No. 2 (Summer 1981), p. 180. This is to draw a fine distinction between *sochiniat'* and *pisat'*, or *scribere*, the verb which Prokopovich twice used when referring to his authorship of his 1722 tract on false martyrdom, (*Ob'iavlenie s uveshchaniem ot sviatogo Sinoda narodu o proderzateliakh, nerassudno na muchenie derzaiushchikh* [Manifesto together with an admonition from the Holy Synod to the people on the impudent persons who attempt

martyrdom for no reason] (letter (in Latin) to Ia. A. Markovich, Pekarskii, pp. 559-60). Defending himself against charges of heresy in 1726, Prokopovich pointed out that works in which he cites the Church Fathers include *Pravda voli monarshei* (*Chteniia v imperatorskom obshchestve istorii i drevnostei rossiskikh* [Lectures in the imperial society of Russian history and antiquities], Moscow, 1852, Book 1, part 2, p. 21). Patristic quotations in fact appear in sections 8 (1 quotation) and 13 (4 quotations). There are also 2 references to Chrysostom in the "examples from sacred history" (nos. 42 and 43, pp. 265, 267). Section 14 also refers to the *Children's Primer* (*Pervoe uchenie otrokam*), an undoubted work of Prokopovich. (Cracraft, "Did Feofan Prokopovich really write *Pravda voli monarshei?*," p. 182; S. M. Solov'ev, book 10, pp. 103, 104; Prince M. M. Shcherbatov, *On the Corruption of Morals in Russia*, pp. 151, 153).

201.   James Cracraft, "Did Feofan Prokopovich really write *Pravda voli monarshei?*," *Slavic Review*, vol. 40 No. 2, (Summer 1951), pp. 173-193.

202.   Cracraft, "Did Feofan Prokopovich really write *Pravda voli monarshei?*," pp. 177-8; A. Titov, "Episkop Afanasii Kondoidi" [Bishop Afanasii Kondoidi], *Russkii Arkhiv*, 1908, Book 3, 1908, pp. 5-24; 'Afanasii Kondoidi' in *Russkii biograficheskii slovar'*, vol. Aleksinskii-Bestuzhev-Riumin, (St Petersburg: tip. glavnogo upravleniia udelov, 1900), p. 371.

203.   Public Record Office, Chancery Lane, Consett to Lord Townshend, 17 July, 1725, State Papers 91/9/407-8.

204.   Cracraft, "Did Feofan Prokopovich really write *Pravda voli monarshei?*," p. 173.

205.   The Latin synopsis of *Pravda voli monarshei* in *Acta eruditorum*, August, 1723, refers to its "author" (autor).

The Synod's overall responsibility for *Pravda voli monarshei*, though not apparent on the face of the book, is nonetheless striking. Peter's order for publication went to the Synod. Orders, suggestions and complaints regarding distribution and translation were addressed to the Synod.

Finally the Synod was made the depot for the handing in of copies of the book when it was proscribed in 1727 (Pekarskii, pp. 664-5). It is clear, as Cracraft argues, that the Synod's importance in its early years lies not "in purely or even largely ecclesiastical or administrative terms," but as "a high-level committee on propaganda and state policy." ("Did Feofan Prokopovich really write *Pravda voli monarshei?*," p. 193).

206.   Consett to Townshend, 24 July 1725, State Papers 91/9/419.

207.   Solov'ev, book 9, p. 607.

208.   A. Titov, pp. 5-6.

209.   e.g. *ne po dostoinstvu glagolemykh veshchei* (Feofan Prokopovich, *Sochineniia* [Works], (ed.) I. P. Eremin, (Moscow: Akademiia Nauk SSSR, 1961), p. 113): *ne nedostoinstvu dostoinstvu rassuzhdaemykh zde veshchei* (p. 126); *estestvennyi zakon, na serdse chelovecheskom napisannyi* (Eremin, p. 82): *estestvennym zakonom, na serdtsakh ikh napisannym* (p. 134); *synove rossistii* (Eremin, p. 129): *synove rossistii* (p. 134); *ves' mir soglasno o sem zasvidetel'stvuet* (Eremin, p. 119): *ves' chestnyi mir est' nam sego svidetel'* (p. 144); *i po otecheskomu svoemu serdoboliiu* (Eremin, p. 138): *i otecheskomu svoemu blagoutrobiiu i serdoboliiu* (p. 174). In my judgment, Prokopovich was probably responsible for including the quotation from Cicero, *Pro Roscio Amerino* (pp. 159-61), a work frequently referred to in his *De arte rhetorica*. (Feofan Prokopovich, *De arte rhetorica*, (ed.) Renate Lachman, *Slavische Forschungen*, 27/11, 1982, pp. 85, ll4, 215, 219, 271, 275).

210.   See A. B. Zaichenko, "Teoriia prosveshchennogo absoliutizma v proizvedeniiakh F. Prokopovicha" [The theory of enlightened absolutism in the works of F. Prokopovich], in *Istoriia razvitiia politiko-pravovykh idei* [From the history of the development of politico-legal ideas], (Moscow, 1984), pp. 76-83. The 1721 tract on intermarriage, traditionally ascribed to Prokopovich, *O brakakh pravovernykh lits s inovernymi. Rassuzhdenie v*

Sviateishem Pravitel'stvuiushchem Sinode sochinennoe [On marriages between Orthodox persons and those of other faiths. A treatise written in the Most Holy Governing Synod], St Petersburg, 1721 (reprinted in P.S.Z., vol. VI, No. 3814), corresponds closely with *Pravda voli monarshei* in style and structure.

1. Stylistic similarities include: *prostoserdechnykh no nemoshchnykh, i v uchenii neiskusnykh chelovek* (P.S.Z., vol. VI, p. 414): *prostoserdechnykh radi, no malovedushchikh chelovek* (p. 120) and *prostoserdechnykh zhe no nevezhlivykh* (p. 126); *da ne rechet kto, chto...* (P.S.Z., ibid.): *da ne rechet kto, chto...* (p. 264); *moshchno nadeiatisia, chto...* (P.S.Z., *loc. cit.* p. 415): *nadeiatisiia sego ne vsegda moshchno* (p. 238); *evreiskii* Iosif (P.S.Z.,loc. cit., p. 417): *Iosif iudei* (p. 248) and *Iosif zhidovin* (p. 222), all three being references to Josephus' *Antiquities.*

2. Like *Pravda voli monarshei*, *O brakakh pravovernykh lits* takes the form of sustained argument, supported by biblical and patristic exegesis (particularly Chrysostom, Ambrose and Theophylact), followed by a list of supporting examples (34) from biblical, Byzantine and Russian history. If, in accordance with Cracraft's criteria, it is admitted that conclusive proof of Prokopovich's sole authorship of *O brakah* is lacking, it is undeniable that both *O brakakh* and *Pravda voli monarshei* were produced under the auspices of the Synod to meet a particular need of the state; and it can be confidently asserted that both were written by the same person or persons. (In support of Cracraft's argument as to the significance of the verb *sochiniat'* and his thesis of a collaborative enterprise by members of the Synod, it may be noted that *O brakakh* is formally entitled *Rassuzhdenie v Sviateishem Sinode sochinennoe*).

211. Cracraft, "Did Feofan Prokopovich really write *Pravda voli monarshei?*," p. 192.

212. Two of the "examples from secular history", numbers 26 and 27, are not, as stated, in chronological order (pp. 255-7); the title of Grotius' work is misquoted at

page 245, though cited correctly at pages 153 and 187; on page 221 the statement is made that the imperial succession can pass in the female line; elsewhere (e.g. page 137) it is assumed that only males can succeed.

213.   See Appendix 1. According to Bernardo Ribera, a Spanish dominican priest resident at St Petersburg, "his [Prokopovich's] library, open to scholars, greatly exceeds the imperial library [of some 1600 books] and that of the Troitskii monastery; for its richness it has no equals in Russia, a country poor in books," (P. Morozov, *Feofan Prokopovich kak pisatel'* [Feofan Prokopovich as a writer], (St Petersburg: tipografiia V. S. Balasheva, 1880), p. 393). The library's contents are itemized by Verkhovskoi, ("Biblioteka Feofana Prokopovicha" [Feofan Prokopovich's library], *Uchrezhdenie dukhovnoi kollegii i dukhovnyi reglament* [The establishment of the Spiritual College and the Spiritual Regulation], vol. 2, (Rostov-on-Don: imperatorskii Varshavskii universitet, 1916), part 5, pp. 1-71. *Pravda voli monarshei* also refers to the existence at St Petersburg of "some three hundred or more law books" relevant to the question of disinheritance (p. 145). This may refer to Prokopovich's library, which included some 500 books on law (Verkhovskoi, *loc. cit.*, pp. 35-43).

214.   Theodor Zwinger, *Theatrum vitae humanae... in XIX libros digestae*, (Basel: per Frobenios fratres, 1565); Johann Jacob Hofmann, *Lexicon universale historico-geographico-chronologico-poetico-philologicum. Continens historiam omnis aevi, geographiam omnium locorum, genealogiam principum familiarum, addita ubique chronologia... mythologiam... discussionem philologicam... aliaque plurima scitu dignissima*, (Basel: typis Jacobi Bertschii & Jon. Rodolphi Genathii, 1677); Sethus Calvisius, *Chronologia, ex autoritate potissimum Sacrae Scripturae, et historicorum fide dignissimorum, ad motum luminarium coelestium, tempora & annos distinguentium, secundum characteres chronologicos contexta & deducta*, (Leipzig: Jacobus Apelius, 1605).

215. As noted by Ribera (footnote 213), Prokopovich's collection became in effect a public library. (Conrad Grau, *Der Wirtschaftsorganisator, Staatsmann und Wissenschaftler Vasilij N. Tatiscev (1686-1750)*, (Berlin: Quellen und Studien zur Geschichte Osteuropas, 1963), pp. 139-141.

216. Cracraft, "Did Feofan Prokopovich really write *Pravda Voli Monarshei?*," p. 176; *For God and Peter the Great. The Works of Thomas Consett*, 1723-1729, p. 8.

217. As noted above (p. 3), Shcherbatov was struck by the 'flattery' and 'fawning' of *Pravda voli monarshei*. Verkhovskoi (vol. 1, p. 87) denies that Peter made any contribution to *Pravda voli monarshei*.

218. Cf. the detailed attention which Peter paid prior to its publication in 1722 of the book which he commissioned from Prokopovich on the Beatitudes (*Khristovy o blazhenstvakh propovedi tolkovanie. Poveleniem vsepresvetleishego derzhavneishego Petra Velikogo, Imperatora i samoderzhtsa vserossiiskogo* [An explanation of Christ's sermon on the Beatitudes. By order of the most serene and mighty Peter the Great, Emperor and sovereign of all the Russias], (St Peterburg: 1722), an apologia of the tsar's absolute control of church affairs. (K. Sivkov, "Petr-pisatel" [Peter the writer], in *Tri veka. Rossia ot Smuty do nashego vremeni. Istoricheskii Sbornik* [Three Centuries. Russia from the Time of Troubles to our Own Time. A Historical Collection], (ed.) V. V. Kallash, (Moscow: izd. t-va I. D. Sytina, 1912), vol. 3, pp. 60-61; Titlinov, p. 427-428).

219. p. 123.

220. *ibid.*

221. *ibid.*

222. pp. 125, 127.

223. p. 135

224. pp. 137, 139.

225. pp. 141-3.

226. pp. 143-5.

227. pp. 145-9.

228. pp. 149-51.
229. pp. 151-3.
230. pp. 153-7.
231. p. 161.
232. p. 163.
233. pp. 169-75.
234. p. 177.
235. p. 181.
236. pp. 183-5.
237. p. 189.
238. pp. 197-203.
239. p. 203.
240. pp. 213-17.
241. pp. 217-27.
242. pp. 227-45.
243. pp. 245-73.
244. p. 279
245. pp. 277-81.
246. *Pravda voli monarshei vo opredelenii naslednika derzhavy svoei. Ustavom derzhavneishego gosudaria nashego, Petra Velikogo, otsa otechestva, imperatora i samoderzhtsa vserossiiskogo, i prochaiia, i prochaia, i prochaia. Sego 1722 godu, fevralia v 11 den' publikovannym utverzhdena i vsenarodnuiu prisiagoiu svidetel'stvovana. Zde prostrannee, prososerdechnykh radi, no malo-vedushchikh chelovek pokazuetsia. V moskovskoi tipografii, avgusta v 7 den'* [The Justice of the Monarch's Right to appoint the heir to his throne. Under the statute of our most mighty sovereign, Peter the Great, Father of his Country, Emperor and Sovereign of all the Russias, etc., etc., etc., published this year, 1722, on 11th day of February, having been confirmed and witnessed on oath by the whole nation, is here demonstrated at greater length for the benefit of honest but ignorant persons. At the Moscow press, on 7th day of August]. The book is in folio, measuring approximately 9" X 5". It consists of a title-page and 3 unnumbered pages, followed by 59 pages of text and 3 unnumbered pages. There are 2 tail-pieces. On the last page

appears *napechatasia v moskovskoi tipografii leta gospodnia 1722, avgusta v 7 den'.*(Pekarskii, II, p. 381; T. A. Bykova and M. M. Gurevich, *Opisanie izdanii napechatannykh pri Petre I. Opisanie izdanii grazhdanskoi pechati (1708-ianvar' 1725g.)*, (Moscow/Leningrad: Akademiia Nauk SSSR, 1955), p. 138). In his letter to Peter of 24 August, Prokopovich referred to it as *O pravde voli monarshei v opredelenie svoikh po sebe naslednikov.* (Voskresenskii, pp. 113-114).

247.   Voskresenskii, pp. 113-114.

248.   The date is given by the Saxon resident, Lefort (*Diplomatische Beiträge zur russischen Geschichte aus dem königlichen Sachsichen Hauptstaatsarchiv zu Dresden*, (ed.) E. Hermann, vol. I, (St Petersburg: Akademiia Nauk, 1868), pp. 36-37.

249.   *Polnoe sobranie postanovlenii i rasporiazhenii po vedomstvu pravoslavnogo ispovedaniia rossiiskoi imperii* [Complete collection of decrees and orders relating to the Orthodox confession in the Russian empire], (St Petersburg, 1874), No. 774, p. 950. From the publication date of 7 August indicated at the end of the book, it may be inferred that Peter approved the text as it stood.

250.   Several versions of the edition in "civil" type are extant, presumably printed on different presses. (T. A. Bykova and M. M. Gurevich, *Opisanie izdanii napechatannykh pri Petre I. Svodnyi katalog. Opisanie izdanii napechatannykh kirillitsei* [Inventory of editions published under Peter I. Union catalogue. Inventory of editions published in church script], (Moscow: Akademiia Nauk SSSR), pp. 251-3; *Opisanie izdanii napechatannykh pri Petre I. Svodnyi katalog. Opisanie izdanii grazhdanskoi pechati (1708-ianvar' 1725g.)* [Inventory of editions published under Peter I. Union catalogue. Inventory of editions of the civil press (1708-January 1725], (Moscow/Leningrad: Akademiia Nauk SSSR, 1955), p. 382.

251.   T. A. Bykova and M. M. Gurevich, *Opisanie izdanii napechatannykh pri Petre I. Svodnyi katalog. Opisanie izdanii grazhdanskoi pechati (1708-ianvar' 1725)* [Inven-

tory of editions published under Peter the Great. Union catalogue. Inventory of editions of the civil press (1708-January 1725)], p. 529.

252. The price of a bound copy was 20 altyns (60 kopecks), and 13 altyns, 2 den'gi (40 kopecks) per unbound copy (Pekarskii, pp. 573-4). According to Consett, the ruble (100 kopecks) was "something less than an English crown" (Cracraft, *For God and Peter the Great*, p. 454). A soldier working on the construction of Peterhof in 1724 earned 3 coppecks a day in the summer. The annual salary of a foreign councillor (sovetnik) in the College of Justice in 1719 was 1200 roubles, that of his Russian counterpart was 800 roubles, and of a middle-grade (Russian) clerk 143 roubles. The price of a copy of the 1718 manifesto on the disinheritance of the Tsarevich Aleksei was 2 altyns. Of 1.341 copies printed 1,329 were sold (Pekarskii, p. 410).

253. *Das Recht der Monarchen, in willkühriger Bestellung der Reichs-folge, durch unsers Grossmächtigsten Landes-Herrn, Petri des Ersten, Vater des Vaterlandes Kaysers und Selbsthalters von allen Reussen, u.u.u. Den 11 Februarii dieses 1722sten Jahres publicirte Verordnung fest gesetzet, und von der ganzen Nation eydlich approbiret; allhier aber ausführlicher denen aufrichtigen, aber einfältigen Menschen zu Liebe dargeleget. Gedrückt in der Buchdruckerei zu Moscau und aus der Rußischen Sprache getreulich ins Teutsche übersetzt. Berlin, bey Ambrosius Haude, kön. Preuß. und der Societät der Wissenschaften priviligirten Buchhändler*, 1724. In the same year Ambrosius Haude also published *Beschreibung der Crönung Ihro Maj. der Kayserinn aller Reussen Catharinae Alexiewnae, so in der Stadt Moscaw d. 7 May 1724 solemniter vollzogen worden. Gedruckt zu St. Petersburg A-o 1724 und aus der Reussischen Sprache übersetzt. Berlin, bey Ambro. Haude, königl. und der Societaet der Wissenschaften Buchhaendler und Factor*, 1724. This was a translation of *Opisanie koronatsii ee Velichestva, Imperatritsy Ekateriny Alekseevny,*

torzhestvenno otpravlennoi v tsarstvuiushchem grade Moskve 7 maia 1724 godu (St Petersburg: 1724).

254.   Pekarskii, p. 665.

255.   P.S.Z., vol. VII, No. 4643; Solov'ev, vol. IX, pp. 554-562; Mardefeld, report of 10 February, 1725, *Sbornik*, vol. 15, pp. 255-6.

256.   According to a sermon given by Thomas Consett at the English church at St Petersburg on 7 February, 1725, there were fears of popular unrest and of demonstrations against Catherine for some days after Peter's death (P. N. Berkov, "Tomas Konsett, kapellan angliiskoi fakturii v Rossii" [Thomas Consett, chaplain to the English factory in Russia], in *Problemy mezhdunarodnykh literaturnykh sviazei v 1720e gody* [Problems of international literary contacts in the 1720s], (ed). B. G. Reizov, (Leningrad: Leningradskii gosudarstvennyi universitet, 1962), p. 13. G. A. Nekrasov (p. 185) quotes a letter of 20 February from the Dutch envoy, W. de Wilde, in which the Chancellor G. I. Golovkin is reported as urging that since Peter I had left no disposition, written or oral, regarding the succession, the people (la nation) should be consulted as to the choice of monarch. This advice was in exact accordance with the course of action laid down in *Pravda voli monarshei* (pp. 217-23)

256.   A decree of January 1726 complained of "unseemly and hostile words" (*nepristoinye i protivnye slova*) used in anonymous letters directed at Catherine and the late Peter the Great by "villains in various cities and districts," (P.S.Z., vol. VII, No. 5004). Campredon reported "qu'on y traitoit la Czarinne d'usurpatrice, qu'on déclamoit vivement contre sa vie," (23 March, 1726, Correspondance Politique, Russie, vol. 19/227). In a book published in 1730, Consett observed: "it is now evident that it [one of the offending letters] contained some severe reflections on his late Majesty's [Peter the Great's] edict, wherein he had made way for the succession of the Empress, and had invested her also with the same power that he asserted to himself of appointing his heir and successor," (Cracraft, *For God and*

Peter the Great, p. lxi). In the same year Prince D. M. Golitsyn observed in the Supreme Privy Council that Catherine had had no right to accede to the throne or to designate a successor. (Korsakov, pp. 4, 13; Magnan, 13 February, 1730, *Sbornik*, vol. 75, p. 477).

257.   P.S.Z., vol. VII, No. 4870

258.   *Pravda voli monarshei vo opredelenii naslednika derzhavy svoei. Ustavom blazhennyia i vechnodostoinyia pamiati derzhavneishego gosudaria nashego Petra Velikogo, otsa otechestva, imperatora i samoderzhtsa vserossiiskogo, i prochaia, i prochaia, i prochaia, preshedshego 1722 goda, fevralia v 11 den' publikovanym utverzhdena, i vsenarodnoiu prisiagoiu svidetel'stvovana, zde prostrannee, prostoserdechnikh radi, no malo vedushchikh chelovek pokazuetsia. Nyne zhe poveleniem blagochestiveishiia velikiia gosudaryni nasheia imperatritsy Ekateriny Alekseevny samoderzhitsy vserossiiskiia, i prochaia, i prochaia, i prochaia. S prilozheniem v nachale ukaza o podkinutykh vorovskikh pis'makh, i vechnogo ustava o nasledii prestola imperii rossiiskoi, i general'nyia prisiagi. Napechatasia v moskovskoi tipografii, 1726 goda, mesiatsia iulia* [The Justice of the Monarch's Right to appoint the heir to his throne. Under the statute of our most mighty sovereign of blessed and eternal memory, Peter the Great, Father of his Country, Emperor and Sovereign of all the Russias, etc., etc., etc., published in the year 1722, on 11th day of February, having been confirmed and witnessed on oath by the whole people, is here demonstrated at greater length for the benefit of honest but ignorant persons. And now by order of our most devout great sovereign lady, empress Catherine Alekseevna, sovereign of all the Russias, etc., etc., etc. it is published at the Moscow press, July, 1726, together with the addition at the beginning of the decree concerning wicked anonymous letters, and the permanent statute concerning the succession to the throne of the Russian empire, and the universal oath]. As with the first edition, several versions are extant. The tail-piece following the Foreword is

identical to that in the first edition. Bykova and Gurevich (p. 253) argue from this that the core of this edition is made from sheets originally printed in 1722.

259.   The St Petersburg edition was entitled *Na pravdu voli monarshei*. (T. A. Bykova and R. I. Kozintseva, *Opisanie izdanii napechatannykh pri Petre I. Svodnyi katalog. Dopolneniia i prilozheniia* [Inventory of editions published under Peter the Great. Union catalogue. Supplements and additions]. (Leningrad: Akademiia Nauk SSSR, 1972), p. 177).

260.   P.S.Z., vol. VI, No. 4879.

261.   Pekarskii, p. 574.

262.   Pekarskii, pp. 573-574. P.S.Z., vol. VI, No. 4879. The order that *Pravda voli monarshei* be recited in church caused problems. (1) The Synod considered it impossible for the whole book to be read in the course of a single church service, and authorized the St Petersburg edition to be divided into "readings" (*chteniia*). Each reading began with a brief recapitulation of the previous reading. (2) Ivan Shuvalov, commander-in-chief of the newly annexed province of Vyborg, reported to the Synod that recitation in the Lutheran churches in that province would be futile, as the inhabitants, mainly Finnish peasants and Swedish pastors, did not understand Russian. According to Morozov (p. 305) the Synod contemplated producing a Swedish translation of *Pravda voli monarshei*. (Pekarskii, pp. 574, 664; T. A. Bykova and R. I. Kozintseva, *Opisanie izdanii napechatannykh pri Petre I. Svodnyi katalog. Dopolneniia i prilozheniia* [Inventory of editions published under Peter I. Complete catalogue. Supplements and additions], (Leningrad: Akademiia Nauk SSSR, 1972), p. 178; Jyrki Paaskoski, "Om privilegierna för Viborgs provins vid freden i Nystad 1721," *Historisk Tidskrift för Finland*, 3, 1993, pp. 361-388).

263.   P.S.Z., vol. VII, No. 5070. Consett had noted that, according to Condoidi, Catherine was expected to nominate Piotr Alekseevich, but emphasized that "she will not be prescribed or compelled, but will vindicate the right" of

nomination vested in her by the statute of 1722 (Consett to Townshend, 17 July 1725, State Papers 91/9/407. Cf. P.S.Z., vol. VII, No. 4870).

264.   P.S.Z., vol. VII, No. 5131; vol. VIII, No. 5909. The publications suppressed were the manifestos of 3 February and 25 June, 1718, concerning Tsarevich Aleksei, described as "of blessed memory," and the manifesto of 5 March, 1718, relating to former Tsarina Evdokiia. A manifesto of 10 October, 1727, announcing Peter's coronation, took a pointedly "legitimist" line. It described the new tsar as "the true and natural sovereign" (*istinnyi i prirodnoi gosudar'*), stated that "God grants the succession to whom He will," stressed that Peter followed the example of his "forbears, crowned by God (*Bogovenchannye*), and [of] all Christ-loving (*Khristoliubivye*) potentates," and described royal power as "a gift, granted to Us by the King of Kings," i.e. by hereditary descent and divine right, not as the result of appointment. (P.S.Z., vol. VII, No. 5179). Cf. p. 23 for similar views expressed by the Tsarevich Aleksei.

265.   Cracraft, *For God and Peter the Great*, p. 8.

266.   Pekarskii, p. 665.

267.   P.S.Z. vol. VIII, No. 5909.

268.   Latkin, pp. 276-277.

269.   Latkin, p. 277.

270.   Latkin, p. 277.

271.   *Dnevnik A. V. Khrapovitskogo* [The Diary of A. V. Khrapovitskii], (ed.) N. Barsukov, (St Petersburg: izd. A. F. Bazunova, 1874), pp. 46-47.

272.   *Sobranie raznykh zapisok i sochinenii, sluzhashchikh k dostavleniiu polnogo svedeniia o zhizni i deianiiakh gosudaria imperatora Petra Velikogo, izdannoe trudami i izhdiveniem Fiodora Tumanskogo* [A Collection of various writings and works serving to provide complete information on the life and actions of the sovereign emperor Peter the Great, published by the efforts and at the expense of Fiodor Tumanskii], Part 10, (St Petersburg: Shnor, 1788), pp. 123-243. Tumanskii slightly reordered the 1726 edition: his version begins with Catherine I's statute of 21

April, 1725; next comes the Statute on the succession, followed by the Foreword. The reversal of the two last, however, contradicts the order announced in the Foreword.

273.   P.S.Z., vol. 24. No. 17,910. Paul explained the principles of the Act as follows: "that the state should never be without an heir; that the heir should always be determined by law; that there should never be the least doubt as to who is to succeed." On Paul's decree and the subsequent line of succession, see *Succession to the Imperial Throne of Russia*, (ed.) Antony, Archbishop of Los Angeles and California, (Bridgeport, Connecticut: The Imperial Union of Russia, 1984).

274.   P.S.Z., vol. VII, No. 4870.

275.   Similar minor inaccuracies in the citation of sources occur in the *Spiritual Regulation*. P. P. Epifanova claims that citation of scholarly sources in Russia began only in 1717 with Shafirov's *Discourse Concerning the Just Causes of the War between Sweden and Russia* ("'Rassuzhdenie' P. P. Shafirova o voine so Shvetsiei" [P. P. Shafirov's "Considerations" on the war with Sweden], in *Problemy obshchestvenno-politicheskoi istorii Rossii i slavianskikh stran. Sbornik statei k 70-letiiu akademika M. N. Tikhonravova* [Problems in the socio-political history of Russia and the Slav countries. A collection of articles to mark the 75th birthday of academic M. N. Tikhonravov], (Moscow: izd. vostochnoi literatury,1963), p. 298)

PRAVDA VOLI MONARSHEI

TEXT AND TRANSLATION

ПРАВДА ВОЛИ МОНАРШЕЙ

ВО ОПРЕДЕЛЕНИИ НАСЛЕДНИКА ДЕРЖАВЫ СВОЕЙ

УСТАВОМ ДЕРЖАВНЕЙШЕГО ГОСУДАРЯ НАШЕГО,

ПЕТРА ВЕЛИКОГО, ОТЦА ОТЕЧЕСТВА,

ИМПЕРАТОРА И САМОДЕРЖЦА ВСЕРОССИЙСКОГО,

И ПРОЧАЯ, И ПРОЧАЯ, И ПРОЧАЯ,

СЕГО 1722 ГОДУ, ФЕВРАЛЯ В 11 ДЕНЬ, ПУБЛИКОВАННЫМ,

УТВЕРЖДЕНА, И ВСЕНАРОДНОЮ ПРИСЯГОЮ

СВИДЕТЕЛЬСТВОВАНА,

ЗДЕ ПРОСТРАННЕЕ, ПРОСТОСЕРДЕЧНЫХ РАДИ,

НО МАЛО ВЕДУЩИХ ЧЕЛОВЕК, ПОКАЗУЕТСЯ

THE JUSTICE OF THE MONARCH'S RIGHT TO APPOINT THE HEIR TO HIS THRONE

UNDER THE STATUTE OF OUR MOST MIGHTY

SOVEREIGN, PETER THE GREAT, FATHER OF HIS

COUNTRY, EMPEROR AND SOVEREIGN OF ALL THE

RUSSIAS, ETCETERA, ETCETERA, ETCETERA

PUBLISHED THIS YEAR, 1722, ON 11th DAY OF

FEBRUARY,

HAVING BEEN CONFIRMED AND WITNESSED ON

OATH BY THE WHOLE NATION,

IS HERE DEMONSTRATED AT GREATER LENGTH,

FOR THE BENEFIT OF HONEST BUT IGNORANT

PERSONS

КО ПРОСТОСЕРДЕЧНОМУ ЧИТАТЕЛЮ ПРЕДИСЛОВИЕ

Известно буди тебе, кто сию книжицу не самого ради любопытства, но яснейшего ради истины познания, прочести пожелаешь, что написанна есть не с таким намерением, да бы ведомый всем, и зде же положенный самодержца нашего, его императорского величества устав, предохранить нам от прекословия некиих в политическом учении сильных противников. Ибо от числа таковых философов, ни единого, который бы устав сей опорочити имел, отнюд не надеемся. Всякому бо от них, дело уставления сего, яко законное и праведное, весьма есть известно. Се же ведаем мы, кроме многих иных любомудрия их изречений, и от сего единого общего им в таковом деле слова, что когда разглагольствуют о наследии, кто ближший к нему, и кто дальший от него, всегда употребляют сего изъятия: *Разве бы родитель инако определил;* чим явно мысль свою показуют, что они о свободной к определению воли родительской ниже мало усумневаются.

Еще же и не того ради книжица сия издается, да бы именуемому уставу монаршему подала некое пособие, ежебы увещать и преклонить подданных к приятию его. Уставы бо и всякие законы, от самодержцев в народ исходящие, у подданных послушания себе не просят, аки бы свободного, но истязуют яко должного: [2] истязуют же не токмо страхом гнева властительского, но и страхом гнева божия, то бо есть, еже глаголет учитель народов, *потреба повиноватися, не токмо за гнев, но и за совесть. (Рим. 13).* Аки бы рекл: не токмо власти предержащей потреба повиноватися бояся гнева его, что есть страх телесный, но и бояся гнева божия, хто душевный на совести страх есть. Сие бо слово

A FOREWORD TO THE HONEST READER

Whoever wishes to read this booklet, not out of idle curiosity, but for a clearer understanding of the truth, take note: it is not written with the intention of defending His Imperial and Sovereign Majesty's statute (which is known to everyone and is set out below) from the objection of any critics versed in political theory. For among such theorists we do not anticipate that there is even one who could find fault with the statute. For they are all well aware that the purpose of this enactment is lawful and just. Apart from many other of their learned observations, we know this from one general expression which they always use when discussing inheritance and who is nearest or furthest in order of succession; for they always make the following exception: *unless the father has decided otherwise;* by which they clearly imply that they do not have the slightest doubt of a father's absolute right to decide the succession.

Nor is this booklet being published to provide some kind of support to the Monarch's statute, in order to exhort and induce the subjects to accept it. For statutes and laws of every kind issuing from sovereigns to people, do not ask obedience of the subjects as a favour, but demand it as a duty; and demand it not only from fear of the ruler's anger, but also from fear of God's anger; for as the Teacher of the Gentiles[1] says: *Ye must needs be subject, not only for wrath, but also for conscience sake* (*Romans,* 13). He said, as it were: we must obey the powers that be, not only through fear of their anger, that is, from bodily fear, but also through fear of God's anger, that is, from spiritual fear and

выводит из преждереченного от себе слова: *несть власть, аще не от бога, сущые же власти от Бога учинены суть. Темже противляяйся власти, божию повелению противляется: противляющиися же, грех себе приемлют.* И того ради не токмо монаршии уставы и законы не требуют себе ни каковой от учительских доводов помощи, силою с вышше себе данною совершенно укрепляемые, но и кто показал бы себе аки помощником властительских определений, тот бы не мало погрешил на безпрекословное повелительство самодержцев, вводя тако их определения в сумнительство помышлений, аки бы оные неизвестной силы суть, аще учительскими доводами утвержденна не будут.

Едина же сочинения книжицы сей вина есть, что понеже в народе нашем обретаются так непокойные головы, и страстию прекословия свербящие сердца, что ни какового уставления от державной власти произносимого похвалити не хотят. Еще же и самое то, что бы они сами собою блажили и почитали, когда видят указом монаршим определяемо, упрямым и злобным сердцем, иногда же и скверноязычным роптанием [3] охуждают; и то делают окаяннии с великим других простосердечных соблазном и смущением совести их, а по тому и с бедством ихъже, временным и вечным; и сеют в отечестве нашем мятежей плевелы, а иностранным подают бесчестное мнение о народе российском, аки бы в нем варварсие нравы, и к государям своим верность притворная, и послушание за гнев токмо, а не за совесть, рабски, а не сыновне творимое: толико зла бессовестные онии ропотники собирают нам.

Того ради судилося за благо, по согласию духовного и мирского главного правительства (к чему и Императорское Величество милостивне склонился) сочинить сию книжицу, в которой сущая в помянутом уставе

124

in our conscience. For he deduces that statement from what he has said in an earlier passage: *There is no power but of God: the powers that be are ordained of God. Whosoever therefore resisteth the power, resisteth the ordinance of God: and they that resist shall receive to themselves damnation.* And therefore not only do a monarch's statutes and laws require no aid from scholarly arguments, being fully sanctioned by a power given to them from above, but whoever held himself out as a supporter of the ruler's decisions would commit no small sin against the incontrovertible authority of sovereigns by thus casting doubt on their decisions, as though they were of uncertain validity unless confirmed by scholarly argument.

The sole reason for writing this booklet is that there are among our people such restless minds, and hearts seething with the passion to contradict, that they will not approve any enactment laid down by the ruling power. Indeed, if there is anything which they themselves have praised and extolled, once they see it laid down by the monarch's decree, they censure it with stubborn and spiteful heart, and sometimes even with abusive complaint; and in so doing, these wretches lead other honest men badly astray and confuse their consciences, to their consequent temporal and eternal ruin; and they sow seeds of rebellion in our country and give foreigners a dishonourable notion of the Russian people as one of barbarous manners, who feign allegiance to their sovereigns, and who obey only from fear, and not for conscience sake, like slaves, and not like sons: so much evil do these unscrupulous complainers store up for us.

Hence it has been thought fit, by consent of the supreme authorities, spiritual and temporal (and with the gracious approval of his Imperial Majesty) for this booklet to be written,[2] in which the justice

монаршем правда, хотя и в самом том уставе довольно показана, яснее нечто и пространнее покажется: да бы безумным но упрямым (аще бы таковии были) прекословцам уста заградить, простосердечных же но невежливых, от вредного оных блазнословия сохранить невредимых, купно же и иностранным порочное о народе нашем мнение отнять, и подать им вину лучших о нас помыслов, да бы ведали, что помянутою проказою нецыи только в России, как и в прочих государствах, а не все общество болезнует.

И се же тебе, любезнейший читателю, в преддверии сем объявляем, что в сочинении слова сего, не токмо правда устава монаршего показуется, но при ней и должности родителей и детей, как простых, так и державных домов, и родительская, [4] и монаршая власть, и самая внутренная, но законная сила монархии, или самодержавства, довольно объясняется; довольно же по силе нашей и по нужде наставления простосердечных невежд, но не совершенно и недостоинству рассуждаемых зде вещей: се же за скудость числа потребных к сему многих книг, и искусства нашего.

Благоволи убо и сим довольствоватися, благосовестный читателю, и аще благоразумен и мудр еси, приими слово сие, яко вину вящшего твоего любомудрия. Аще же не много искусна и ведуща тебе знаешь, не отрини сего, хотя несовершенного поучения. [5]

of the Monarch's statute, though amply demonstrated in the statute itself, is expounded somewhat more clearly and at greater length, in order to silence foolish but stubborn critics, if such there be, and to safeguard honest but ignorant persons from their harmful sophistry; and also to disabuse foreigners of their false opinion of our people, and to give them reason to think better of us, so that they may know that in Russia, as in other states, only a few suffer from that plague of which we spoke, and not the whole of society.

And therefore, dear reader, we declare to you in this preface that not only is the justice of the Monarch's statute demonstrated in this work; but the duties of parents and children, both in ordinary households and in ruling households, the authority of parents and of monarchs, and the inherent but lawful power of monarchy, or sovereignty, are also amply explained: amply, that is, in relation to our ability and to the need to instruct honest but ignorant people; but not explained to perfection, or in accordance with the importance of the topics under discussion: this for lack of the many books necessary for the task, and because of our lack of skill.

Pray be content with it, therefore, honest reader, and if you are sensible and wise, accept this work as an opportunity to increase your wisdom. And if you know yourself to have little learning or knowledge, do not reject this piece of instruction, imperfect though it is.

Peter the Great's Law - Text

Мы, Петр Первый, Император и Самодержец
Всероссийский, и протчая, и протчая, и протчая,

Объявляем: Понеже всем ведомо есть, какою авессаломскою злостию надмен был сын наш Алексей, и что не раскаянием его оное намерение, но милостию божиею ко всему нашему отечеству пресеклося, (что довольно из манифеста о том деле видимо есть). А сие ни для чего иного у него взросло, токмо от обычая старого, что большому сыну наследство давали: к томуж один он тогда мужеска полу нашей фамилии был, и для того ни на какое отеческое наказание смотрети не хотел. Сей не добрый обычай, не знаю чего для был так затвержен: ибо не точию в людях по рассуждению умных родителей бывали отмены, но и в святом писании видим, когда исаакова жена состаревшуся ее мужу, меньшому сыну наследство исходатайствовала; и что еще удивительнее, что и божие благословение тому следовало. Ещеж и в наших предках оное видим, когда блаженныя и вечнодостойныя памяти, Великий Князь Иоанн Васильевич, и поистине великий, не словом, но делом: ибо оный рассыпанное разделением детей владимировых наше отечество собрал и утвердил, который не по первенству но по воли сие чинил, и дважды отменял, усматривая достойного наследника, который бы собранное и утвержденное наше отечество паки в расточение не упустил. Перво мимо сыновей отдал внуку, а по том отставил внука уже венчанного, и

[THE STATUTE ON THE SUCCESSION]

We, Peter the First, Emperor and Sovereign of All the Russias, etcetera, etcetera, etcetera,

Declare: Whereas it is known to all with what wickedness, namely, that of an Absalom,[3] our son Aleksei was filled, and that his plans were cut short, not by his repentance, but by God's mercy towards our entire country (as is clear enough from the Manifesto concerning that matter).[4] Now this arose in him for no reason other than the old custom of granting the succession to the eldest son; and as he was then the only male member of our family, he would take no heed of any fatherly chastisement. I do not know why this evil custom was so deeply rooted: for not only has it been done away with among men in general, according as wise parents judged best, but we see the same thing in Holy Writ, when Isaac's wife persuaded her aged husband to give his inheritance to his younger son, and, what is still more wonderful, God's blessing followed. Moreover, we also see it among our own forbears, in the case of the Grand Duke Ivan Vasil'evich,[5] of blessed and eternal memory, and truly, a man great not only in name, but also in deed: for he reunited and strengthened our country, dismembered as it was through its division among the sons of Vladimir;[6] and he did so not according to the right of birth, but according to his own will, and he twice changed the order of succcession in his search for a worthy heir who would not let our country, once united and strengthened, fall back into ruin. First, passing over his sons, he bestowed the succession upon his grandson; and later he deposed his

129

отдал сыну свое наследство (о чем ясно из степенной книги видеть возможно) а имянно, в лето 7006, февраля в 4 день, Князь Великий Иоанн Васильевич учинил по себе наследника внука своего, Князя Димитриа Ивановича, и венчан был на Москве на великом княжении княжеским венщем Митрополитом Симоном. А в лето 7010, апреля в 11 день, Великий Князь Иоанн Васильевич разгневался на внука своего Князя Димитриа, и не велел его поминать в церквах [6] Великим Князем, и посадил его за караул. И тогож апреля в 14 день учинил наследником сына своего Василиа Иоанновича. И венчан был оным же Митрополитом Симоном. На что и другие сему подобные есть довольные примеры, о которых краткости ради времене, ныне здесь не упоминаем: но впредь оные особливо выданы будут в печать.

В таком же рассуждении, в прошлом 1714 году, милосердуя мы о наших подданных, чтоб и партикулярные их домы не приходили от недостойных наследников в разорение, хотя и учинили мы устав, чтоб недвижимое имение отдавать одному сыну, однакож отдали то в волю родительскую, которому сыну похотят отдать, усмотря достойного, хотя и меньшему мимо больших, признавая удобного, который бы не расточил наследства. Кольми же паче должни мы иметь попечение о целости всего нашего государства, которое с помощию божиею ныне паче распространено, как всем видимо есть; чего для за благо рассудили мы сей устав учинить, да бы сие было всегда в воле правительствующего государя, кому оный хощет, тому и определить наследство; и определенному, видя какое непотребство, паки отменить, да бы дети и потомки не впали в такую злость, как выше писано, имея сию узду на себе. Того ради повелеваем, да бы все наши верные подданные, духовные

grandson, who had already been crowned, and gave it to his son. This may clearly be seen from the Chronicles,[7] as follows: in the year 7006,[8] on the 4th day of February, the Grand Duke Ivan Vasil'evich appointed as successor his grandson, Prince Dimitrii Ivanovich, and he was crowned in Moscow as Grand Duke by the Metropolitan Simon; and in the year 7010,[9] on the 11th day of April, the Grand Duke Ivan Vasil'evich was angry with his grandson, Prince Dimitrii, and forbade him to be mentioned in the churches as Grand Duke, and placed him under guard. And on 14th day of April he made his son, Vasilii Ivanovich, successor, and he was crowned by that same Metropolitan Simon. There are many similar examples, which for lack of time we do not mention here: but they will be published separately at a future date.

With this in mind, in the year 1714, taking pity on our subjects, in order that private families should not be brought to ruin by unworthy heirs, we laid down a statute that immoveable property should be left to one son only;[10] but we left it to the fathers' discretion to leave it to whichever son they think fit, according to merit, even if it be to a younger son, passing over the elder sons, if they acknowledge him to be a worthy successor, who would not dissipate the inheritance. How much greater, then, must be our concern for the preservation of our whole State, which, with God's help, is today greatly expanded, as is evident to all. For this reason we have thought fit to lay down this statute, whereby it should always be in the power of the reigning monarch to appoint whomsoever he wishes as his successor; and if he sees any fault in him whom he has appointed, to revoke the succession, so that his children and descendants may not fall into such wickedness as was described above, with this to curb them. We therefore

и мирские, без изъятия сей наш устав пред Богом и его Евангелием утвердили на таком основании: что всяк, кто сему будет противен, или инако как толковать станет, тот за изменника почтен, смертной казни и церковной клятве подлежать будет. оный подлинный устав в Сенате подписан его Императорского Величества собственною рукою, тако, Петр

В Преображенском в 5 день февраля, 1722 году. Печатано в Московской Типографии, 1722 февраля в 8 день. [7]

Клятвенное обещание

Я нижеименованный обещаюсь и клянусь пред всемогущим Богом и святым его Евангелием, в том, что по объявленному его пресветлейшего и державнейшего Петра Великого, Императора и Самодержца Всероссийского, нашего всемилостивейшего государя, о наследствии уставу, сего настоящего 1722 года, февраля 15 дня, по которому, ежели его Величество по своей высокой воле, и по нем правительствующии государи российского престола, кого похотят учинить наследником, то в их величества воле да будет. А ежели же и определенного в наследники, видя какие непотребства, паки отменить изволят, и то в ихже величества воле да будет.

И тот его Величества устав, истинный и праведный признаваю, и по силе того устава, определенному в наследство, во всем повиноватися, и по нем за истинного наследника, и себе за государя признавать, и во всяком случае за оного стоять, с положением живота своего буду, и против тех которые и сему противно поступать будут. А ежели я сему явлюсь противен, или инако противное что помянутому уставу толковать стану, то за изменника почтен, и смертной казни, и церковной клятве подлежать буду. И во утверждение сей моей клятвы целую слова и крест Спасителя моего, и подписуюсь. [8]

command all our true subjects, spiritual and lay, without exception, to confirm this our statute before God and his Gospel in such a way that any who opposes it or interprets it differently shall be deemed a traitor, and be liable to the death penalty and to excommunication.

The original statute was signed in the Senate in his Imperial Majesty's own hand thus - Peter

At Preobrazhenskoe, the 5th day of February, 1722. Printed at the Moscow Publishing-House, the 8th day of February, 1722.

THE OATH

I, the undersigned, promise and swear by Almighty God and His Holy Gospel, in accordance with the statute on the succession, decreed by His Most Serene and Potent Majesty, Peter the Great, Emperor and Sovereign of all the Russias, our most gracious lord, on 5th day of February, 1722, whereby His Majesty, according to his sublime pleasure, and likewise those who reign after him on the throne of Russia, are free to appoint as successor whomsoever they wish. And if they see any faults in the appointed successor, their Majesties are also free to revoke the appointment.

And I acknowledge that statute of His Majesty as true and just, and by virtue of that statute I shall submit in everything to his designated successor, and after his death I shall acknowledge him as the true successor and my sovereign, and shall support him at all times with my life against those who oppose it. And if I oppose it or interpret anything otherwise than according to the aforementioned statute, I shall be deemed a traitor and shall be liable to the death penalty and to excommunication. And in confirmation of this my oath, I kiss the words and the cross of my Saviour and I subscribe my name.[11]

ПРАВДА ВОЛИ МОНАРШЕЙ
ВО ОПРЕДЕЛЕНИИ НАСЛЕДНИКА ДЕРЖАВЫ СВОЕЙ

Главный устав императорского величества Петра Великого, государя нашего милостивейшего, сего 1722 года, февраля в 11 день, славно публикованый, от всего всех чинов народа слышан есть, любовно принят, благодарно похвален, и присягою, или клятвенным обещанием, яко праведный свидетельствован. Праведно се и достодолжно: аще бо и всякие частные законы или уставы верховных властей, одну некую в народе пользу творящие, или един вред некий из отечества истребляющие, со усердием принимать и верно сохранять подданнии долженствуют, понуждаеми на то, как божиим в священном писании повелением, так и естественным законом, на сердцах их написанным: то кольми паче долженствуем вышепомянутый Монарха нашего устав нелицемерно лобызать, и со всяким тщанием, по крайней возможности соблюдать и содержать, который не часть добра некоего, но вся отечеству нашему требуемая благая приносит, и не часть некоего зла, но вся злая предварительне отсецает. Ибо, понеже всего отечества состояние на высочайшей власти висит, как на доброй доброе, так на худой худое: устав же сей предоберегает, да бы в российском государстве монаршескую власть наследствовали самые лучшие, и к толь высокому и трудному правительству угоднейшие лица, от благоразумных самодержцев [9] благовременне усмотренные и определенные.

Того ради устав сей есть всероссийской монархии аки презерватива, или предохранительное врачевство, и к получению доброго, и ко отдалению злого состояния преполезнейшее. И по тому не только содержать оный, и вечно сохранять, но и не забвенно, от всего сердца благодарствовать законодателю нашему и самодержцу должни суть сынове российстии, яко истинному отцу отечества, который по крайнем

THE JUSTICE OF THE MONARCH'S RIGHT TO APPOINT THE HEIR TO HIS THRONE

The basic statute of His Imperial Majesty, Peter the Great, our most gracious sovereign, promulgated on the 11th day of February this year, 1722, has been heard by all ranks of the whole nation, lovingly received, gratefully acclaimed and acknowledged as just by an oath, or sworn promise. That is right and proper: for if all individual laws or statutes of the ruling powers, which bring any single advantage to the nation or rid the country of any single evil, must be zealously received and loyally observed by the subjects, who are bound to do so both by God's command in Holy Writ and by natural law, which is written in their hearts, how much more, then, must we sincerely praise this abovementioned statute of the Monarch, and make every effort to observe and maintain it to the utmost of our ability; for it brings with it not a part of some benefit, but all the blessings which our country needs; and it eliminates in advance not a part of some evil, but all evils. For since the condition of the whole country, for better or for worse, depends on the supreme power, so this statute provides that those who succeed to monarchical power in the Russian State shall be the best and most qualified persons for this lofty and onerous office, persons sought out in good time and nominated by right-minded sovereigns.

Hence this statute is a kind of prophylactic or preventative medicine for the monarchy of all the Russias, most conducive to its welfare and most effective in averting evil. Russia's sons must therefore not only keep it and maintain it forever, but must be unfailingly and wholeheartedly grateful to our Lawgiver and Sovereign, as a true

135

своем к отечеству благоутробии, за малое дело себе почитал, толикими попечении, и трудами собственными, не токмо целое сохранить, но и широко распространить; еще же и гражданскими и воинскими исправлении, и исправлений крепостьми, то есть и здравнейшими уставами и законами утвердить, и на толикую высоту славы вывесть, аще бы всего того и на предбудущие времена известною некоею силою не укрепил, что и благопромыслительно сделал сим препрезнейшим уставом, о свободном себе, и будущим по себе самодержцам избрании и наречении державы российской наследника, не по естественном первенстве, яко погрешительном правиле, но по усмотрении добродетельного превосходства. И не чаем, дабы кто ведая сие и рассуждая, прекословить толь премудрому уставлению восхотел, или возмогл, разве бы общего отечеству своему, яко враг домашний, и по тому и собственного себе самому добра завидел, яко пребезумнейший от человек.

Но понеже могут обрестися невежливии, и не далече видящии человецы, котории недоумения ради своего, или и от злобных прекословников смущаеми, усумневатися будут, не противно ли се сущей правде, да первородный [10] самодержца некоего сын, аще бы и неугоден был к толь высокому правительству, не наследит родительского скипетра, а другий меньший его брат, или и от иного рода некий искусный и добродетельный, и добре царствовати могущий, определением самодержца, наследие на престол его получит. Того ради за благо судилося подручным Монарха нашего управителям, на конференции или собеседовании Святейшего Синода, и Правительствующего Сената, показать всякому, изданною в народ книжицею, как вышепомянутый императорского величества устав, не токмо никоемуже о неправде подозрению не подлежит, но как здравому естественному разуму, так и самого Бога неложному слову согласует, и государству российскому весьма нужный и препрезный является. Аще же и сам устава сего автор,

Father of his Country, who, in his great zeal for the country, has thought little of his own great pains and efforts not only to preserve it but also to expand it greatly; and to strengthen it with civil and military reforms, and with the bastions of reform, namely, with most excellent statutes and laws, and to raise it to such a height of glory, that if he had not manifestly consolidated all this for the future, he has providently done so by this most useful statute, whereby he and the sovereigns who come after him may freely choose and nominate the heir to the Russian throne, not according to natural birthright - a bad rule - but in accordance with moral excellence. We do not suppose that anyone who knows this and considers it, either would or could oppose so wise an ordinance, unless it be that most foolish of men, an internal enemy, jealous of his country's general good and hence of his own.

There may, however, be ignorant and short-sighted men who, through their lack of understanding, or prompted by malicious critics, will wonder whether it is not contrary to true justice for a sovereign's first-born son, even though he may be unfit for such high office, not to inherit his father's sceptre, while another, his younger brother, or even someone from another family, who is skilled and virtuous and capable of ruling well, succeeds to the throne at the sovereign's behest. For this reason, our Sovereign's chief ministers, at a conference or meeting of the Most Holy Synod and of the Governing Senate,[12] have thought fit to demonstrate to all by means of a published booklet, that His Imperial Majesty's aforementioned Statute not only admits of no suspicion of injustice, but accords both with natural common sense and with the infallible word of God himself, and is most necessary and useful to the Russian State. Although the author of this statute,

всероссийский император, не просто устав сей издал, но с крепкими резонами или доводами, також и с образами или примерами свободного монархом определения в наследники их, и показание того довольное изъявил; однакож, да и последний сумнительства сучец от мысли невежливых истребится, и место недоумению не останется, издается сие рассудительное слово в народ, которое первее ясными доводами, по том же и многими примерами известно покажет, како вышепомянутый монарший устав, и праведный, и зело полезный, паче же и всему отечеству весьма нужный есть. И тако первее предлагаются зде

РЕЗОНЫ ИЛИ ДОВОДЫ

Резоны или доводы сему предложению служащие видим быти сугубые: одни от рассуждения законов общих о власти родительской, коеголибо чина человек; а другие собственно [11] от рассуждения высочайшей власти, императоров, царей, и прочиих коейлибо титлы самодержцев.

Первые доводы от рассуждения власти всех обще родителей

1.

И первее рассуждая законы общие власти и долженства родительского, видим сей естественный закон, что хотя и должни родители рожденным от себе детям равное как себе давать прекормление. Подобает бо тому, кто кого в жизнь сию произвел, промышлять ему и содержание жизни, инако того ради только родил бы, да бы рожденный от него умерл. И се было бы не только бесчеловечие, но и бессловесных естеству противное: и

the Emperor of all the Russias, has not only himself promulgated this Statute but has given ample proof, with cogent reasons or arguments and also with instances or examples, that monarchs are free to appoint their successors, nevertheless, in order to remove the least trace of doubt from the minds of the ignorant, and to leave no room for misunderstanding, this treatise is being published, wherein will be plainly shown, first by means of clear arguments and then with numerous examples, how just, how extremely useful and, above all, how very necessary to the entire country the Monarch's abovementioned statute is. First, therefore, there follow:

Reasons or Arguments

We see that there are are two kinds of reasons or arguments which support our proposition. Some derive from a consideration of the laws concerning parental authority in general, whatever the class of persons; while others derive strictly from a consideration of the supreme authority of emperors, kings and other sovereigns, whatever their title.

First series of arguments concerning the power of parents generally
1.

First, when we consider the general laws concerning the power and duty of parents generally, we see that there is a natural law that parents must willingly provide equal sustenance for their own begotten children as for themselves. For he who has brought someone into this world must provide him with the means to live; otherwise he would have begotten him only for his offspring to die. And this would not only be inhuman, but

скотина бо кормит исчадия своя, покамест возрастут, и своею силою пищи себе искати возмогут; и понеже в детях плоть и кровь родителей содержится, того ради и равную им как себе пищу должни родители. Сей закон воспоминая утверждает и Апостол. *Не должна суть, рече, чада родителем снискати имения, но родители чадом, (2 Коринф, гла. 12).*

Однакож видим и пределы закона сего, и самый естественный разум толкует нам его с некиим договором, то есть: аще сын будет благонравный, и к родителям своим благовейный, тому и прекормление от родителей и наследие имения их должно есть; аще же сын явится злонравен, непокорив родителям, наставление отметающий, дому своему бесчестие, или и разорение наводящий, того снабдевати родители не суть должни, и праведно могут лишати наследия. Понеже бо якоже родители должни суть снабдевати чада, тако и чада законом природным, и в десятословии от Бога утвержденным, должни суть всякую честь и повиновение родителям, то когда чада долженство свое злонравием [12] разоряют, освобождают тогда и родителей своих от должного им призрения. Сын непокорный и злонравный перестает быти сын, аще не естественным, обаче законным образом, (якоже и оный блудный сын, в притче евангельской, недостойна себе глаголет нарещися сыном отца своего, но желает принят быти яко един от наемник его). Вопреки убо и отец перестает быти отец ему, то есть, от долженства своего к нему разрешается, и аще не отринет его вовсе, не видя в нем надежды исправления, то сделает по долготерпению, по природной милости и сердоболию своему, но не по долгу. Утверждается сие и от слова божия: Вседержитель бо Господь, укоряя за беззаконие иудеев, и устрашая их клятвою и всеконечным от себе отвержением, приводит на пример

contrary even to the nature of dumb beasts: for even cattle feed their young until they grow up and can seek sustenance for themselves; and since children are their parents' flesh and blood, parents must provide them with equal sustenance as for themselves. The Apostle reminds us of this law, when he states: *The children ought not to lay up for the parents, but the parents for the children* (2 *Corinthians*, 12).

However, we see that there are also limits to this law, and natural reason itself makes clear to us that it is conditional, that is, if a son is virtuous, and respectful to his parents, he is entitled to receive sustenance from his parents and to inherit their property. But if a son proves wicked and disobedient to his parents, rejects their instruction, and brings disgrace or even ruin on his house, his parents are not bound to provide for him and may rightly disinherit him. For just as parents must provide for their children, so children, by the law of nature, confirmed by God in the Ten Commandments, owe their parents all honour and obedience; so when children, by their wickedness, violate their duty, they release their parents from the duty to look after them. A disobedient and wicked son ceases to be a son, in law if not in fact, (just as the prodigal son in the parable in the Gospels says that he is unworthy to be called his father's son, but still wishes to be accepted as one of his heirs). Conversely, the father ceases to be a father to him, that is, he is released from his duty to him; and if he does not disown him outright when he sees in him no hope of improvement, he acts out of patience and natural mercy and compassion, and not out of duty. This is also confirmed by the word of God: for Almighty God, upbraiding the Jews for their transgression and threatening them with his curse and his eternal rejection, cites the example of a

господина и отца, от рабов, или от сынов прогневанного, у пророка Малахии, *Сын*, рече, *славит отца, и раб господина своего боится: то аще отец есмь аз, то где слава моя? и аще господь есмь аз, то где есть боязнь моя? (Малах. гл. 1)*. Сим же словом показует нам Бог, что отец, от сына бесчествуемый, может отринути от себе сына, то есть изгнати из дому, и лишити прекормления и наследия своего: понеже и сам Бог Израиля (которого у Исаии сыном нарицает, и сыном перворродным в книзе Исхода) за беззаконие отринул (*Исаиа, гл. 1; Исход, 4)*.

2.

Сказуем же еще, что за нераскаянное злонравие сыновнее, могут родители отвергать от себе сынов своих: а и се ведати подобает, что иногда родители и не могут не отвергати сынов, понуждаеми или совестию пред Богом, или и страхом суда человеческого. Понеже бо выше речеся, что отцы, яко виновники жизни сыновней, должни суть [13] промышлять сынам своим содержание жизни: бывают же сыны таковые, которым лучше было не родитися, не токмо непокоривыи, но и родителей в смертную печаль и бедство воводящии, не токмо отечеству весьма непотребныи, но и вредныи, и потому или лучше бы не жити им, или поне лучше жити в скудости оставленным, нежели в довольстве содержимым: довольство бо готовое творит таковых ленивыми, свирепыми, и на всякое зло дерзкими, а скудость и лишение много к злу оружия отъемлет им, востягает же и обуздовает их; того ради, когда родитель никаким наказанием не успевает, и весьма не видит надежды исправления в таковом сыне своем, должен есть прочее востягнути и смирити его тем, что едино останется или к исправлению его, или поне ко укрощению

master angered by his servants, or a father angered by his sons. In the Prophet Malachi He says: *A son honoureth his father, and a servant his master; if then I be a father, where is mine honour? and if I be a master, where is my fear? (Malachi, 1).* In this passage, then, God shows us that a father dishonoured by his son can disown his son, that is, cast him out of his house, and deprive him of his sustenance and inheritance. For God himself disowned Israel for its wickedness, (Israel, whom in Isaiah he calls his son and in the book of Exodus - his first-born son (*Isaiah,* 1^{13}; *Exodus,* 4).

2.

We may add that parents can disown their sons for their inveterate wickedness; and indeed it should be understood that sometimes they have no alternative, but are compelled to do so either by their conscience before God or from fear of men's judgement. It was said above that fathers, being the cause of their sons' existence, must provide their sons with the means to live. There are such sons, however, for whom it would be better had they never been born, who are not only disobedient, but also bring upon their parents mortal grief and misery, and who are not merely quite useless to the country, but are positively harmful to it, and for whom therefore it would be better for them either not to live at all, or at least to be left to live in need, than to be maintained in abundance. For ready abundance makes such sons indolent, reckless and ripe for every kind of mischief, while need and deprivation remove from them many instruments of evil, and restrain and control them. So when a father does not prevail through any kind of chastisement, and sees no hope at all of improvement in such a son, he must further restrain and control him by the sole remaining means of correcting him or at least of mitigating

злонравия его, то есть отринути от себе, и наследия своего лишити; тако бо он оставлен и лишен, аще и не покается, то поне не возможет прочее сильно свирепствовати, яко безоружен уже, и нищетою аки бы связанный. Таяжде бо вина которая одолжает родителя к содержанию жизни сыновней, когда в отраву злому и неудобь исправляемому сыну стала, разрушается уже, и не токмо не одолжает родителя к содержанию жизни просто сыновней, или честной и угодной жизни, но паче одолжает отъяти угодие и довольство сыну, которое ему есть вина злого жития.

3.

И сия вышепредложенная рассуждения суть, аки законыестественные, сама собою крепкая: не может бо здравый разум человеческий инако рассуждати. Посмотрим еще, не тожде ли утверждают и изданные в народах законы, такожде и законоучительных философов писания. [14] Бесчисленные суть, тако рещи, книги от многих авторов сочиненные, о уставах и законах гражданских, а нигде в них не полагается сумнительство о сем, может ли родитель сына лишити своего наследия; только рассуждают учители, а законодавцы государи и определяют разные вины, коих ради может родитель отринути сына от наследия своего: и тако весь честный мир есть нам сего свидетель. И естьлибы кто о толиком учителей и законоположников множестве усумневался, то мощно ему показать и у нас в России, а наипаче в царствующем Санктпитербурхе, до трех сот, и вящше, законных книг, в которых рассуждается о винах и обстоятельствах такового то сынов не добрых отвержения, то что, естли бы нам вникнути в славные и великие по Европе книгохранительницы? Довольно же зде един воспомянути устав Иустиниана царя, числом междо Новеллами его сто пятыйнадесять, в главе третией, где Иустиниан, запрещая родителям, да бы без вины сынов своих из наследия не отвергали, именует вину правильного отвержения,

his wickedness, namely, by disowning and disinheriting him;[14] for once abandoned and destitute, even if he does not repent, at least he can no longer run wild, being now as it were disarmed and restrained by poverty. For the principle which obliges a father to maintain his son no longer applies when it serves to corrupt a wicked and recalcitrant son; and not only does it not oblige the father to maintain his son, or to maintain him in an honourable and comfortable style of life, but rather it obliges him to deprive the son of the comfort and abundance which are the cause of his evil way of life.

3.

These foregoing considerations, like the laws of nature, are self-evident: for man's common sense can reach no other conclusion. Let us now see whether the same is not also confirmed by the laws laid down among the nations and likewise by the writings of jurists. There are, so to speak, innumerable books, by many authors, concerning statutes and civil laws,[15] and nowhere in them is any doubt raised as to whether a father can disinherit his son: the jurists simply discuss, and the sovereign legislators lay down, the various grounds on which a father can disinherit his son; thus the whole civilised world is our witness. Should anyone doubt the existence of so many jurists and legislators, one can show him, even here in Russia, and in particular at the capital, St Petersburg, some three hundred or more law books, in which are discussed the reasons and circumstances relating to the disinheriting of unworthy sons; what should we find, then, if we could enter the great and famous libraries of Europe? It suffices here to mention one statute of the emperor Justinian, number 115, in chapter three of his *Novellae,* where Justinian, forbidding parents to disinherit their sons without

сыновнее неблагодарствие. И понеже неблагодарствие есть имя не весьма ясное, и толку требующее, того ради исчисляет четыренадесять вин, которыми сыновнее к родителям своим неблагодарствие означается, а именно:

1. Аще сын родители бить дерзнет.

2. Аще тяжелую и бесчестную обиду им сделает.

3. Аще их в криминальном некоем деле (которое не было бы против государя) на суд позовет.

4. Аще с злодеями в злодействии их сообщается. [15]

5. Аще умышлял на житие родительское, отравою, или иным каковым либо образом.

6. Аще с мачехою своею, или и подложницею родительскою плотско вмешается.

7. Аще доношение на отца подав, убыток ему знатный сделает.

8. Аще за родителем арестантом не восхощет ручитися.

9. Аще не допускает родителей завет или духовную писать.

10. Аще в чин позорных поединщиков или скоморохов, без воли родительской вступит, разве и родитель тогожде промысла употреблял бы.

11. Аще родителям хотящим дщерь свою, в подобающую пору браком мужеви сочетати, она, не соизволяя, блудно жити станет.

12. Аще родителям, ума лишившимся, не прилежит сын помоществуя им в таковом бедствии, и пещися об них вознерадит.

13. Аще родителя в плен отведенна, не потщится сын скоро искупити, то отец инако свободившийся, на воле своей имеет лишити или не лишити сына наследия. Но аще за сыновним нерадением, умрет в пленении отец его, таковаго сына Иустиниан велит не допускать до родительского наследия.

cause, names filial ingratitude as a just cause for disinheriting. Since ingratitude is not a very precise term and requires interpretation, he lists fourteen definitions of filial ingratitude, namely:

1. If a son dares to assault his parents.

2. If he does them some grave and disgraceful wrong.

3. If he lays some criminal charge against them (other than treason).

4. If he becomes an accomplice of evildoers in their wrongdoing.

5. If he has conspired against a parent's life, by poison or by any other means.

6. If he has carnal knowledge of his stepmother or even his father's concubine.

7. If, by bringing information against his father, he causes him significant loss.

8. If he refuses to stand bail for a parent under arrest.

9. If he prevents his parents from writing a testament or will.

10. If he becomes a base gladiator or actor against his parents' will, unless his father follows the same profession.

11. If a daughter, when her parents wish her to marry at an appropriate time, refuses to do so, and lives in sin.

12. If his parents lose their sanity, and a son does not come to their assistance in such a misfortune, and neglects to take care of them.

13. If a father is taken prisoner, and his son does not endeavour to ransome him promptly, then the father, having been liberated by some other means, is free to disinherit his son, or not, as he pleases. But if, through the son's neglect, the father dies in captivity, Justinian forbids such a son to succeed to his patrimony.

14. Аще родитель усмотрит сына еретичествующа, и святей церкви не сообщающася, свободен есть лишити его наследия.

Сия четыренадесять вины от Иустиниана именованные, и от нас сокращенно предложенные, утверждают и прочии [16] законоучители, но сверх сих вин, и иные многие изобретают. И по сему известно, как волен родитель есть и должен смотрети за сыном, каков быти он хощет, и тако или не допустити его до наследия своего, или аще уже и именовал бы его наследником, то за вышепомянутую некую, или и иную важную вину переменив завет свой, лишити наследия.

4.

Но что большее есть, согласует закону сему и священное писание. Что бо в переводе славенском в притчах соломоновых так написано: *раб смыслен удержит господина несмысленна, во братию же разделит имение на части (притчи, 17),* то в еврейском первоначальном составе, так яснее чтется: *раб смыслен погосподствует над студным сыном, и с братиею разделит имение,* то есть, получит часть наследия с прочею братиею, аки брат, вместо оного брата студного: и невозможно сего толковать в таком разуме, аки бы смысленный раб насильством или коварством часть сына несмысленного наследил. Глаголет бо зде дух святый о таком рабе наследнице с похвалою его, предпочитая его паче сына студного, и таковое наследие зрится зде яко благословенное.

Но яснее сие от писания утвердится нижше, где будет речь о образах: там бо довольно покажется, что святии патриархи и цари благочестивии не всегда смотрели на первородство сынов своих, но и первенство иногда переносили на меньших сынов, якоже Исаак перенесл первенство от Исава на Иакова; или и на внучат своих, [17] якоже Иаков перенесл первенство

14.   If a father discovers that his son is a heretic and not in communion with Holy Church, he is free to disinherit him.[16]

These fourteen reasons set forth by Justinian and presented by us in shortened form are confirmed by other jurists; but they also find many other reasons besides. It is therefore clear that a father has the right and duty to see how his son turns out, and accordingly either to bar him from his inheritance, or, if he has already named him as his heir, then, for one of the abovementioned reasons or for some other valid reason, to change his will and disinherit him.

4.

Moreover, Holy Writ also concurs with this law. For in the Slavonic translation of the Proverbs of Solomon it is written: *A wise servant shall have rule over a master that causeth shame, and shall have part of the inheritance among the brethren* (*Proverbs,* 17). This reads more clearly in the original Hebrew text, as follows: *a clever servant shall prevail over a foolish son and shall share the inheritance with the brethren,* that is, he will receive part of the inheritance together with the other brothers, as if he were a brother, instead of the foolish brother. This cannot be interpreted as meaning that the clever servant should inherit the foolish son's portion by force or trickery. For the Holy Spirit here speaks in praise of such a servant and heir, preferring him to the foolish son, and such an inheritance is seen here as a blessing.

But this will be more clearly confirmed below, when we come to examples from Scripture. For there it will be amply demonstrated that the holy patriarchs and devout kings did not always consider their sons' birthright, but sometimes transferred the birthright to their younger sons, as Isaac did, when he transferred it from Esau to Jacob; or even

от сынов рувимлих на сынов сына своего Иосифа; и прочии наследие свое мимо больших сынов малейшим давали, якоже Давид; от чего явно есть, что закон оный, чрез Моисеа данный Израилю, в книгах числ *(числ. 27 и 36)*, который наследие определяет сынам, а у кого нет сынов, дочерям, и прочая, разумеется с договором тайным, аще сыны или дщери, и прочии ближшии кровию родителям, не явятся наследия весьма недостойнии.

5.

Утверждается тожде и от усыновления. Частый у древних обычай был, умотря некоего честного и великия надежды на себе являющего юношу, усыновлять себе, кто хощет, и имения своего всецелого или от части творити его наследником. Образы усыновления многие обретаются во историах: тако Иулий Кесарь усыновил себе Августа, Август Тивериа *(Севтоний)*; и у христиан Иустин царь не отрицал, на желание Кавада царя перского, принять себе в сына племянника его Хозроа, под некиим договором, якоже пишет Прокопий кесарийский *(Прок., о войне персид., книга 1)*; и Иустиниан усыновил себе Аталарика, якоже пишет Кассиодор *(Кассиодор., 8)*; и тожде является от законов царских, о чине и правилах усыновления изданных, якоже видим в кодексе иустиниановом, в книзе 8, в титле 48, один закон Гордиана императора, осмь законов Диоклитиана и Максимина, два иустинианова; и в новеллах царя Леона конституциа, или устав двадцать четвертый. Но и в священном писании, [18] усыновил себе Иаков внучат своих Ефрема и Манассию, яко Рувима и Симеона *(Бытия, 48)*; фараонова дщерь отрока Моисеа *(исход, 2)*; Мардохей сестру

150

to their grandsons, as Jacob did, when he transferred it from the sons of Reuben to the sons of his son Joseph; while others, passing over their elder sons, granted the succession to their youngest, as did David; from which it is plain that the law which Moses gave to Israel in the Book of Numbers (*Numbers*, 27 and 36), which assigns the inher-itance to sons, and in the absence of sons, to daughters, and so on, is to be understood with the tacit proviso that the sons or daughters and other kinsfolk of the parents shall not prove wholly unworthy to inherit.

5.

The same is also confirmed by the practice of adoption. It was a frequent custom among the Ancients for a man, if he saw an honourable youth of great promise, to adopt him as his own, if he wished, and make him heir to all or part of his estate. There are many examples of adoption in history. Thus Julius Caesar adopted Augustus, Augustus adopted Tiberius (*Suetonius*); and in the Christian era, the Emperor Justin did not refuse, at the request of Kavad, king of Persia, to adopt as his son Kavad's nephew, Chosroes, on certain conditions, as Procopius of Caesarea writes (Procopius, *On the Persian War*, 1); likewise Justinian adopted Athalaric, as Cassiodorus writes (Cassiodorus, 8). The same emerges from the imperial laws concerning the procedure and rules of adoption, as we see from the Codex of Justinian, book 8, title 48, from one law of the emperor Gordian, from eight laws of Diocletian and Maximian, from two of Justinian; and from the twenty-fourth constitution, or statute in the *Novellae* of the Emperor Leo. In Holy Writ too, Jacob adopted his grandsons Ephraim and Manasseh on a level with Reuben and Simeon (*Genesis,* 48); Pharaoh's daughter adopted the boy Moses (*Exodus,*

свою двоеродную Есфиру принял во дщерь себе *(Есфир, 21)*. Усыновление же не только творили людие бесчаднии, исполняя недостаток естества своего, сынов избранием, но инии и чада имущии, усыновляли себе других, и к числу детей своих принимали, якоже известно является от вышеименованного устава Леона царя: в том бо уставе Леон запрещает, да бы впредь дети усыновленнии не сочетовалися браком с детьми естественными, как то прежде бывало.

В таковом же усыновлении явно видим, что отец, благословных ради вин, или все свое имение или поне часть его может свободно и праведно отлучити от наследия естественного сына своего. Ибо когда, имея сына своего естественного, усыновляет себе другого, не может не определити наследником своим усыновленного, но и самым усыновлением творит его наследника себе; и тако сын естественный, хотя и не винный и добрый, праведно лишается части наследия своего. Кольми же паче злонравного и неудобь исправляемого сына волен и силен отец есть отлучити от первенства, от лучшей части наследия, или и всего наследия лишити.

6.

А когда еще посмотрим на великую родителей власть собственную в наказании и казне детей своих, то и вящше слово наше укрепится. Гугон Гротий, славный законоучитель, в премудром своем рассуждении о правде мира и войны, в книге второй, [19] под числом пятым и седьмым, с древних авторов показует, что у многих народов, а именно: у фиваидов, финикиан, фригов, готфов, мексиканов, персов, и у самых древних римлян, власть была родителям, нужды ради, продавать дети своя; а собственно у римлян, власть родители имели и смертию казнить сынов своих за вину, яко тойже Гротий показует, на томже месте. Не не знаем же, что помянутые разных народов обычаи и уставы не весьма достохвальны суть, и суду философов политических яко сумненные подлежат. Оная бо детей

2); Mordechai adopted his cousin Esther (*Esther,* 2). Moreover, not only was adoption practised by childless people, thereby fulfilling a natural need, but some who already had children adopted others in addition to their own, as is clear from the abovementioned statute of the emperor Leo: for in that statute Leo forbids marriage between adopted children and natural children, as formerly happened.

From this practice of adoption, then, we clearly see that a father, for good reasons, can freely and justly bar his natural son from all or at least part of his inheritance.[17] For when a man with a son of his own adopts another, he cannot refuse to make the adopted son his heir, but by the very act of adoption he makes him his heir; and so his own son, though innocent and virtuous, righly forfeits part of his inheritance. How much greater, then, is a father's right and power to deprive a wicked and recalcitrant son of his birthright, and to bar him from most or even all of his inheritance.

6.

Moreover, when we consider the great authority which parents have to chastise and punish their children, our argument will be still further strengthened. Hugo Grotius, the eminent jurist, in his sagacious treatise on the law of war and peace (book two, article five and seven) shows from the ancient authors that among many nations (namely, the Thebans, Phoenicians, Phrygians, Goths, Mexicans, Persians and the ancient Romans themselves), parents had the right, in case of need, to sell their children; and among the Romans, in particular, they even had the right, for good cause, to put their sons to death, as Grotius shows in the same passage. We are well aware that these customs and statutes of the various peoples are not particularly commendable, and it is for political

продажа являет некое неблагоутробие лицу родительскому поносное, и ушесам человеческим не приятное; а смертная детей казнь по тому подозренная, что мимо главный суд деялась, и могла иногда сделатися по страсти. И того ради лучший иных народов устав велит родителям непокорных и пакостных детей судиам представляти, якоже узаконили римские цари в иустиниановом кодексе, книга 8, титла 47; император Александер, под числом 3; да Валерий и Галлиен императори под числом 4. И тожде указал сам Бог в законе моисееве, в книгах второзакония *(второзак., глава 21).* Разве когда родитель есть сам власть верховная, суд и меч от Бога имущая, и тогда сын может от отца, не яко от отца, но яко от государя своего, казнен быти смертию, якоже первый консуль римский, Брут, казнил сынов своих смертию за измену *(Ливий, книг. 2, гла. 5);* и Манлий диктатор римский своего сына смерти предал за преслушание указа его *(Ливий, книг. 8, гла. 7).*

Но хотя вышепомянутый народов обычай, [20] о продаже и о смертной казни детей, первый яко зверость некую в родителях являющий, а другий яко в страсти подозренный, и не от всех приятый, от иных же и отверженый видим, однакож рассуждение нам подают о великой власти родительской над детьми своими. Ибо в народах оных, которые держалися помянутых обычаев, никто не мог сему прекословити, что отец без всякого сумнительства может сына своего за вину изринути из наследия, понеже может и смертию сам казнити его: не подобает бо возбраняти ему власти меньшей, который имеет большую, якоже пишет в пандектах иустиниановых, книга 8, титла 17, закон 21. А в народах прочиих, которые именованных обычаев не приняли, самые вины, коих ради не

theorists to adjudge these doubtful matters. For the sale of children shows a certain lack of compassion, shameful in a parent and unpleasant to men's ears; while the execution of children is suspect, as having taken place without reference to the supreme court, and because it may sometimes have been done in passion. Hence the statute in force among some nations is best, which commands parents to bring their disobedient and delinquent children before the judges, as was laid down by the Roman emperors in the Codex of Justinian, Book 8, article 47, by the emperor Alexander, article 3 and the emperors Valerius and Gallienus, article 4. The same thing was enjoined by God himself in the law of Moses in the book of Deuteronomy (*Deuteronomy*, 21). Only when a father is himself the supreme authority, and wields justice and the sword from God, can a son be put to death by his father, not in his capacity as a father, but as his sovereign; as when the first Roman consul, Brutus, put his sons to death for treason (*Livy, 2, 5*), and when the Roman dictator, Manlius, had his son put to death for disobeying his order (*Livy, 8, 7*).

Now, although we see that the custom among some nations of selling or putting to death their children has not been accepted by all nations, and indeed has been rejected by some (the former, because it shows a certain cruelty in parents, the latter, because of the suspicion that it was done in passion), nonetheless it gives us an idea of the great authority which parents have over their children. For among the peoples who practised those customs, no-one could deny that a father could undoubtedly disinherit his son if he had cause, since he could even put him to death: for a lesser right may not be denied to him who has a greater, as is written in the Pandects of Justinian, (Book 8, article 17, law 21). As for the other nations who did not adopt these

приняли, показуют великую власть родительскую. Не приняли обычаев оных того ради, что продавать детей противно есть утробе отеческой, так, что родители, дети своя продающии, являют себе или весьма не имевших, и скотам природного, чадолюбия, или оное из утробы своей извергших; а смертию самим родителям дети своя казнить (аще суть человецы и сами подвластни) подозренно есть правильному суду, не по страсти ли некоей деется, якоже выше упомянулося.

Сия же вины явственно показуют, что родители имеют власть над детьми своими, делать с ними по воле своей, только бы не студное и неподозрительное их дело было. Еще же и сие, что единые помянутые обычаи о продаже и смертной казни детей, от честных народов не приняты, явно показуют, что всякая прочая власть, [21] и последовательне лишение наследия, в воле родительской осталося. Зде бо место подозрения не остается, понеже живу сущу сыну, которого лишил отец наследия, не может утаитися вина, праведно ли или неправедно лишил его наследие.

7.

Посмотрим еще на родительскую честь, и зде явится нам великое предложения нашего утверждение. О детях, которые уже из власти родительской вышли и своею волею живут, есть ли и тогда явятся родителям неблагодарни, а именно, есть ли словом ругательным или некою жестокою обидою раздражат родителей, узаконено в уставах римских лишить таковые дети свободы своей, и подвергнуть оные паки под власть родителей своих. Так узаконяют Валентиниан, Валент и Гратиан императоры, в кодексе, книга осьмая, титла 8; и не просто и не первее они узаконили сие, но утвердили древний закон, якоже речь их

customs, the very reasons why they did not do so demonstrate the great authority of parents. They did not do so for this reason: that to sell one's children is contrary to fatherly compassion; so that fathers who do sell their children show either that they altogether lack that love of their offspring which is natural even to cattle, or else that they have cast it out of their hearts; while if parents (if they themselves are subjects) put their children to death, it may be suspected by a regular court that this was done in passion, as was said above.[18]

These arguments, then, clearly show that parents have authority over their children to deal with them as they think fit, provided that their conduct is not shameful or suspect. Moreover, the fact that it is only the customs involving the sale or execution of children that have not been accepted by civilised peoples, clearly shows that every other right, and consequently the right to disinherit, remains within a parent's power. Here there remains no room for suspicion: for if a father has disinherited his son, then as long as the son lives, the cause of his disinheritance and whether it was just or unjust, cannot be concealed.

7.

Let us now consider the honour due to parents, and here too we shall find much support for our proposition. Concerning children who have already left their parents' authority and live inde-pendently, even then, if they prove ungrateful to their parents, that is, if they vex their parents by abusive language or by some grave affront, it is laid down in the Roman statutes that such children shall forfeit their freedom and be restored to their parents' authority. This is laid down by the emperors Valentinian, Valens and Gratian, in the Codex, book 3, article 8; nor were they the only ones or the first to enact this, but rather they confirmed

являет. А хотя и противный сему устав обретается Леона царя, числом в уставах его двадесятьпятый, однакож толковник уставов оных и прочиих цесарских законов, Дионисий Годефред, показует, что устав тот леонов весьма испорчен. Но что большее, в священном писании смертная казнь сыну указана, а именно, укаменовать повелено того сына, о котором донесут родители его судиам, что родителям непокорив есть и наказанием их не исправляется *(второзак., глава 21)*. Мощно от сего знать, коликая честь родительская. Не за пианство бо и иные злонравия, за которые ни у иудей, ниже у иных народов [22] никого на смерть не сужено, но за едино родителям непокорение, и за презрение наставления их, толь жестокой казне предать повелел Бог. Еще же и за злословие, отцу или матери от сына изреченное, смертную же казнь указал, в книгах левитсих *(Левит., глава 20)*.

Что же речем о отцеубийстве, так страшное сие и у самых язык неверных было беззаконие, что законоположник афинейский, Солон, не написал ему и казни в законах своих; и вопрошен, для чего умолчал и не определил, как казнить отцеубийцу, отвещал, что толикого злодеяния во всем мире не надеялся *(Цицерон в слове за Росциа америна)*. А у римлян древних, отцеубийцев так казнено, в кожаный мех зашитого вергали в воду *(Цицерон, там же)*, о которой казни так рассуждает Цицерон: *о великой премудрости! не является ли, что (отцы наши) такого человека всего добра естественного лишили, когда ему одним временем воздух, солнце, воду и землю отняли, да убивый рождшего себе лишился бы всех тех вещей, от которых вся прочая рожденна быти сказуется? Не хотели такового поврещи зверям на снедение, да бы и звери, толикого злодея*

an ancient law, as their words indicate. And although there is a statute of the emperor Leo which contradicts this (number 25 in his statutes), the commentator on these and other imperial laws, Dionysius Gothofredus,[19] shows that that statute of Leo is very corrupt. Moreover, in Holy Writ the penalty of death by stoning is prescribed for a son of whom his parents report to the judges that he is disobedient to them and is not improved by their chastisement (*Deuteronomy,* 21). From this we may acknowledge how great is the honour due to parents. For no-one was sentenced to death for drunkenness or for other vices, whether among the Jews or among other peoples: it was only for disobedience to parents and disregard of their instruction that God laid down so harsh a penalty. Indeed, in the book of Leviticus, he even prescribed the death penalty for a son who curses his father or mother (*Leviticus,* 20).

What, then, shall we say of parricide, which was deemed such a heinous crime even among the pagans themselves, that the Athenian lawgiver, Solon, did not even prescribe a penalty for it in his laws; and when asked why he had omitted to make any provision for it, he replied that he had not imagined that such wickedness could exist any-where in the world (*Cicero, in his speech for Roscius of Ameria*). Among the ancient Romans, the penalty for patricides was to be sewn up in a leather sack and thrown into the water (*Cicero, ibid.*), which penalty Cicero discusses as follows: *O excellent wisdom! Is it not clear that (our ancestors) deprived such a man of every natural good, when they took from him simultaneously air, sun, water and earth, so that he who killed him who begat him, should forfeit all those elements to which all other things are said to owe their birth? They did not want to throw such a man as prey to*

159

причастившеся, не стали нам лютейшии. Не хотели нагого воврещи в реку, дабы доплывше моря, не осквернили его, которым прочая оскверненная очищаема мнятся быти. Но и ничтоже есть так маловажное и так общее, чего бы (таковому злодею) не отняли. Что бо так общее есть, яко воздух живущим, земля умершим, море утопающим, берег изверженым из моря? Обаче таковии так живут, донележе могут, [23] *что никогдаже воздуха дыханием не приемлют, так умирают, что костей их земля не коснет, так обуреваются в воде, что вода их не омывает, так, на конец, из воды извергаются, что и при камени, покоя мертвии не обретают (Цицерон в слове за Росциа америна).* Доселе ритор римский. А до помянутой казни еще лютейшее мучение придал Константин Великий, который собственным законом повелел в мех с отцеубийцем заключать пса, змиа, петуха и обезъяну, якоже видим в кодексе иустиниановом, книга 9, титла 17.

Естьли же толь высокую честь родителям должны дети, есть ли за преслушание их и злословие лишаются свободы по уставам гражданским, а по закону божию и на смерть осуждаются, есть ли убити родителя зло, отнюд быти не могущее, судилося Солону премудрому, а прочии за такое злодейство указали страшную вышепомянутую казнь: то кто усумневатися может, что вольно и свободно всякому родителю, злонравного сына изгнати от наследия? Кому бо должна есть честь великая, тому и малое бесчестие сделанное жестоко осуждается. Кольми же паче сын непокорством и неблагодарствием своим, великое родителям (которым всякую возможную честь должен) бесчестие творящий, и за тое и смерти достоин, праведно может благодеяния лишен быти.

wild beasts, lest the beasts themselves, having partaken of so great a malefactor, should become more savage towards us. They did not want to throw him naked into a river, lest, he having floated out to sea, they should pollute that by which other polluted things are thought to be cleansed. Indeed, there is nothing so mean or common of which they did not deprive (such a miscreant). For what is as common as air to the living, earth to the dead, the sea to the drowning, the shore to those cast up by the sea? But such men live, (while they can), without ever breathing the air; when they die, the earth will not receive their bones; they are tossed on the water, without being cleansed by it, and finally, when they are cast ashore dead, they do not even find rest upon a rock (Cicero in his speech for Roscius of Ameria).[20] So spake the Roman orator, and to the penalty already mentioned a still harsher torment was added by Constantine the Great, who laid down by special decree that there should be put in the sack together with the patricide a dog, a snake, a cock and an ape, as we see in the Codex of Justinian, Book 9, article 17.

Now if children owe their parents such great respect, if for disobeying or cursing them they forfeit their freedom under civil law and are condemned to death under God's law, if to kill a parent is an evil which the wise Solon considered impossible, and for which others laid down the terrible penalty mentioned above: then who can doubt that every father has an absolute right to disinherit a wicked son? For where great honour is due, even a slight affront is harshly condemned. How much more so, then, may a son justly forfeit his parents' favour, who by his disobedience and ingratitude does grave dishonour to those to whom he owes all possible honour, and for which alone he deserves death.

8.

На конец и сие ведати подобает, что наследие имений родительских, и доброму сыну туне, а не по долгу дается. Должны родители чадам снискати имения, якоже выше под числом первым от нас показано. [24] Но рассудити подобает, кто одолжил родителей к таковому о детях своих промыслу. Не одолжили их дети: что бо дети дарили или взаим дали родителям своим, или чим у них имение аки бы должную себе мзду заслужили, когда еще не родилися от них, но и по рождении своем первее бесчисленные от них приемлют благодеяния, нежели и могут благодарити, не токмо служити им. И самое бо рождение, кто не наречет благодеяние? И коликое благодеяние! Родивший бо мене, самого мене дал мне. Что же речем о следующем, по рождении, долгом и многотрудном и сердобольном попечении, которым иссыхают, тако рещи, родители, дожидался совершенного возраста детей своих? Не токмо убо дети ничего не дарили, ниже взаим дали родителям, ниже заслужили что у них, и по тому и не одолжили их к отданию себе имений их, но и никогда не возмогут по достоянию благодарити, и отслужити им за приятые от них благодеяния, якоже согласно мудрствуют как политическии философи, так и богослови. Кто же родителей одолжил к толикому о детях своих промыслу? Одолжил во первых естества создатель, не токмо написанным на сердцах человеческих законом, но и природным к детям своим сердца склонением, которое влиял и в бессловесные животные. Одолжают же и сами себе родители, толикую в утробе своей ощущающе к детям своим любовь, яко вящше и добром их радуются, и злоключением уязвляются, нежели своим. И по тому когда отвергают от себе детей, мощно знать, [25] что нестерпимую уже злобу

8.

Finally, it should also be understood that a patrimony is bequeathed, even to a worthy son, out of good will, not out of duty. Parents must acquire goods for their children, as we showed above under number 1. We should consider, however, who it was who obliged parents to make such provision for their children. It was not the children: for what did children ever give or lend to their parents, or how did they earn the right to their property, as if it were some recompense owed to them, when they had not even been born, but rather first received at their birth countless blessings from them, for which they can never thank them enough, let alone deserve them? For who will not call birth itself a blessing? And how great a blessing! For he who begat me gave me to myself. And what shall we say of the long, laborious and anxious care which follows birth, with which parents, so to speak, exhaust themselves while waiting for their children to grow up? For not only have children neither given nor lent anything to their parents, nor deserved anything from them, and so have not obliged them to give them their property, but rather they can never sufficiently thank them and repay them for the blessings which they have received from them, as both political theorists and theologians agree. Who, then, obliged fathers to make such provision for their children? In the first place, it was the Creator of Nature, not only through the law that is written in men's hearts but also through the innate affection for their offspring with which he has inspired even dumb animals. Parents, then take this obligation on themselves, feeling in their hearts such love for their children, that they rejoice more at their success and grieve more at their ill fortune, than at their own. When, therefore, they disown their children, it may be

163

усмотрили в них.

Утверждают долг тот и гражданские законы, да никогда разрушится чин естественный, и да не явится крайнего бесчеловечия образ: отец или матерь, детей своих ненавидящии туне; хотя больше не надеятися да бы родители без вины когда возненавидели чад своих, нежели не надеялся Солон, да бы когда сын на родителя руку поднесл. Должни убо родители снабдевати всячески детей своих, но видим от кого долг тот наложен на них, а от детей не наложен; и по тому наследие полагается в числе туне творимых благодеяний, что является от такового судебного случая: когда умрет некто, который займом одолжился, и до смерти своей долгов не заплатил заимодавцу, тогда сын должника оного, наследствовав имения родительские, должен от тех имений платить заимодавцу до исполнения всего долга; и естьли не может исполнитися долг, разве отданием всего имения, то и все имение сын заимодавцу отдать принужден будет судом; от чего знать мощно, что имения оные не так были должные сыну, как заимодавцу. Ибо естьли бы так должные были сыну, как и заимодавцу, то подобало бы оные разделити между сыном и заимодавцем, хотя бы заимодавцу и не весь долг выплачен был, так, как когда умрет кто многим заимодавцам одолжен, разделяются его имения заимодавцам по пропорции или по размеру долгов, хотя бы им и не дополнилися взаим данные деньги. [26] Но наследник сын не может так делитися с родительским заимодавцем имениями родительскими, донележе не дополнит всего, что взаим дано было отцу его. Да и по тому тожде известно, что отец до смерти своей при себе держит, аще хощет, имения своя, и когда наставит и понудит сына своим промыслом (достиг довольных к тому лет) питатися, творит достохвально. По смерти же его, есть ли нет заимодавцев, наследует сын родительские имения, что нет

concluded that they have discerned in them some intolerable evil.

This duty is also confirmed by civil laws, which forbid the violation of the natural order or the occurrence of any kind of gross inhumanity, such as a father or mother hating their children without cause; though we have no more reason to expect a parent ever to hate his children without cause than Solon had to expect a son ever to raise his hand against his father. So while parents are bound to provide for their children in every way, we see by whom that duty is imposed on them: it is not imposed by the children; and therefore inheritance is reckoned among the blessings granted out of good will, as is clear from the following legal case: when a man dies in debt without having paid his creditor, the son, on inheriting his father's estate, must repay the creditor in full out of the estate; and if the debt cannot be discharged except by surrendering the whole estate, the son will be compelled by law to surrender the whole estate to the creditor; from which we may conclude that the son did not have as much right to the estate as the creditor. For if the son had as much right to it as the creditor, it should be divided between son and creditor, even though the whole debt might not be repaid to the creditor, just as, when a man dies in debt to many creditors, his goods are divided among the creditors in proportion to the debts, even though the debts may not be fully discharged. But a son who inherits cannot divide his father's goods with his creditor in this way until he has discharged his father's debt in full. Hence it also follows that a father, if he wishes, retains control of his property for as long as he lives; and if, when his son is of age, he tells him to earn his own sustenance, and makes him do so, he does a praiseworthy act. On his death, however, if

другого ближшего к наследию их.

Еще же и в священном писании оная благая от Бога нам подаваемая наследием нарицаются, которые туне и благодатно подает Бог. Слыши апостольское слово: *аще от закона наследие, не к тому уже от обетования: Аврааму же обетованием дарова Бог (галат., 3).* И учители древнии толкуют *наследие* в разуме туне подаваемых благ. Златоустый на сие апостольское слово, в посланиих к Колоссаем, в главе первой, *благодаряще Бога и отца, призвавшего вас в причастие наследия святых в свете,* тако рассуждает: *Чего ради нарицает наследием? Да покажет, что от благих своих дел никтоже получает царствие; но якоже наследие есть паче благого случая, тако и зде. Никтоже бо такое жития исправление показует, да бы достоин царствия явился, но все дара его есть. Того бо ради глаголет: "егда вся сотворите, глаголите, яко раби непотребни есмы, яже бо должни бехом сотворити, сотворихом."* Тойжде толк на помянутое слово апостольское предлагают [27] Феофилакт и Екумений.

От сего же кто не видит, что родитель может праведно сына, когда не благодарен явитя, лишити наследия своего? Не свое его добро отнимает ему; не задолжился родитель сыну займом его или заслугою, но естественным законом должен был воскормити его до возраста; по благоутробию же родительскому одолжил сам себе (которое одолжение неистотное и непрямое, и не подлежащее правильной тяжбе одолжение есть) и отписать ему по себе имения. Но когда сын злонравием раздражит утробу отеческую, и еще является по себе, что наследствованные имения на

there are no creditors, a son inherits his father's property, because there is no-one with a better right to it.

Moreover, in Holy Writ, the blessings bestowed on us by God are called an inheritance, which God gives of his own free will and grace. Hear the word of the Apostle: *For if the inheritance be of the law, it is no more of promise: but God gave it to Abraham by promise* (*Galatians,* 3). The Early Fathers interpret *inheritance* in the sense of blessings freely granted. Chrysostom, discussing these words of the Apostle in the Epistle to the Colossians, chapter one, *Giving thanks unto God the Father, which hath made ye meet to be partakers of the inheritance of the saints in light,* reasons as follows: *Why does he call it an inheritance? To show that no one obtains the Kingdom by his good works; but as an inheritance is rather the result of good fortune, so it is here. For no one shows such improvement in his life as to be worthy of the Kingdom, but all is of His free gift. Therefore he says: 'When you have done all, say, we are unprofitable servants, for we have done that which was our duty to do.'* Theophylact and Ecumenius place the same interpretation on the Apostle's words.

Who, then, does not see from this that a father can rightly disinherit his son, if he proves ungrateful? The benefit of which he deprives him is not the son's by right; the father has not put himself in his debt through some loan or service from the latter; he was obliged by natural law only to provide for him until his majority; but out of fatherly affection he took upon himself an obligation (not a true and genuine obligation, or one enforceable by legal action) to bequeath his property to him. But when the son by his unworthiness breaks his father's heart and also makes it plain that he will put his

зло употребит, не одолжается прочее родитель снабдевать, или творить наследником, но может, иногда же и долженствует отчуждить его от себе и от своего наследия.

Сия обще о законе власти родительской довольна суть к ясному и несумненному познанию и самим невежам, како всяк родитель волен есть сына своего, аще неблагодарна, и наставление отеческое отметающа, и надежды покаяния не являюща усмотрит, низринути из первенства, отъяти часть наследия, или и всего наследия лишити.

9.

Сие же ведая, кто уже усумневатися может о отцах государях самодержавных? Аще бо простый родитель, человек подвластный, такую власть над сыном имеет, то как бы не имел той родитель, который купно и государь есть? Самодержавный бо государь не только подданному народу, но и своим детям государь есть. И что большее, есть ли будет сын государь, [28] а не государь отец его (что может прилучитися в государстве не наследственном или и в наследственном, когда от государя деда наследствовал бы государство внук, мимо сына его а своего отца), тогда сын государь и отцу своему государь будет, и сын по естеству будет уже отцу своему отец по высочайшей власти своей. Кольми же паче и родитель и государь волен, свободен и праведно силен есть в устроении детей своих, усмотревая их добронравие или злонравие, ум или малоумие, охоту к высокой правительства философии, или леность и небрежение, должное себе яко отцу и государю повиновение, или непокорство, неблагодарствие и противность, определять себе в наследники, или лишать наследия. Все бо что выше показано обще о родителях, в родителях государях сугубо содержится. Возвратимся мало на предреченная, и скоро пробежим оныя.

inheritance to bad use, his father is no longer bound to provide for him or to make him his heir, but can and indeed sometimes must disown and disinherit him.

These facts about the law concerning parental authority in general are enough for even the most ignorant to understand clearly and without doubt that every father, if he sees that his son is ungrateful, rejects his fatherly instruction and shows no hope of repentance, is entitled to deprive him of his birthright, and of part or all of his inheritance.

9.

Knowing this, therefore, who now can have any doubt concerning fathers who are sovereign monarchs? For if an ordinary father, a subject, has such authority over his son, how could a father who is also a monarch, not have it? For a sovereign monarch is sovereign not only over his people but also over his children. Moreover, if a son is monarch, and his father is not (which can happen in a non-hereditary state, or even in an hereditary state, when a grandson succeeds to his grand-father's throne, passing over his father), then the son will also be his father's sovereign, and although a son by nature, he will be a father to his father by virtue of his supreme power. How much more, then, does he who is both father and monarch wield absolute power and just authority in the directing of his children, to appoint as heir or to disinherit according to their good or bad character, their intelligence or lack of it, their zeal for the lofty science of government or their indolence and neglect, their due obedience to himself as father and sovereign, or their insubordination, ingra-titude and resistence. For all that was shown above about fathers in general hold doubly good for fathers who are monarchs. Let us return briefly to

Показалося под первым числом, как волен есть сына за нераскаянную злобу его отогнать от себе и наследия своего. Сугубая тая свобода есть самодержавному родителю: волен он есть над детьми своими яко отец их, волен есть и яко государь их. Не может бо никтоже помыслить, что государевы дети не суть его подданнии: понеже были бы они весьма не подвластнии в мире сем, что никому же от Бога дано, кроме самых высочайших самодержавных властей. [29]

Показалося под другим числом, что иногда родители нетокмо могут, но и должни суть злонравных детей отчуждати: и сия должность сугубая есть на самодержавных родителях: должен есть государь смотреть за сыном, да не будет вредливый дому своему, и се должен яко родитель; но яко государь должен смотреть, да не будет вредлив сын его добру общему и всему отечеству, или делом или образом, или обоима тема, что яснее нижше покажется.

Показалося под числом третьим, какую родителям к извержению из наследия детей власть дают законы гражданские: как же сей власти не сугубо имеет государь родитель? Аще бы не имели государи власти над детьми своими, данной всем родителям, были бы они родители от простых родителей меньшии; и аще бы коей власти при себе не имели, якобую они же дают прочим, не имели бы государи того, что прочиим дают, и как бы могли давати прочиим, чего сами не имели бы?

Показалося под числом четвертым, как и слово божие глаголемою зде властию вооружает родителей: а ктож не видит, что слово божие самодержавных родителей сугубо же оною властию укрепляет? Не отъемлет бо Бог родителям самодержцам, что дает простым родителям; а сверх того, и всякую душу, и тако и детей их, полной и совершенной

the points made earlier, and quickly summarize them.

1.   Under No. 1 we showed that a father is free to disown and disinherit a son for inveterate wickedness; a father who is a sovereign is doubly so entitled: he has authority over his children as their father and also as their sovereign. No one can suppose that a monarch's children are not his subjects; for then they would not be subject to any authority in the world, which God grants to no-one apart from the supreme sovereign authorities themselves.

2.   Under No. 2 we showed that sometimes fathers not only may but must disown their unworthy children; and this obligation holds doubly good for fathers who are sovereigns:as a father, a monarch must see that his son does not become a danger to his house; but as a monarch, he must see that his son does not become a danger to the public good and to the whole country, by deed or by example, or both, as will be shown more clearly below.

3.   Under No. 3 we showed the authority which the civil laws give to parents to disinherit their children: does not a father who is a monarch possess this authority twice over? If monarchs did not have the authority over their children which is granted to all fathers, they would, as fathers, be inferior to ordinary fathers; and if they themselves lacked the authority which they give to others, monarchs would not have what they give to others; and how could that be?

4.   Under No. 4 we showed how the word of God also invests parents with the authority of which we speak; and who can fail to see that it doubly invests sovereigns with that authority? For God does not take from sovereigns what he gives to ordinary fathers; moreover he subjects everyone, including, therefore, their children, to their complete and

воле их подвергает, якоже учит Апостол в послании к римлянам. *(рим, 13)* [30]

Показалося под числом пятым, что волен всяк родитель и не бесчадный, благословных вин ради, творити усыновление, и по тому наследие свое разделяти. Сугубо и сие может родитель государь, по сугубому попечению своему, и высокого своего дому и всего государства; что бо на пример, когда будут некоему государю дети не злы нравом, но зело скудоумнии, еще же и вельми немощнии, и отчаянной болезни подлежащии, и весьма ко владению неугоднии, не может ли государь усыновить себе, и к числу их принять честного и умного юношу?

Показалося под числом шестым, какая собственная власть родителям к наказанию, у многих же народов и к смертной казне детей своих. Сугубая власть сия у родителя самодержца без всякого прекословия. Кто бо речет, что не может он и детей своих судить на смерть, яко государь? Но и яко отец тожде может, того ради, что таковый отец не имеет вышшего суда, которому бы представил винного сына; в чем от простых родителей весьма отличен есть. Аще же то может, то кольми паче может первенство, или часть наследия, или и все наследие отнять сыну своему.

Показалося под числом седьмым, как высокую везде и всегда честь должни дети родителям своим, и коликой казни достойны суть за бесчестие или нападение их, и по тому без сумнения отчуждению подпадают. То кто всего того сугубо и без сравнения не видит на детях государей самодержавных? [31] Аще бо сын государев обесчестит отца своего, в едином человеце сугубую честь разрушит, высокую родительскую и высочайшую монаршую. И что государи злонравных и

absolute authority, as the Apostle teaches in the Epistle to the Romans (*Romans,* 13).[21]

5. Under No. 5 we showed that every father, even if he already has children, is free to adopt for good reason, and hence to divide the property which he bequeathes. A monarch is doubly entitled to do so by virtue of his twofold concern, both for his own eminent house and for the entire State; for example, when a monarch has children who, though not of bad character, are of very low intelligence, physically weak, suffering from some hopeless disease and wholly unfit to rule, can the monarch not adopt and add to their number some honest and intelligent young man?

6. Under No. 6 we showed the special authority which parents have to punish their children, including, among many peoples, the power to put them to death. Incontrovertibly, this is a twofold power in the case of a father who is a sovereign. For who will deny that, as a monarch, he can condemn his children to death? But he can also do so as a father: for in his case he has no higher court before which to present his guilty son; in which respect he is quite different from ordinary fathers. If, then, he can do that, how much more can he deprive his son of his birthright, or of part or all of his inheritance.

7. Under No. 7 we showed the great honour which children everywhere and at all times owe to their parents, and how great a punishment they deserve for dishonouring or injuring them, and hence that they are undoubtedly liable to be disowned. Who, then, does not see that all this holds doubly good, indeed incomparably more so, for the children of sovereign monarchs? For if a monarch's son dishonours his father, he violates the twofold honour due to one man: the great honour owed to fathers and the supreme honour

противных себе детей своих наказуют или казнят обычно меньше и кротчае, нежели подданных прочиих, дают то чести крове своея и отеческому своему благоутробию и сердоболию, а не аки бы меньшая их, нежели прочиих подданных вина была.

Показалось на конец под числом осьмым, что наследие, не яко некая прямая мзда, но яко туне даемое благодеяние детям дается от родителей, не детьми своими, но естественным законом к тому одолжаемых, и что долженство тое неблагодарствием детей разрушается. И сие все в лицах родителей самодержавных усугубляемо видим. Не заслужили у отца государя дети его, что прекормление не токмо во всем изобильное, но и высокочестное имеют; но за сие и Богу и родителеви своему безмерно должни благодарны быти. Кольми же паче ни у кого они сами собою не заслужили того, что родитель их государь есть: како бо и когда заслужити сие могли?

Но уже приступим к собственному рассуждению монаршей власти, и что оное покажет к предложенному слову, увидим.

Вторые доводы от рассуждения власти родителей государей

10.

И сами государи никаковой заслузе своей толь высокого сана восписати не могут. Ни которая бо заслуга не может так высоко оценена быть, да бы ей монаршеская корона, яко прямая мзда, должна была. Может кто в избирательном, а не в наследном государстве, [32] того дослужити, что по смерти государя будет пред прочиими достоин короны; но оной себе яко должной мзды домогатися не может. Но всякий

owed to monarchs. If monarchs usually chastise or punish their rebellious and recalcitrant children less often and more mildly than they do their other subjects, they do so for the sake of their family honour and out of fatherly affection and compassion, and not because their children's guilt is less than that of other subjects.

Finally, under No. 8, we showed that an inheritance is bestowed by parents on their children not as a just reward, but as a blessing granted of their own free will; that this obligation is placed upon them not by their children, but by natural law, and that it is rescinded if the children prove ungrateful. We see that all this holds doubly good in the case of fathers who are sovereigns. The children of a monarch did nothing to deserve from their father the fact that they enjoy not merely abundant but princely provision in everything; in return, however, they owe both to God and to their father an immeasurable debt of gratitude. How much less, then, did they themselves do anything to deserve from anyone the fact that their father is a monarch: for how and when could they have done so?

Let us now proceed, however, to consider monarchical power in particular, and see what it adds to what has gone before.

Second series of arguments concerning the power of parents who are monarchs
10.

Not even monarchs themselves can ascribe their lofty rank to any merit of their own. For no merit can be accounted so high as to claim the monarch's crown as its just reward. In an elective, though not in an hereditary state, a man can through his merit bring it about that, on the monarch's death, he will be deemed worthier of the crown than others; but

государь, наследием ли или избранием скипетр получивший, от Бога оное приемлет: Богом бо *царие царствуют и сильнии пишут правду (притч., 8); от Господа дается им держава, и сила от Вышнего (прем., 6); владеет вышний царством человечим, и емуже восхощет, дает е (даниел, 4).* То како может государев сын у родителя своего короны, аки бы некоего долга, истязати? В наследном государстве по смерти государевой, должна корона сыну его, аще тому не явилася противная воля государева, даже до смерти его: но по чему корона должна сыну государеву, о том нижше сего будет рассуждение. Но хотя народ сыну государеву, от родителя неотлученному, по смерти родительской и должен корону, но сам родитель государь весьма недолжен, по предложенным доводам, но и последующим.

11.

Ведаем, что монарх родитель сугубою властию содержит под собою сына своего, то есть, яко родитель сына и яко государь подданного, о чем выше упомянулося. Яко родитель, должен рожденному от себе сыну честное, и своей толь высокой фамилии подобающее прекормление; а како, и доколе сие должен, уже выше, в общем о власти родительской рассуждении изъяснилося. А яко государь подданному наследие государства своего, по чему бы должен был, трудно сказать, понеже прочим своим подданным сего не должен. И есть ли кто скажет, [33] что подобает родителю пещися по всякой возможности, дабы сын его был во всем подобный ему, (ибо сын есть образ родителя своего, и аки бы другий он), и по тому подобает родителю, да аще сам монарх есть, и сына бы во свое время толикой чести не лишил: ответствуем на сие не

he cannot claim it as his due reward. Rather, every monarch, whether he receives his sceptre through inheritance or by election, receives it from God: for it is through God that *kings reign and princes decree justice* (*Proverbs*, 8); *power is given them by the Lord and strength from the Most High* (*The Wisdom of Solomon*, 6); *the most High ruleth in the kingdom of men, and giveth it to whomsoever he will*, (*Daniel*, 4). How, then, can a monarch's son demand the throne from his father as of right? In an hereditary State, on the monarch's death, the crown must pass to his son, unless the monarch decided otherwise before his death: why the crown must pass to the monarch's son will be considered below. However, although the people must confer the crown on the monarch's son on his father's death, provided that he was not disowned by his father, the monarch himself is under no such obligation, for the reasons already stated and also for the following reasons.

11.

We know that a monarch who is a father has a twofold authority over his son, namely, as a father over his son and as a monarch over his subject, as was mentioned above. As a father, he owes his son an honourable provision and one befitting his eminent family; what form of provision and for how long he owes it has already been explained above in the discussion of parental authority generally. But why, as a monarch, he should owe to him, as a subject, the succession to his throne, is difficult to say: for he does not owe it to his other subjects. And if anyone says that a father should make every possible effort to make his son resemble him in everything (for a son is the image of his father and, as it were, his other self), and that therefore a father, even if he is the monarch himself, should in his turn not deprive his son of

177

единократно.

И первее, не противимся тому, что подобает родителю прилежно пещися, дабы во всем ему уподобился сын его; но токмо во всем том, что лицу сыновнему прилично, то есть, в мудрости, добронравии и во всех добродетелях, а не и в самой верховной власти и чести; инако подобало бы сыну от рождения своего, или поне от совершенного смысла и возраства, действительно соцарствовати отцу своему государю, не дожидаяся смерти его: что ни где не деется.

И зде воспомянути приличествует, что честнии христианстии историки предали нам о царе Феодосии Великом. Вручал он сынов своих Аркадиа и Онориа, Арсению, мудростию и честным житием свидетельствованному, в наставление. Надсматривал же сам Феодосий явно и тайно, как их Арсений учит; и когда увидел, что Арсений стоя, царевичам седящим, предает учение, разгневался за сие на Арсениа, аки бы на соблазняющего детей своих. Когда же Арсений извиняяся сказал, что таковая честь им достойна яко царям, словом сим паче осорблен Феодосий рекл: *ты ли и поставляеши царями? Силен есть царь небесный дати им царство на земле, будут ли того достойни; аще же обрящутся зли* [34] *и недостойни, то лучше им пребыти без царствования, нежели царствовати с безумием.* Кто такового феодосиева любомудрия с удивлением не похвалит? И кто не возжелает, да бы вси государи тако мудрствовали? Видим же от сего, что достохвальный оный монарх тщался прилежно, да бы сыны его подобны ему были, и хотел, чаю, да бы были и лучшии от него, понеже бодро промышлял о добром их наставлении; но уподобляти их честию себе не хотел, и издалече не допускал, и не в своей, но в божии то силе

this great honour: to this we have more than one answer.

1.   First, we shall not deny that a father should diligently strive to make his son resemble him in everything; but only in everything proper to a son, that is, in wisdom, goodness and all the virtues, but not in supreme power and honour; otherwise, it would be right for a son, as soon as he was born, or at least was of full age and understanding, actually to reign together with his father, without waiting for the latter's death; which is nowhere the case.

It is appropriate here to recall what reliable Christian historians have passed down to us concerning the emperor Theodosius the Great. He entrusted the upbringing of his sons, Arcadius and Honorius, to Arsenius, a man known for his wisdom and honourable way of life. Theodosius himself, however, kept watch, both openly and secretly, to see how Arsenius taught them; and when he saw that Arsenius delivered his instruction standing up, while the princes remained seated, he was angry with Arsenius for what he regarded as leading his children astray. When Arsenius, in excuse, said that as emperors, they were entitled to this honour, Theodosius, still more offended at these words, said: *Do you, then, make them emperors? The King of Heaven has power to grant them a kingdom on earth, if they are worthy of it; but if they prove wicked and unworthy, it were better for them to live without ruling, than to rule without understanding.* Who will not admire and praise such wisdom in Theodosius? And who will not wish that all monarchs reasoned as he did? So we see from this that that praiseworthy monarch strove diligently to make his sons resemble him, and, indeed, wished them to surpass him, since he took such pains over their upbringing; but he did not wish to make them his equals in honour, and he

полагал, и то с договором, аще достойни будут .

Другий ответ наш от образов прочиих чинов, например: священник не должен пещися, да бы сын его был священник; тако и воевода, и градоначальник, и философский учитель, и прочии, имея на себе долженство от Бога и от естества положенное, пещися, да бы их дети были умнии, добрии, и чести достоинии, не имеют долженства тщатися весьма, детей своих в чин себе подобный выводити. То для чего бы цари родители обязаны были долженством, которое на прочиих родителях не лежит?

Третий ответ: должни цари родители, так наставляти сыны своя, да бы они явилися достойни царствования, и тако да бы могли быти им подобны достоинством своим; но сие самое долженство являет, что царь родитель не должен сына поставляти с собою, или по себе царем; понеже бо должен есть наставляти сына к достоинству царствования, то просто на царство возводити его не должен. [35]

Четвертый ответ наш, что мы зде рассуждаем сие наипаче: весьма ли должен, как простый родитель, так и родитель государь, сына своего подобна и равна себе творити, не смотря на его достоинство; так, что хотя бы негоден и непотребен сын, то должен был бы отец, есть ли не лучший от себе, то поне не меньший чин ему дати. И в таковом договорном а не простом рассуждении, не видим того на родителях долженства, понеже его не показуют нам ни естественные, ни божественные, ниже гражданские законы; но еще показуют все противное, как то уже известно есть и от вышепредложенных доселе доводов, и от следующих доводов же и образов яснее известится.

kept them far from that, and left it to God's will, not his own, and even then only on condition that they should prove worthy of it.

2.   Our second answer is taken from the example of other callings: for example, a priest need not see that his son becomes a priest; likewise a general, a mayor, a teacher of philosophy, and so on, though they do have a duty, placed on them by God and nature, to see that their children are intelligent, virtuous and worthy of honour, they are not bound to make special efforts to raise their children to a calling like their own. Why, then, should kings be under an obligation which is not incumbent on other fathers?

3.   Our third answer is as follows: kings must bring up their sons to be fit to rule and thus to be their equals in worth; but this very obligation shows that a king is not bound to make his son co-ruler, or king after his death; precisely because he must bring up his son to be worthy of ruling, he is not bound to raise him to the throne in any event.

4.   Our fourth answer, which is the particular subject of our present treatise, is to ask whether a father, be he an ordinary father or a monarch, is really bound to make his son similar and equal to himself, regardless of his merit; so that, even though the son is unfit and unworthy, the father would still be bound to give him a rank, if not superior, at least not inferior to his own. Even under such hypothetical circumstances, we see no such obligation incumbent on fathers; for there is no mention of it in natural, divine or civil law; but rather they show the very opposite, as is clear from the preceding arguments, and as will become still clearer from the following arguments and examples.

12.

Пособствует же нам к сему жалостное пререкание премудрого Екклисиаста на неизвестных наследников; которое пререкание, хотя и обще родителям служит, однак яко от царя изреченное, и вину вящшую в царской фамилии имеющее, вящше самим государям годствует. Есть же таковое: повествует первее Соломон, как много промыслом, тщанием и трудом своим собрал себе стяжания царского, так что всех прежде его бывших в Иерусалиме превозшел; по том же не известен сый, кто и каков оные трудов его плоды наследит, тако сетует: *и возненавидех аз всяческая мира, и труд мой, в немже трудихся аз под солнцем, яко оставляю его человеку будущему по мне. и кто весть, мудр ли будет, или безумен?* [36] *и обладати имать всем трудом, в немже трудихся, и мудровах под солнцем, и се же суета. и обратихся аз отрещися сердцу моему о всем труде, в немже трудихся под солнцем: яко есть человек, егоже труд его в мудрости и в разуме и в мужестве: и человек, иже не трудится о нем, даст ему часть его: и сие есть суета и лукавство велие, яко бывает человеку в сем труде его, и во изволении сердца его, иже труждается под солнцем. (екклисиаст., глава 2).*

Когда же сие пререкание, духом святым от Соломона изреченное, слышим, можем ли не совоздыхать и не соболезновати царям, таковую иногда трудов своих тщету терпящим в наследниках своих, яковой бояся, Соломон отреклся всея своея радости, которую плодами трудов своих получил? И сталося то, чего он боялся. Не известен был, каков наследник его будет, мудр ли, или безумен; и боялся, не безумен ли будет. Явился же его наследник Ровоам безумен: презрев бо искусных министров совет,

12.

We receive guidance here from the pitiful lament of the wise Ecclesiastes against unknown heirs; which lament, although it applies to fathers in general, yet, coming as it does from a king and having greatest relevance in a royal family, is most apposite to monarchs. It is as follows: Solomon first tells how, through his industry, zeal and toil, he has amassed a kingly fortune, so that he has surpassed all his predecessors in Jerusalem; but then, not knowing who and what kind of man will inherit the fruits of his labours, he laments as follows: *Yea, I hated all my labour which I had taken under the sun: because I should leave it unto the man that shall be after me. And who knoweth whether he shall be a wise man or a fool? Yet shall he have rule over all my labour wherein I have laboured, and wherein I have showed myself wise under the sun. This is also vanity. Therefore I went about to cause my heart to despair of all the labour which I took under the sun. For there is a man whose labour is in wisdom and in knowledge and in equity; yet to a man who hath not laboured therein shall he leave it for his portion. This also is vanity and a great evil. For what hath man of all his labour and of the vexation of his heart wherein he hath laboured under the sun?* (*Ecclesiastes, 2*).

Now when we hear this lament, uttered by the Holy Spirit through Solomon, how can we fail to condole and sympathise with kings who sometimes endure just such a reversal of their labours by their successors as Solomon feared, when he renounced all the joy which he had received from the fruits of his labours? And it turned out as he feared. He did not know what kind of man his successor would be, a wise man or a fool; and he feared that he would be a fool. And his successor, Jeroboam, turned out to be a fool: for spurning the counsel of experienced

и послушав совета малоумных человек, раздражил народ израильский, и десять колен отстало от него, и тако труды отца своего мало не доконца разорил, о чем пишется в книгах третиих царств *(3 книга царств, глава 12).* Есть ли же бы известен был Соломон, что так безумный наследник его будет, то как бы не промыслил иного себе наследника, аще бы Ровоама исправити прежде не возмогл, или и увидел бы его к исправлению отнюд неугодна и отчаянна? Ктож уже сказати может, что государи должни [37] суть просто и без рассуждения ума и нравов сыновних, сыны своя творити по себе наследники? И естьли бы кто упрямо сие твердил, тот понужден самим собою был бы сказать и сие, что государи не должни смотреть, да бы государства трудом их добре исправленные и утвержденные, не приходили в бедство крайнего своего разорения: и тако уподобилися бы государи малым отрокам, которые на улицы строеньишка своя из песка созидают, и тотчас отшедше от них, оставляют оные в растоптание мимоходящим.

13.

Приступим еще ближше к престолу царскому, и вопросим, что значит оная славная царей титла, *величество,* или, якоже прочии европейские народы с латинска нарицают, *маестат* или *маестет.* Наречие сие просто, само собою в употреблении грамматическом, значит всякое вещи единой пред другими превосходство, хотя речь есть о словесных животных, хотя о бессловесных и о не живущих. Но не в сем тако пространном разуме рассуждаем зде *величество,* но токмо в разуме философии политической. Но и в той еще философии, двойственный разум обретается имени сего *величество.* Иногда бо свободнейшим употреблением приемлется за превосходную, но не за верховную честь коего либо честного лица: обретаются такового употребления имени сего примеры, хотя не многие, у некиих древних римских писателей; но обще у всех народов как славенских, так и прочих, сие наречие [38] *маестет* или *величество* употребляется за самую крайне превосходную честь, и единым токмо верховным властям подается, и значит не токмо достоинство их

ministers and hearkening to that of men of little understanding, he angered the people of Israel, and the ten tribes abandoned him, and so he all but destroyed his father's labours, as is written in the third Book of Kings, chapter 12. Now if Solomon had known that his successor would be such a fool, would he not have provided himself with another successor, :f he could not first make Jeroboam mend his ways, or if he saw that he was utterly incorrigible? Who can say now that monarchs are bound, under all circumstances and regardless of their sons' intellect and morals, to make them their successors? If anyone were to insist that this is so, he would also have to say that monarchs need not trouble to prevent their kingdoms, reformed and strengthened by their toil, from going to wrack and ruin; and so monarchs would be like small boys who build sandcastles in the streets, and leave them, as soon as they have gone, to be trodden down by passers-by.

13.

Let us approach still closer to the royal throne, and ask the meaning of that glorious royal title, *majesty,* or, as other European peoples call it, from the Latin, *majestas* or *Majestät.* The word itself, in its grammatical usage, simply means any kind of superiority of one object over others, be they human, animal or inanimate. But we are not here considering *majesty* in this broad sense, but only in the sense in which it is used in political theory. But even there, the word *majesty* has a double meaning. For sometimes, in very free usage, it denotes the special, though not supreme honour of some worthy person: a few rare examples of this use of the word are to be found in certain ancient Roman authors; in general, however, among all peoples, Slavic and others, the word *Majestät* or *majesty* is used of the supreme honour; it refers to the supreme

185

превысокое, и которого, по Бозе, большего нет в мире, но и власть законодательную крайне действительную, крайный суд износящую, повеление неотрицаемое издающую, а самую ни каковым же законам не подлежащую. Тако изряднейшии законоучители описуют *величество,* между которыми Гугон Гроций именно так глаголет: *высочайшая власть (величество нарицаемая) есть, которой деяния ни чией же власти не подлежат, так да бы могли уничтоженная быти изволением другого человека; когда же глаголю другого, изъемлю самого его, кто такую власть высочайшую имеет: ему бо волю свою переменити мощно. (Гугон, о правде войны и мира, книга 1, глава 3, число 7).*

Разумети же подобает, что когда глаголют законоучители, что власть высочайшая, *величеством* нарицаемая, не подлежит ни коей же другой власти, слово есть только о власти человеческой; божией бо власти подлежит, и законам от Бога, яко на сердцах человеческих написанным, тако и в десятословии преданным повиноватися долженствует; законам же от человек, аще и добрым, яко к общей пользе служащим, не подлежит. Но и закону божию так подлежит, что за преступление того божию токмо, а не человеческому суду повинна: и тако всяк самодержавный государь человеческого закона хранити не должен. Кольми же паче за преступление [39] закона человеческого не судим есть: заповеди же божие хранити должен, но за преступление их самому токмо Богу ответ даст, а от человек судим быти не может; что все довольно покажем и от разума естественного и от слова божия, и древних учителей свидетельством.

Ведаем сие во первых от естественного разума: понеже бо нарицается и есть верховная, высочайшая и крайняя власть, то како может законам человеческим подлежати? Аще бы подлежала, не была бы верховная. А когда и сами государи творят то, что гражданские уставы повелевают,

authorities alone, and it denotes not only their high dignity, than which, after God, there is none greater in the world, but also the supreme legislative, judicial and executive power, that power which is itself not subject to any laws whatsoever. Such is the definition of *majesty* given by the most eminent jurists, including Hugo Grotius, who says as follows: *The supreme power* (*called majesty*) *is that whose actions are not subject to the power of anyone so as to be annulled at the will of another; when I say another, I exclude him who wields this supreme power; for he is free to change his mind.* (*Hugo Grotius, On the law of war and peace, book 1, chapter 3, no. 7*).[22]

It must be understood, however, that when the jurists say that the supreme power called *majesty* is not subject to any other power, they mean any human power; for it is subject to God's power, and it must obey the laws of God, both those which he has written in men's hearts and those which he has handed down in the Decalogue; but it is not subject to the laws of man, even if they are good and promote the general welfare. But it is subject to God's law only in the sense that it is answerable for transgressing it to God's judgement alone, and not to man's: and so no sovereign monarch is obliged to observe man-made law. How much less, then, can he be judged for transgressing it: he must keep God's commandments, but he will answer to God alone for transgressing them, and he cannot be judged by men; as to all of which we shall give ample proof from natural reason, from the word of God and from the testimony of the Early Fathers.

We know this, first, from natural reason: for since this power is called, and is, the supreme, highest and utmost power, how can it be subject to man-made laws? If it were subject to them, it would not be supreme. Even when monarchs themselves do

творят по воле, а не по нужде: се же или образом своим поощряя подданных к доброхотному законохранению, или и утверждая законы, яко добрые и полезные.

Ведаем паки тожде от священноно писания: явственнно учит нас о сем дух святый у Екклисиаста: *уста царя сохрани, и о словесех клятвы Божия не тщися* (не тощ являйся в клятве твоей пред Богом, о твоем царю подчинении изреченной). *От лица бо его пойдеши, не стани в словеси лукавне; яко вся яже аще восхощет сотворит, якоже царь совладе. И кто речет ему, что твориши? (Екклисиаст, 8).* Явственно дух святый, научая подданных совершенного царям своим повиновения, показует, что власть царская весьма в повелениях и деяниях своих свободна есть, и ни чиему истязанию о делах своих не подлежит. И видим зде царей выше достоинства всех прочиих человек возведенных: [40] что бо в помянутом Екклисиаста слове глаголется о царе, *и кто речет ему, что твориши?* то ни о коем же другом чину в писании не обретается, токмо о едином Бозе. Тако о власти и силе божией рассуждая, Иов, между иными рассужденьми глаголет: *аще изменит, кто возвратит, или кто речет ему, что сотворил еси? (Иов, глава 9).* И Исаиа: *еда речет глина скудельнику, что твориши? (Исаиа, 45);* которое слово повторяет и Апостол в послании своем к римлянам *(рим.,9).* И тожде чтем у Даниила пророка о Бозе: *Несть иже сопротивится руце его, и речет ему, что сотворил еси? (Даниел, глава 4).*

И не возможно толковати слова екклисиастова, аки бы того ради, никтоже речет цареви, *что твориши?* что гнева его и силы боится; могут бо глаголати, и глаголют цареви, *что твориши?* оные злодеи, которые

what the civil statutes command, they do so of their own freewill, not out of necessity, in order by their example either to encourage their subjects to obey the law willingly, or else in order to confirm that the laws are good and useful.

We also know this from Holy Writ: for the Holy Spirit teaches us this clearly in Ecclesiastes: *Keep the King's commandment, and that in regard of the oath of God* (that is, do not be false to the oath of allegiance to the king, which you have sworn before God). *Be not hasty to go out of his sight: stand not in an evil thing; for he doeth whatsoever pleaseth him. Where the word of a king is, there is power: and who may say unto him, what doest thou?* (*Ecclesiastes*, 8). Clearly, the Holy Spirit, in teaching subjects the duty of perfect obedience to their kings, shows that the king's power to command and to act is absolute, and is not subject to anyone's scrutiny. We also see here that kings are exalted in honour above all other men: for what is said of the king in the passage from Ecclesiastes, *and who may say unto him, what doest thou?* is not found in Scripture in reference to any other authority, apart from God alone. Thus Job, when he considers God's power and strength, among other reflections, says: *Behold, he taketh away, who can hinder him? or who will say unto him, what doest thou?* (*Job*, 9). Likewise Isaiah: *Shall the clay say to him that fashioneth it, what doest thou?* (*Isaiah*, 45); which expression is repeated by the Apostle in his Epistle to the Romans (*Romans*, 9); and we read the same concerning God in the Prophet Daniel: *None can stay his hand, or say unto him, what does thou?* (*Daniel*, 4).

The words of Ecclesiastes cannot be understood to mean that no-one shall say to a king, *what doest thou?* out of fear of his anger and strength; for there are those who can and do say to a king, *What*

мятеж на царя воздвизают. И дух святый, повелевая усты Екклисиаста своего совершенно повиноватися царю, и воспоминая изреченную к повиновению клятву, не телесным страхом повеление свое утверждает, егда глаголет *и кто речет ему, что твориши?* Но толикую от Бога данную царям власть показует, яко никтоже не имеет власти истязати царя о делах его, и вопрошати его, *что твориши?* Подобне якоже и у Апостола, велит властям предержащим повиноватися, *не токмо за гнев, но и за совесть (рим., 13);* чему согласно и другое тогожде Екклисиаста слово: *в совести твоей не клени царя (екклисиаст., глава 10);* и третие тогожде в притчах его: *слава Божия крыти слово; слава же царева, чтити повеления его. Небо высоко, земля же глубока,* [41] *сердще же царево необлично (притч., глава 25).* Где не о простом сердца царева закрытии речь есть; тако бо закрытое сердце есть и всякого человека; глаголет бо Псаломник: *приступит человек и сердце глубоко;* и Апостол: *Кто весть о человек, яже в человеце, точию дух человека живущий в нем? (1 коринф., глава 2).* Чего ради и един сердцевидец нарицается Бог. Но в притчах сердце царево *необлично* нарицается собственной ради вины, что всяк подданный долженствует творити повелаемая от царя, не истязуя советов и намерений его, якоже явно есть из союза слова: сказав бо приточник, что слава царева есть в почтении повелений его, наводит: *небо высоко, земля же глубока, сердще же царево необлично,* аки бы рекл: *чти всяк царева повеления, и не испытуй, чего ради сие или оное повелевает или*

doest thou?, namely evildoers, who stir up rebellion against him. The Holy Spirit, in enjoining through the lips of Ecclesiastes perfect obedience to the king, and reminding us of our sworn oath of allegiance, does not sanction his command through bodily fear, when he says: *and who may say unto him, what doest thou?* He shows rather that so great is the power which God grants to kings, that no one has the power to question a king about his deeds and to ask him, *what doest thou?* Likewise he also commands through the Apostle obedience to the powers that be, *not only for wrath but also for conscience sake (Romans, 13)*. There is a second passage by that same Ecclesiastes which corresponds with this: *Curse not the king, no not in thy thought (Ecclesiastes, 10)*; and a third by the same author in his Proverbs: *It is the glory of God to conceal a thing: but a king's glory is in respecting his commands. The heaven for height, and the earth for depth, and the heart of kings is unsearchable (Proverbs, 25)*. This does not simply means that a king's heart is hidden; for the heart of every man is hidden; for the Psalmist says: *Man shall come and his heart is deep;*[23] and the Apostle says: *What man knoweth the things of a man, save the spirit of man which is in him? (I Corinthians, 2)*. For this reason God alone is called he who *knoweth the secrets of the heart.*[24] But in Proverbs, the heart of kings is called *unsearchable* for a special reason, namely that every subject must carry out the king's orders without questioning his designs and intentions, as is clear from the context: for the author of Proverbs, after saying that a king's glory lies in respecting his commands, adds: *The heaven for height, and the earth for depth, and the heart of kings is unsearchable*, as if to say: *let every man honour the king's commands, and not seek to know why he commands or ordains this or*

191

уставляет: якоже бо высоты небесной и глубины земной испытати невозможно, тако не подобает испытовати царева сердца. Сей разум есть слова приточникова; и не токмо утверждается от союза речей своих, и от другой вины, зде же от нас предложенной, но и от согласия с вышепомянутым тогожде и Приточника и Екклисиаста словом: *и кто речет ему, что твориши?*

Ведали сие добре древнии церковнии учители, которые слово оное кающегося царя Давида, *Тебе единому согреших (Псалом 50),* в таком разуме толковали, что царь и в преступлении самого закона божия (божий бо закон убийством и прелюбодеянием преступив Давид, глаголет к Богу [42] *Тебе единому согреших*) не судим есть от человек, но единого Бога суду подлежит. Златоустый помянутое Псаломника слово тако изъясняет: *Царь бех, тебе единого бояхся (Златоуст на псалом 50),* подобне и равновременный в древности Златоустому Иероним сказует: *царь бех, и иного не бояхся (Иероним в послании 46 к Рустику).* Пространее же и яснее толкует Амвросий Святый, медиоланский епископ : *царь он был, ни киим же законам не подлежащий: свободни бо суть царие от уз на преступники устроенных; ниже бо киим либо законом позываеми суть казнь прияти, ограждени суще самодержавия своего властию. Того ради (согрешивший Давид) человеку не согрешил, не повинен быв суду человеческому (Амвросий на псалом 50).* Согласно мудрствует и древнейший от вышеименованых христианский во Африке учитель Арновый: *всяк под судом живущий, согрешая, согрешает на Бога, согрешает и на закон мира; сей же царь, под властию единого Бога пребывающий, и его единого яко власть над властию царскою имущего, боящийся, единому Богу согрешил (Арновый на псалом 50).*

that: for just as the height of heaven and the depth of the earth cannot be probed, so it is not meet to probe into the heart of a king. This is the meaning of the passage in Proverbs; and it is confirmed not only by the context and by the other reason which we have given here, but also because it corresponds with the earlier passage by that same author of Proverbs and Ecclesiastes: *And who may say unto him, What doest thou?*

This was well known to the Early Church Fathers, who interpreted the words of the repentant King David, *Against thee, thee only, have I sinned* (*Psalm* 50), (which David says to God, having transgressed God's law through murder and adultery)[25] to mean that a king, even when he transgresses God's law, cannot be judged by men, but is subject only to God's judgement. Chrysostom explains the words of the Psalmist as follows: *I was a king, and feared thee alone* (*Chrysostom on Psalm* 50), And likewise Chrysostom's contemporary, Jerome, says: *I was a king, and feared no other man* (*Jerome, Epistle* 46 *to Rusticus*). This is explained more fully and clearly by Saint Ambrose, Bishop of Milan: *He was a king, and therefore subject to no laws: for kings are free from the bonds prescribed for transgressors; for by no law are they liable to punishment, being protected by their sovereign power. Therefore he (David) did not sin against man, not being subject to man's judgment* (*Ambrose on Psalm* 50). The earliest of these Church Fathers, the Christian Father in Africa, Arnobius, reasons likewise: *Every man who lives under law, when he sins, sins against God and sins against the world's law; but this king, who was under the power of God alone, and feared Him alone, as one who has power over the power of kings, sinned only against God* (*Arnobius on Psalm* 50).

Мощно зде видети от согласия древних сих учителей, каковое тогда было учение о самодержавном величестве, что власть его есть неподвластная, ни которому же суду человеческому не подлежащая, и весьма не прикосновенная. Но и в позднейшие времена живо и действительно было тоежде мудрование. Ибо Феодор Балсамон (который по тысяща двосодном году преставился), патриарх антиохийский, в толковании на канон шестьнадесятый собора карфагенского *(Балсамон в толковании правила 16 карфагенского* - канон есть правило церковное, закон же устав гражданский), и своим, и других тогдашних учителей именем, [43] сей яко общий догмат воспоминает, что царь ниже каноном, ниже законом подвержен есть.

Вся сия доселе предложенные о несудимой от человек власти доводы заключим словом Петра Святого, который велит властям повиноватися, *не токмо благим и кротким, но и строптивым (1 послание Петра, глава 2).* Аще же и строптивым повиноватися подобает, то и грехов их, не токмо дел правительских, судити не возможно: судящий бо другого не повинующийся уже есть, но властительствующий; якоже вопреки, повинующийся кому, не может судити того, которому повинуется. И уже довольно разумеем, како сильна, законами не связуема, и суду человеческому отнюд неподлежащая есть самодержавная власть, и сия то оной сила в славной своей титле *маестет* или *величество* содержится.

Сие же уразумевше, без сумнения разумеем, и без всякого прекословия исповести долженствуем, что всяк самодержец, как во всех прочиих, так и в сем (о немже речь сия) деле своем, то есть в определении наследника на престол свой, весьма волен и свободен есть. Вышеположенные бо доводы учат нас, во первых, что хотя бы грех был самодержцам определяти в наследники меньшего сына, мимо старейшего, или и мимо сынов, иного

We can see here, from the unanimity of these Early Fathers, what the doctrine was in those days regarding sovereign majesty, namely, that its power is subject to no other power, is subject to no human judgment, and is quite unimpeachable. But the same doctrine also held good in later times. For Theodore Balsamon, Patriarch of Antioch (who died after the year 1200), in his commentary on the sixteenth canon of the Council of Carthage (*Balsamon, Commentary on the sixteenth Carthaginian canon*) both in his own name and in that of the other Fathers of that time, states as a general dogma that a king is subject neither to canon law nor to civil law. (A canon is an ecclesiastical rule, a law is a civil statute).

Let us conclude all the foregoing arguments that sovereign power cannot be judged by men, with the words of Saint Peter, who enjoins submission to the authorities, *not only to the good and gentle, but also to the froward* (I, *Peter*, 2). If, therefore, obedience is due even to the froward, then we cannot judge even their sins, let alone their political actions: for he who judges another is no longer a subject, but a ruler; conversely, he who is a subject cannot judge him whose subject he is. We now understand well enough the strength of sovereign power: that it is not bound by the laws or in any way subject to human judgment; and this strength is contained in its glorious title of *Majestät* or *majesty*.

Now if we have understood this, we understand beyond a doubt and must unreservedly acknowledge, that every sovereign, in all his other deeds as in that which is our present subject, namely the appointment of the heir to his throne, is absolutely free to act as he chooses. For the preceding arguments teach us, first, that even if it were a sin for sovereigns to appoint a younger son as heir, passing over an elder son, or even to pass

кого от чуждых себе усыновленного, по усмотрении оных непотребства, сего же добродетелей, то однакож монаршей в том воле должни суть повиноватися подданнии, не токмо без явного прекословия, но и без тайного роптания, еще же и без суждения в помыслах. Но и тыяжде доводы ясно показуют, [44] что всякому наследному самодержцу (о яковом наипаче речь нам есть) определяти короны своея наследника, которого сына ни похощет, или коголибо похощет, весьма есть безгрешно. Человеческий бо закон о сем не может быти, понеже явственно показалося, что самодержцы законам человеческим не подлежат; закона же божия на сие собственного не обретаем, якоже от нижеписанных доводов и прикладов еще вящше уведаем.

14.

А еще, когда рассудим, кое долженство на царях лежит, от самого Бога возложенное на них, то не токмо и от того познаем, что не грех им, по воле своей избирать себе наследника, но и грех есть не избирать. Царей должность есть (якоже и в *Учении отроческом,* в пятой заповеди положено) содержать подданных своих в беспечалии, и промышлять им всякое лучшее наставление как к благочестию, так и к честному жительству. Да будут же подданнии в беспечалии, должен царь пещися, да будет истинное в государстве правосудие, на охранение обидимых от обидящих подданных себе; також и да будет крепкое и искусное воинство, на защищение всего отечества от неприятелей. А что бы было и всякое лучшее наставление, должен царь смотреть, что б были искуснии учители, как духовнии, так и гражданстии, довольное число.

О таковых своих должностях много имеют государи учения в священных писаниях. На всех бо местах оных писания, на которых или желаемая царям от Бога помощь в правительстве их, [45] или

196

over their sons altogether and appoint some stranger whom they had adopted, having regard to the unfitness of the former and the virtues of the latter, even then the subjects must obey the monarch's will, not only without open criticism but also without secret grumbling, and even without mental reservations. But these same arguments also show clearly that for any hereditary sovereign (the main subject of our discussion) to appoint as heir to his throne whichever son he wishes or whomever else he wishes, is no sin at all. There can be no man-made law on this, for it has been clearly shown that sovereigns are not subject to man-made law; and we find no particular divine law against it, as we shall learn still more from the following arguments and examples.

14.

Moreover, when we consider the duty incumbent upon kings, and imposed on them by God himself, we shall learn that not only is it no sin for them to choose a successor at their will, but indeed it is a sin not to do so. It is the duty of kings (as is also laid down in the *Children's Catechism,*[26] at the fifth commandment) to maintain their subjects in safety, and to provide them with the best instruction of every kind for a way of life both devout and honourable. For his subjects to live in safety, a king must ensure that there shall be true justice in the state to protect his subjects from offenders; and likewise that there shall be a strong and skilful army to defend the whole country from its enemies. And for there to be the best instruction of every kind, a king must see that there are expert teachers, both spiritual and secular, in sufficient number.

Monarchs find much instruction concerning these duties in Holy Writ. For in all passages of Scripture where mention is made of the desire of kings for help from God in their rule, or for the

правительста их польза и похвала воспоминается, воспоминаются должности их. Предложим зде некие священных писаний места:

Боже, суд твой цареви даждь, и правду твою сыну цареву. Судити людем твоим в правде, и нищым твоим в суде. Да восприимут горы мир людем, и холми правду. Судит нищым людским, и спасет сыны убогих, и смирит клеветника. (Псалом 72).

Божий слуга есть, тебе в благое. Аще же злое твориши, бойся: не бо без ума меч носит: божий бо слуга есть, отмститель в гнев злое творящему. (Римл. 13).

Князи от царей посылаются во отмщение убо злодеем, в похвалу же благотворцем. Яко тако есть воля божия, благотворящым обуздовати безумных человек невежество. (I Послан. Петра, глава 2).

Мерзкость цареви творяй злая: с правдою бо готовается престол начала. (Притчи, 16).

Егда царь праведен на престоле сядет, не станет противо очию его ничтоже лукаво. (Притчи, 20).

Дух пред лицем нашим, благ господь (в еврейском христос господень) ят бысть в рассыпанных наших, о нем же рехом, в сени его поживем в странах. (Плач Иеремиин, глава 4, под словом реш. О царе Седекии глаголет сие Иеремиа, 2 книг. царств, 25).

Светильник израилев, царь израилев нарицается.

И когда повелевает Апостол молитися *за царя, и за вся иже во власти суть,* нужду того показует сию: *да тихое и безмолвное житие поживем. (I, Тимоф., глава 2).*

prosperity and glory of their rule, mention is also made of their duties. We shall here set forth several passages from Holy Writ:

Give the king thy judgements, O God, and thy righteousness unto the king's son. He shall judge thy people with righteousness, and thy poor with judgement. The mountains shall bring peace to the people, and the little hills, by righteousness. He shall judge the poor of the people, he shall save the children of the needy, and shall break in pieces the oppressor (Psalm 72).

He is the minister of God for good. But if thou do that which is evil, be afraid: for he beareth not the sword in vain: for he is the minister of God, a revenger to execute wrath upon him that doeth evil (Romans, 13).

Princes are sent by kings *for the punishment of evildoers, and for the praise of them that do well. For so is the will of God, that with well doing ye may put to silence the ignorance of foolish men (I, Peter, 2).*

It is an abomination to kings to commit wickedness: for the throne is established by righteousness (Proverbs, 16).

A king that sitteth in the throne of judgement scattereth away all evil with his eyes (Proverbs, 20).

The breath of our nostrils, the blessed of the Lord (in Hebrew, *the anointed of the Lord*) *was taken in their pits, of whom we said, Under his shadow we shall live among the heathens (Lamentations, 4, under resh.* Jeremiah says this of King Zedekiah, *2 Kings, 25).*

The King of Israel is called *the Light of Israel.*[27]

And when *the Apostle commands us to pray for kings and for all that are in authority*, he gives this reason: *that we may lead a quiet and peaceable life* (I, *Timothy, 2).*

199

От сих и прочиих писаний явно есть царского сана долженство, еже есть сохраняти, защищати, во всяком беспечалии содержати, наставляти же и исправляти [46] подданных своих, якоже выше речено.

А есть ли о добре общем народа себе подданного толико пещися должен есть самодержец, то како не должен есть прилежно смотрети, дабы по нем наследник был добрый, бодрый, искусный, и таковый, который бы доброе отечества состояние не токмо сохранил в целости, но и паче бы утвердил, и укрепил; и естьли бы что не довершенное застал, тщался бы привести в совершенство. Есть ли же сам добре государство управив, оставит оное негодному, неискусному, ленивому, и не утверждати, но разве рассыпати общее добро могущему, то что пользовало его попечение? Не сам ли виновен будет всему нестроению и гибели, худым наследником сделанной? Что пользует, что сам много добра отечеству промыслил, есть ли сам же чрез наследника непотребного все тое разрушит? Воистинну каковой похвалы достоин искусный кормчий, который добре правив корабль, отлучаяся же от корабля, посадит на кормиле, вместо себе, человека к тому отнюд необученного, таковой достоин и монарх, который управленное от себе государство худому и разорительному отдаст наследнику.

Аще же должен монарх усматривати по себе наследника доброго, то како может смотрети на первородство между сынами своими? Должен паче он и на сыновство не смотрети детей своих, но обучати оные всяким, державному правительству подобающим, искусствам, долженствует. И есть ли все сыны равносильни явятся, и не будет ни на едином от них [47] никакой вины порока и зазора, отдаст скипетр в наследие первородному, или старейшему, по чину естественном; есть ли же старейший сын или к царствованию неугодный, или злонравный, и родителям неблагодарный покажется, и отпадет вся надежда исправления его, тогда государь не токмо может, но по совести своей и должен есть, миновать сына старейшего, а меньшего в наследие произвесть, дабы

From these and other passages it is clear what the duty of kings is, namely, to keep and protect their subjects, to maintain them in all safety and to instruct and improve them, as was said above.

Now if a sovereign must take such pains for the common good of his people, surely he must strive diligently to see that his successor is virtuous, brave, skilful and such as would not only maintain the country's welfare, but would consolidate and strengthen it still more; and who, if he found something incomplete, would strive to complete it. Now if a monarch, having ruled the state well, leaves it to one who is unfit, unskilled, lazy, and liable not to consolidate but only to dissipate the common good, of what use was his diligence? Will he himself not be to blame for all the disorder and ruin brought about by a weak successor? Of what avail is it that he has done much good for the country, if he himself, through a worthless heir, undoes it all? Indeed a monarch who leaves the State which he has ruled to a weak and spendthrift successor, is as praiseworthy as a skilful pilot, who, having steered a ship well, on disembarking, puts in his place at the helm a man utterly untrained for it.

If, then, a monarch must seek out a worthy successor, is he really to consider the question of primogeniture? Rather he must ignore the fact that his sons are his children, but must instruct them in all the skills proper to a sovereign monarchy. And if all his sons prove equally able, and if none of them shows any sign of vice or blame, he will assign the succession to the first-born or eldest, following the natural order; but if the eldest son proves either unfit to rule or of bad character and ungrateful to his parents, and all hope fails of his improvement, then the monarch not only may, but must in conscience pass over the eldest son and

старейший он, или и не хотя, не повредил трудов родительских, есть ли не искусен есть к толикому делу, или и нарочно не рассыпал бы, есть ли зол есть, и родителеве не приязнен. А когда бы так несчаслив в сынах своих был монарх, что ни единого бы от них не видел к царствованию устроенна и угодна, то должен пред Богом, яко о приставничестве своем слово ему воздати имущий, должен есть и с стороны усмотрети искусного и благонравного, и того написати наследником. Сия бо должность происходит от вышеписанных должностей, самого Бога повелением наложенных царям.

15.

Но туюжде и вольность и должность царей увидим, когда рассудим еще всенародное намерение, которым монархиа введена и содержима быти разумеется. От чего покажется и должное народа воле царской во всем повиновение.

Всем известно, что не един по всем мире образ есть высочайшего правительства: но инде главные всего отечества дела управляются согласием всех жителей, яковое правительство было прежде у многих народов еллинских, [48] и долго пребывало у римлян. А в наша времена есть такое правительство в Венеции, Голландии и в Польщи: и сие нарицается димократиа, то есть народодержавство.

Инде же не всего народа, но и не единого лица волею, но несколько избранных мужей сословием правится отечество, яковый правления образ был в Риме при десяти правителях не долгое время: и сие правительство нарицается аристократиа.

Инде же вся держава в руках единого лица держится: и сия именуется монархиа, то есть самодержавство.

raise a younger son to the succession, lest the eldest should either unwittingly impair his father's achievements, if he is unfit for so great a task, or should deliberately undo them, if he is wicked and hostile to his father. And if a monarch should be so unfortunate in his sons that he could not see even one fit and able to rule, then, before God, to whom he is accountable for his stewardship, he must seek out a fit and virtuous stranger, and appoint him as his successor.[28] For this duty stems from the duties described above, which are laid on kings by God's own command.

15.

But we shall note this same right and duty of kings when we also go on to consider the general will of the people, by which monarchy is understood to be established and upheld; and from this will also be shown the people's duty to submit in everything to the king's will.

Everyone knows that no one form of government prevails throughout the world: in some places the country's affairs are administered through the consent of all the inhabitants, which form of government formerly existed among many of the peoples of Greece and long prevailed among the Romans. In our day such a form of government exists in Venice, Holland and Poland, and is called democracy, that is, rule by the people.[29]

Elsewhere the country is ruled neither by the will of all the people nor by that of one man, but by a small body of elected men; which form of government existed for a short time in Rome under the Decemviri: and this form of government is called aristocracy.[30]

Elsewhere, all power is in the hands of one person: and this is called monarchy, that is, rule by one man.

Но и сверх сих образов правления, бывают правительства отличные от всех сих именованных, которые с сих же троих или двоих, аки бы смешанный состав свой имеют.

Еще монархиа двойственного вида есть: в иной бо монархии не наследный скипетр содержится, но по смерти монарха единого, избирает народ монарха по согласию своему, не смотря на дети монарха умершего. Таковая аки бы была монархиа римская от Кесаря Иулиа до Константина Палеолога, и ныне монархиа германоримская аки бы таковая.

Иная же монархиа наследная есть, в которой по отце сын, или по брате брат, иногда же по отце и дщерь царствует; и тако в одном дому содержится скипетр, из рук в руки до сынов и внуков переходит, и разве пресечется линия крови самодержавной, в то время народа согласием монарх новый избирается. Таковые монархии многие прежде были, и ныне суть, между которыми есть сия, преславно ныне процветшая монархиа всероссийская. [49]

От сего же правительств разнообразия показуется ясно, что всякий правления образ, и сама наследная монархиа, имеет начало от первого в сем или оном народе согласия, всегда и везде по воле своей, премудро действующу смотрению божию. Сие же глаголем о честном и правильном начале монархии, не воспоминая зде монархий оных, которые начало приняли от некоего превозмогающего в народе человека, насильствием народ себе покорившего, яковое начало имела монархиа ассирийская от Немрода, хотя и в таковых монархиах, когда уже народ непрекословно, безмятежно, еще же и доброхотно повиноватися самодержцу своему приобыкл, разумети подобает, что дом монарший, не к тому насильствием своим похищенное, но всенародною волею отданное себе скипетро держит:

In addition to these forms of government, however, there are others, which differ from all the above-mentioned and which constitute a mixed form of government, consisting of two or three of them.

There are also two kinds of monarchy: in one the sceptre is not hereditary, but on a monarch's death, the people elects a monarch of its own choice, without regard to the children of the late monarch. Such or similar was the Roman monarchy from Julius Caesar to Constantine Palaeologus,[31] and the Germano-Roman monarchy today.[32]

The other form of monarchy is hereditary, in which son succeeds to father, or brother to brother, and sometimes even daughter to father; thus the sceptre remains in one family, and is handed down to sons and grandsons, unless the reigning dynasty is cut short, when a new monarch is elected by the people. Many such monarchies existed formerly and exist today, including this monarchy of all the Russias, which today flourishes so gloriously.

From this variety of forms of government it is clear that every form of government, including hereditary monarchy itself, derives its origin from an initial agreement among this or that people, in every case at God's volition and under his wise and active providence. We are speaking here of the true and proper origin of monarchy, and not of those monarchies which originated from some man who prevailed among the people by forcibly subduing it, as with the Assyrian monarchy which began with Nimrod;[33] though even in monarchies such as these, once the people has grown accustomed to submit to its sovereign without complaint or unrest and indeed voluntarily, it should be understood that the royal house wields the sceptre not as something usurped by force but as conferred on it by the general will of the people:

сам бо народ доброхотным своим повиновением являет на тое преклоненную волю свою.

Еще же рассудити подобает, каковая воля народная в начале монархии избирательной разумеется, и какова в начале монархии наследной; от таковых бо воли народной толков прямых и истинных много света получим и о свободной или не свободной воли монархов в определении наследников своих.

Не мощно же инако толковать народной воли, только от самого вида и образа монархии; какова бо где монархиа есть, таковую и волю народную в начале тоя монархии бывшую разумети подобает.

Тако в начале монархии избирательной, какова была воля народная, сими словесы изобразити можем: [50] *согласно вси хощем,* глаголет народ к монарху первому, *да ты владееши нами к общей пользе нашей, донежеле жив пребываеши; и мы вси совлекаемся воли нашей, и тебе повинуемся, не оставляюще нам себе самим ни какой свободности к общим определениям: но токмо до смерти твоей; по твоей же смерти будет паки при нас воля наша, кому высочайшую над нами власть отдати, по усмотрении достоинства и по нашем согласии.*

В монархии же наследной, таковая была к первому монарху воля народная, аще и не словом, но делом изъявленная: *согласно вси хощем, да ты к общей нашей пользе владееши над нами вечно, то есть, понеже смертен еси; то да по тебе, ты же сам впредь да оставляеши нам наследного владетеля; мы же единожды воли нашей совлекшеся, никогда же оной впредь, ниже по смерти твоей употребляти будем; но как тебе, так и наследникам твоим по тебе повиноватися клятвенным обещанием одолжаемся, и наших по нас наследников тымже долженством обязуем.* Таковый же толк воли народной в наследуемой монархии, не токмо от

for the people itself, by its voluntary submission, shows that such is its will.

We should also consider how the will of the people at the origin of an elective monarchy and of an hereditary monarchy is to be understood; for from a true and correct understanding of the will of the people, we shall also shed much light on whether or not monarchs are free to appoint their successors.

Now the will of the people can only be interpreted from the type and form of the monarchy itself; for it should be understood that, whatever the form of any monarchy, it corresponds to the will of the people, which was present at its origin.

Thus we can formulate the will of the people at the origin of an elective monarchy in these words: *We all unanimously desire,* says the people to its first monarch, *that you rule over us for our common good for as long as you shall live; and we all renounce our freedom and submit to you, without leaving ourselves any freedom to decide the common weal: but only during your lifetime; and on your death we shall again be free to decide on whom to bestow supreme power over us, having regard to his worth and by our common agreement.*

In an hereditary monarchy, however, the people's will with respect to its first monarch was expressed as follows, in fact if not in word: *We all unanimously desire you to rule over us for our common good for ever, that is, for as long as you shall live; and you yourself shall leave a n hereditary successor to rule over us after you; and we, having once renounced our freedom, will never avail ourselves of it hereafter, not even after your death; but we bind ourselves by a solemn oath to submit to you and after you to your successors, and we bind our heirs after us by the same obligation.* That such is the explanation of the people's will in an hereditary monarchy is not only confirmed by

вида самой монархии утверждается (яковая бо где монархиа есть, такой себе исперва похотел народ), но и по тому известен есть, что когда народ монархам наследным клятву свою, для некоей важной вины, обновляет, не иных упоотребляет слов, только вышеположенных или им   подобных и равносильных к изъявлению клятвенного своего обещания. [51]

Ведати же подобает, что народная воля, как в избирательной, так и в наследной монархии, и в протчих правительства образах, бывает не без собственного смотрения божия (как о сем и выше помянулося), но божиим мановением движима действует; понеже ясно учит священное писание, якоже выше сего довольно мы видели, что *несть власть аще не от Бога*. И того ради вся долженства, как подданных к государю своему, так и государя к добру общему подданных своих, не от единой воли народной, но и от воли божией происходят.

Посмотрим же, какая долженства подданных, и какая государей являются в наследной монархии, и с вышеположенного толкования воли народной, разумей же купно и божией, и что может и что не может творити народ и государь.

Долженства народа подданного сия суть:

1. Должен народ без прекословия и роптания вся от самодержца повелеваемая творити, что и выше, под числом тринадесятым, от слова божия показано, зде же и от толкования воли народной явно показуется: аще бо народ воли общей своей совлекся и отдал оную монарху своему, то како не должен хранити его повеления, законы и уставы, без всякой оговорки?

2. И по тому не может народ судити дела государя своего, инако бо имел бы еще при себе волю общего правления, которую весьма отложил, и отдал государю своему. И того ради пребеззаконное дело было

the form of the monarchy itself (for the form of any monarchy is that which the people first chose for itself), but is also evident from the fact that whenever the people for some important reason renews its oath of allegiance to its hereditary monarchs, it uses words identical or similar and equivalent to those set out above.

It should also be understood that the will of the people, both in an elective and in an hereditary monarchy and in the other forms of government, does not make itself felt without God's special providence (as was mentioned above), but operates at God's instigation; for Holy Writ clearly teaches, as was amply shown above, that *there is no power but of God.* Hence all duties, both those of the subjects towards their sovereign and those of the sovereign in respect of his subjects' common good, derive not only from the will of the people but also from the will of God.

Let us see, therefore, what the duties of subjects and of sovereigns are in an hereditary monarchy, and from our explanation above of the will of the people, which is also that of God, let us see what people and monarch can and cannot do.

The duties of the people are as follows:

1.   The people must do all that the sovereign commands without criticism or complaint, as was shown from Scripture under number 13 above, and as also clearly emerges here from our explanation of the will of the people: for if the people has renounced its common freedom and has conferred it on its sovereign, then it must surely obey his commands, laws and statutes, without reservation.

2.   And therefore the people cannot judge its sovereign's actions, for otherwise it would still retain the right to decide the common weal which it altogether renounced and conferred on its sovereign. A most heinous deed, therefore, was that

209

сильных некиих изменников от парламента великобританского, [52] над королем своим Каролом Первым, 1649 года сделанное, от всех проклинаемое, и от самых англичан уставленным на то повсегодно слезным праздником, весьма хулимое, нам же и воспоминания недостойное.

3. Кольми же паче не может народ повелевати что либо монарху своему: како бо повелевати может тому, которому отдал волю свою? Достойное памяти слово есть Валентиниана, которого когда воинство избрало императором, и стали вопить, домогаяся, дабы он в товарищи себе другого нарекл, отвещал им тако: *Мене, рече, избрати императором было в вашей воле; но когда уже избрали есте мене, сие, чего желаете, не в вашей, но в моей воле есть. Вам яко подданным подобает тихо, мирно пребывать, мне же яко император смотрети надлежит, что есть на потребу (Созомен, книга 6).* Естьли же так свободен монарх избранный (какова была римская монархиа), то кольми паче наследный, которому народ волю свою и власть над собою во веки отдал.

4. Хотя народ из начала наследной монархии и усмотревает мужа доброго, который бы с великою отечества пользою царствовати мог, однакож, когда уже избрал его самодержцем своим, а он не таков, какова его надеялся, покажется, или и быв на время добр, переменится в злого, не может уже народ отставити его: не может бо отданной ему воли своей отняти: коею бо волею мог бы сие творити, понеже воли своей и власти лишился. Но когда бы и хотел упрямо отменити волю свою народ [53] (что было бы великое непостоянство, и никогда бы так монархиа наследная быть не могла), но не может отменити воли

done in the year 1649 by some powerful traitors in the Parliament of Great Britain against their king, Charles I: a deed cursed by all men and abhorred by the English themselves by the establishment of an annual day of mourning, and as far as we are concerned, a deed unworthy even to be remembered.[34]

3. Still less, then, can the people command anything of its monarch: for how can it command him to whom it has yielded its freedom? Memorable are the words of Valentinian, who, when the army had chosen him as emperor, and the men began to harangue him, demanding that he nominate another as his colleague, answered them as follows: *You were free,* he said, *to choose me as emperor; but once you chose me, what you now desire lies not in your power, but in mine. It is for you, as subjects, to act quietly and peaceably, and for me, as emperor, to see what needs to be done* (Sozomen, *Book* 6). If an elected monarch has such power, (and the Roman monarchy was elective), how much more has an hereditary monarch, to whom the people has yielded in perpetuity its freedom and the power to rule over it.

4. Although the people, at the origin of an hereditary monarchy, seeks out a worthy man, capable of ruling with great advantage to the country, nevertheless, once it has chosen him as its sovereign, if he proves other than was hoped, or if, having proved worthy for a time, he changes for the worse, the people cannot now depose him: for it cannot take back the freedom which it bestowed on him and by virtue of which it might have deposed him: for it has forfeited its freedom and power. Even if the people insisted on changing its mind (which would be highly inconsistent, and a hereditary monarchy could never subsist under such circumstances), it cannot change the will of

божией, которая и волю народную двинула, и купно с оною сама действовала в уставлении такой монархии и первого монарха избрании, якоже выше довольно показано. Но должен терпеть народ коелибо монарха своего нестроение и злонравие, (якоже и дух святый повелевает, *не токмо благим и кротким, но и строптивым* повиноватися); разве бы при первого монарха избрании были положенные некие договоры, самого монарха соизволением, или и клятвою утвержденные, которых за не исполнение, уставлено бы монарха оставляти; но тая монархиа не прямая была бы монархиа, еще же и непрестанным бедствиям подлежащая (мощно бо злым человекам и добрые дела монаршие толковати на зло), и весьма не таковая, о яковой нам слово сие.

5. Следует убо и сие, что нам зде розыскуется, что должен народ имети за прямого и законного себе государя, кого наследником по себе наречет старейший государь, не смотря, первородного ли сына, или меньшего, или и не сына. Есть ли бо волю свою о владении над собою отдал ему, ведати же должен, что на то и воля божия была; то како может противитися, когда государь не большого, но меньшего сына, или и не сына нарицает наследником? Воли в том своей народ лишился, и всю волю возложил на монарха: то есть ли бы хотел монарху прекословити в наречении наследника, сам бы себе прекословил, [54] и клятву свою разрушил бы народ.

Мнят же нецыи, что может народ дати скипетр первому монарху, купно и будущим по нем сынам, внукам, правнукам, и всей его снисходящей линии, а не положити на воли его избрание наследника; и показуют того образ в писании, в судейских книгах, где израильтяне тако власть над

God, which inspired the will of the people and acted in concert with it in establishing the monarchy and in the election of the first monarch, as was amply shown above. Rather the people must endure any failing and vice in its sovereign (for the Holy Spirit commands us to submit *not only to the good and gentle, but also to the froward*), unless, at the election of the first monarch, certain conditions were laid down with his consent or were confirmed by him on oath, whereby it was stipulated that if the monarch did not fulfil them, he would be deposed; such a monarchy, however, would not be a true monarchy, and would indeed be subject to continual misfortunes (for it would be open to wicked men to misrepresent even the monarch's good deeds), and is certainly not the kind of monarchy which forms our present subject.

5.   For it also follows, and this is the subject of our present enquiry, that the people must accept as its true and lawful sovereign whomsoever the monarch names as his successor, regardless of whether it be his first-born son, a younger son, or not his son at all. For if the people conferred on him the right to rule over it, it must know that this too was by the will of God; how, then, can it resist, when the monarch names as his successor not his eldest son, but a younger son or someone not his son? The people forfeited its freedom in the matter, and conferred it all on the monarch: so if it sought to oppose the monarch in his nomination of a successor, the people would contradict itself and violate its oath.

Some suppose that the people can give the sceptre to the first monarch and also to his future sons, grandsons, great-grandsons and all his descendants, without conferring on him the right to choose his successor; and they point to an example of this in Scripture, in the book of Judges, where the

собою предают Гедеону: *владей ты в нас, и сынове сынов твоих, яко ты спасл еси нас от руку мадиамлю (Судие, глава 8).* И такое власти даяние сказуют быти аки бы привязаное до сынов государевых, так что государь не силен есть наследия скипетра отняти сыну своему, яко не в своей воле лежащее, но от народа сыну его из начала, хотя он еще и не родился, отданное. Но сие мнение весьма не крепкое, паче же и суетное есть. Который бо народ так слепо отдал бы себе в владение тех человек, которых не ведает, каковы будут, понеже они еще и не родилися? И для чего бы сие делал народ? Пользы ли ради своея? Но кая надежда пользы в не известии будущих владетелей? Не так, как в монархе свободном на все, и на избрание наследника своего: в том бо надежда есть, что естьли сын его неподобен ему, и к правлению не угоден явится, изберет он кого усмотрит доброго и искусного в наследие. Но и для благодарствия своего к монарху не может делати то народ: кое бо се благодарствие, давати ему и его сынам владетельство, да так, что монарх не волен есть утвердити, или отняти сыну наследие?

И от сего мощно толковать, в какой силе [55] народ израильтеский отдавал над собою власть Гедеону и сынам и внукам его: не отдавал так, да бы Гедеон весьма не волен был рассуждать о достойнстве и непотребствии детей своих; тако бо народ сделал бы нечто и себе не полезное, и Гедеону не благоприятное, которому отдавал над собою власть, благодарящ за избавление от руку мадиамлю; того ради слово народа израильтеского к Гедеону *владей ты над нами, и сынове сынов твоих* с таким договором разумети подобает: *владей ты над нами*

Israelites give Gideon power over them in these words: *Rule thou over us, both thou, and thy son, and thy sons' sons also: for thou hast delivered us from the hand of Midian (Judges,* 8). Such a conferment of power, they say, also attaches, as it were, to the monarch's sons, so that the monarch has no right to deprive his son of the succession, since this allegedly does not lie within his power, but was originally bestowed by the people on his son, even though the latter was not yet born. But this view is most unsound and indeed nonsensical. For what people would so blindly surrender itself to the rule of persons whose character it does not know, because they have not yet even been born? And why would the people do so? For its own advantage? But what advantage could it hope for from not knowing its future rulers? Not as much as from a monarch with absolute power, including the power to choose his successor: for in his case there is hope that, if his son is unlike him and proves unfit to rule, he will choose as his successor someone whom he sees to be a good and worthy candidate. But the people cannot do this, even out of gratitude to the monarch: for what sort of gratitude would it be to grant to him and his sons the power to rule, but in such a way that that the monarch has no right to confirm or to revoke a son's succession?

We can therefore explain in what sense the people of Israel gave to Gideon and his sons and grandsons power to rule over them: they did not give it in such a way that Gideon had no right to consider the worth or unfitness of his children; for then the people would have done something without advantage to itself and ungracious to Gideon, to whom it gave power to rule over it in gratitude for its deliverance from the hand of Midian; therefore the words of the people of Israel to Gideon, *Rule thou over us, both thou and thy son and thy sons'*

совершенною и вечною волею, так, чтоб и сыны и внуки твои наследно туюжде над нами власть имели, есть ли ты или по тебе наставший владетель не отставит сына своего от наследия. Который слова израильтеского толк и по сему известен, что Гедеон, не приемля подаемой власти, так народу отвещал: *не владею аз вами, ни возвладеет сын мой вами.* Есть ли бы не на воле гедеоновой было отрешить от власти детей своих, то себе самого токмо отрешил бы, а детей своих отрешити не мог бы; видим же, что с собою и дети своя отрешил. Сия бо есть прямая и совершенная наследная монархиа, а монархиа помянутым мнением мечтаемая, ни наследная, ни избирательная есть: не наследная, понеже, есть ли бы народ и мимо воли монарха первого отдал власть сынам и внукам его, то их на власть сам народ избрал бы; однакож и избирательная таковая монархиа наренщися не может: каковое бо се избрание, избирать кого на власть прежде рождения его? [56]

6. Но что делать народу, когда государь умрет, не оставив по себе, ни на словах ни на письме, определенного наследника? Ответсвуем на сие: народ, понеже волю свою вечно отдал государю своему, и на его волю весьма себе возложил, и содействовало в том божие смотрение, то и по смерти государя своего, должен есть его волею управлятися. И понеже в таковом случае не явно известна народу воля государя умершего, яко ни словами сказана, ни письмом объявлена, того ради должен народ всякими правильными догадами испытовать, какова была, или быти могла воля государева, и которого бы из сынов, своим нарекл он наследником, есть

sons also, should be understood with this qualification: *Rule over us absolutely and for ever, so that your sons and grandsons successively may have the same power over us, unless you or the ruler who follows you shall remove his son from the succession.* That this is the meaning of the words of the Israelites is also clear from the fact that Gideon, refusing the proffered power, answered the people as follows: *I will not rule over you, neither shall my son rule over you.* Had Gideon not had the right to exclude his children from power, he would have excluded himself alone, but could not have excluded them; but we see that he renounced it for himself and for his children. For such is the nature of a true and perfect hereditary monarchy; but the kind of monarchy supposed in the opinion cited is neither hereditary nor elective: it is not hereditary, because if the people, despite the wishes of the first monarch, had conferred the power on his sons and grandsons, then the people itself would have elected them to power; but neither can such a monarchy be called elective: for what kind of election is it to elect someone to power before he is born?

6.   But what should the people do, when the monarch dies without designating his successor, whether orally or in writing? Our answer is as follows: because the people has conferred its freedom on the monarch in perpetuity and has submitted itself entirely to his will, and God's providence was also operative in this, then, even on the monarch's death, it must be governed by his will. And since in this case the late monarch's wish is not clearly evident to the people, having been expressed neither orally nor in writing, the people must try to ascertain, by all manner of just conjectures, what it was or might have been, and which of his sons he would have named as his

ли бы о том дело было. Волю же умершего государя мощно испытовать и толковать двема сима ведении:

Первое, какого нрава был государь, и к чему наипаче склонен? другое, равно ли, или не равно дети своя любил? Неравенство же зде разумеется знатное и великое, так, что одного сына любя паче другого, другого аки бы не любил, и не благоволил о нем; есть ли известно, что сего сына вельми любил, а о другом не благоволил, то и воля его известна, что любимому сыну отдал бы наследие; и весьма того подобает имети за наследного государя, только бы сие могло остаться без мятежа и смущения, и не смотрети, добрый ли есть, или злый сын любимый: должен был смотрети сие родитель его государь; а народ, не смотря на то, должен имети за наследника, восписуя наследие его самой воле божией, [57] и яко крест и наказание от Бога приемля без роптания, есть ли злонравен наследник явился, так, как и выше речено о самом первом монархе, который по восприятии скипетра зол покажется.

Есть ли же неизвестно, равно ли или не равно сыны своя любил государь, то смотрети на нравы его: на пример, был государь тщательный, трудолюбивый, военный, учения любящий, всякого добра отечеству своему с ревностию желающий; а от сынов его един есть подобонравен ему, а другой весьма отличен от его, ленивый, недоброрадетельный, к воинскому подвигу неугодный, и не охотный учения, и прочее добро общее или презирающий, или пещися о том не могущий, то по сему знать мощно, что первого любил родитель, а о сем не благоволил, и не хотел быть сему наследником по себе. Есть ли же не известно, что государь равно любил дети своя, то не известно которого из них хотел нарещи

successor, if it had come to that. Now the late monarch's wish can be ascertained and interpreted from two kinds of information.

First, what was the monarch's character and what were his main preferences? Second, did he love his children equally or not? By this is meant a significant and marked inequality, so that loving one son more than another, he plainly disliked the other and disapproved of him; if it is clear that he greatly loved the former and disapproved of the latter, then it was clearly his will to grant the succession to the favourite son, and provided this can be done without rebellion or unrest, this son should certainly be accepted as the hereditary monarch, without considering whether he is good or bad: it was for his father, the late monarch, to consider this; the people must accept him as the successor regardless, ascribing his succession to the will of God, and accepting it without complaint as a cross and a punishment from God if the successor has proved to be a bad man, as was said above about the first monarch, who, on taking up the sceptre, turns out to be an evil man.

If, however, it is not known whether the monarch loved his sons equally or not, then his character should be considered: for example, if the monarch was zealous and hardworking and a soldier, if he favoured learning and keenly aspired to every good for his country; and if one of his sons resembles him in character, while the other is very different, indolent, careless, unsuited to military feats, indifferent to learning and otherwise either contemptuous of the common good or incapable of striving for it, then it may be concluded that the father loved the former and disapproved of the latter, and did not wish him to be his successor. If it is not known whether the monarch loved his children equally and hence which of them he

наследником, и в таковом случае должен народ, храня чин естественный, имети за государя себе сына государева первородного, или старейшего; и не смотрети каков ни есть он.

Тожде подобает хранити, есть ли государь, хотя и не равно любил дети своя, да не знатным неравенством. Есть ли же один сын остался по государе, а наследия волею родительскою не отрешен, то, хотя бы он и злонравен, и известно, что от родителя не любим был, должен народ иметь его за наследного государя; понеже вероятнее есть, что умерший без завета государь, хотя и не любил сына, однакож наследия его [58] лишити не хотел, желая не испустити короны из дому своего; а народ должен поступати по воле государя своего, естьли не по известной, то хотя по толкуемой; понеже отдав ему вечную и наследную над собою власть, обещался с клятвою воле его повиноватися. И се, а не иное есть наследия монаршего основание: что, отдав себе вечно народ властительской воле монарха, должен впредь имети за наследного государя того, кого монарх наследником наречет; естьли же не нарек, умрет без завета, то о детях его, воли его испытовати подобает так, как выше рассудилося; а естьли один сын остался, то народ не может знать, что не хотел ему родитель быти наследником, и так, аки бы известной воле умершего монарха повинуяся, должен сына принимать себе за монарха.

А что зде рассуждается о сынах монарших, тожде разумети подобает, во оскудении сынов, и о дщерях монарших (где женская власть не отставлена, как отставлена во Франции) и о монаршей братии, и о прочей ближайшей и единодомовной фамилии, по беззаветной смерти монаршей. Когда же оскудеет вся ближайшая фамилиа, а последний в ней государь

wished to name as his successor, then the people must observe the natural order, and accept the monarch's first-born or eldest son as its sovereign, regardless of his character.

It should do likewise if, even though the monarch did not love his children equally, the inequality was not significant. And if only one son remains at the monarch's death, and was not barred from the succession by his father, then, even if he is of bad character and it is known that he was disliked by his father, the people must accept him as its hereditary sovereign; for it is more likely that a monarch who died intestate, even though he disliked his son, nevertheless had no wish to bar him from the succession and let the crown pass from his family; and the people must act according to the monarch's will, express or implied; because, having conferred on him perpetual hereditary rule over itself, it has sworn to obey his will. This, and none other is the foundation of monarchical succession: that the people, having once surrendered itself in perpetuity to the monarch's will, must henceforth accept as its hereditary sovereign him whom the monarch names as his successor; and if he dies intestate without naming a successor, his wishes concerning his children should be ascertained in the manner discussed above; and if only one son remains, the people cannot infer that his father did not wish him to be the successor, and must accept him as its sovereign. as though in obedience to the late monarch's known wish.

These considerations concerning a monarch's sons should also be understood to apply, in the absence of sons, to his daughters (where female rule is not excluded, as in France);[35] and to his brothers and other immediate members of his family, if the monarch dies intestate. But when the

никого в наследники не определил, и без завета преставился, тогда воля, бывшим монархам отданная, возвращается к народу. Но и зде ведати подобает, что естьли последний монарх, не определив именно наследника, определение оставил бы, из которой фамилии, или из которого чина людей избирать [59] или не избирать монарха нового, то народ и тое хранити должен чисто и свято; се же того ради, понеже воле монаршей вечно себе повинул, и тако, донележе может воля монаршая быти являема, дотоль оную исполняти народ должен.

Показаны доселе должности народные в монархии наследуемой, и от оных довольно показалося, что в такой монархии государь весьма волен и свободен есть определяти себе наследника. Еще в кратце рассмотрим, есть ли некие должности, и на самом государе лежащие, в таковой то монархии: но зде опасно познавати подобает, что может, и что долженствует государь, и сие от оного отлично есть.

Может монарх государь законно повелевати народу не только все, что к знатной пользе отечества своего потребно, но и все, что ему ни понравится, только бы народу не вредно и воле божией не противно было. Сему же могуществу его основание есть вышепомянутое, что народ правительской воли своей совлекся пред ним, и всю власть над собою отдал ему: и сюды надлежат всякие обряды гражданскии и церковныи, перемены обычаев, употребление платья, домов строения, чины и церемонии в пированиах, свадьбах, погребениях, и прочая, и прочая, и прочая.

Может государь сам себе отрешить царствования, якоже отрешили себе иногда Птолемей Филомитор, восточный царь, якоже о нем пишет Иосиф жидовин *(книга 13, глава 7, древностей)*, Диоклитиан, и

entire family dies out, and the last monarch of that house has not appointed any successor and has died intestate, then the freedom conferred on the previous monarchs reverts to the people. But even then it should be understood that if the last monarch, without appointing a successor by name, left orders as to the family or class of men from which the new monarch should or should not be chosen, the people must observe them strictly and faithfully, because it submitted itself in perpetuity to the monarch's will, and so as long as the monarch's will can be elucidated, the people must carry it out.

So far, we have shown the duties of the people in an hereditary monarchy, and from these it has been amply demonstrated that in such a monarchy the monarch is absolutely free to appoint his successor. Let us now briefly consider whether any duties are incumbent on the monarch himself in such a monarchy; but here we should carefully distinguish what a monarch can do and what he is obliged to do, for there is a difference between the two.

A sovereign monarch can lawfully command of the people not only whatever is necessary for the obvious good of his country, but indeed whatever he pleases, provided that it is not harmful to the people and not contrary to the will of God. The foundation of this power, as stated above, is the fact that the people has renounced in his favour its right to decide the common weal, and has conferred on him all power over itself: this includes civil and ecclesiastical ordinances of every kind, changes in customs and dress, house-building, procedures and ceremonies at feasts, weddings, funerals, etc., etc., etc.[36]

A monarch can abdicate, as did the eastern king Ptolomy Philometor, as Josephus the Jew writes

Максимиан, и Карол Пятый, кесари, и прочии в историах. [60] Вина могущества сего есть, что народ, отдая всю волю свою государю своему, не отнял от него в замену никоейже воли. А от сего известно, что естьли самого себе от короны, то кольми паче сына своего может отрешити от наследия короны.

Может государь приняти себе другого в товарищи, что многии творили государи римстии; и сами государи нарицалися Августи Кесари, а товарищи их просто Кесари. А от сего паки утверждается, что и наследника по себе определяти на воле государевой лежит.

Может государь товарища своего отринуть, якоже отринул Константин Великий Ликиниа; из которого могущества подается нам новый довод, что и сына может лишити наследия.

А долженство на монархах лежит тое, которое выше под числом четыренадесятым описалося. Но там показано оное из священных писаний; зде же показуется от самого монархии народного уставления. Всякая бо, коего либо от вышеименованных образа власть верховная, едину своего уставления вину конечную имеет, всенародную пользу. Сие только ведати народ должен, что государь его должен о его пользе общей пещися, но в делах попечения своего не народу, но единому Богу стоит или падает, и того единого суду подлежит, о чем выше под числом тринадесятым довольно показано.

Сие же царей долженство не токмо свободных творит их в определении наследников своих, но и одолжает усмотревати такового наследника, [61] который бы пользы народной не разрушил; чего ради не должен монарх ни единому из сынов своих скипетра наследия; но паче должен есть по своему званию нарицати наследника между сынами своими не старейшего,

(*Antiquities,* Book 13, *chapter* 7), the emperors Diocletian, Maximian, Charles V, and others in history. The origin of this right is that the people, in conferring all its freedom on the monarch, did not take from him any freedom in exchange. It is also clear from this that if he himself can renounce the crown, how much more can he bar his son from the succession to the crown.

A monarch can take another as his colleague, as did many Roman emperors. The emperors them-selves were called Augustus Caesar, while their colleagues were simply called Caesar. This again confirms that it also lies within a monarch's power to appoint his successor.

A monarch can depose his colleague, as Constantine the Great did to Licinius; which prerogative gives us further proof that he can also deprive his son of the succession.

As for the duties incumbent on monarchs, there is that which was described above under number 14. There it was demonstrated from Holy Writ; here it is demonstrated from the very establishment of monarchy by the people. For each and every one of the forms of government mentioned above has one ultimate reason for its establishment, namely, the common good of the people. The people need only know that the monarch is obliged to strive for its common good; in the exercize of his care, however he is answerable not to the people, but to God alone. and is subject only to His judgement, as was amply demonstrated above under number 13.

This duty incumbent on kings not only gives them absolute power in the appointment of their successors, but also obliges them to seek out a successor who will not undermine the public good; hence the monarch is not obliged to grant the succession to any of his sons; rather he is obliged by his calling to name as successor not the eldest,

но лучшего. А естьли ни един сын угоден к тому явится, то и не сына, но или иного от крови своея, или и отвне дому и фамилии своей. И тако довольно разумеем от уставления монархии, как государи в определении наследников своих свободни суть, паче же и званием своим к определению добрых наследников одолжаеми, и как народ определение без роптания и прекословия принимати долженствует.

16.

Еще нечто на конец предложим, что по мнению нашему к утверждению вещи зде рассуждаемой вельми угодно, и вместо крепкого заключения и нерушимой печати будет.

Изначала вышеписанного под числом пятнадесятым довода, помянулося, что монархиа есть двойственного вида: иная монархиа избирательная, иная же наследная, о которой нам речь сия есть.

Есть же у политических философов рассуждение, которая монархиа, избирательная или наследная, лучшая и полезнейшая. Предлагаем зде вократце рассудительные о обоих монархиах доводы.

За монархию избирательную против наследной сия нецыи предлагают:

1. Что в монархии избирательной, дети благородные поощряются всяким лучшим учениям навыкати, другдруга превзыти желая, да бы мог иногда [62] избиранием народа добродетельми его удивленного, удостоится престола монаршего; а в наследной монархии, монарший сын, яко беспечально и известно скипетра себе ожидающий, не хощет честным и к высокому правительству должным искусствам прилежати; подданных же дети, отсечены суще от надежды толь высокого достоинства, не видят, для чего бы им неленостно во учении и добродетелях упражнятися.

but the best, of his sons. And if not one son proves worthy, then he must not nominate a son, but someone else, either from his own kin or even from outside his house and family. Thus we can clearly understand, from the establishment of monarchy, that monarchs are free to appoint their successors, and indeed are obliged by their calling to appoint worthy successors; and that the people must accept their decision without complaint or criticism.

16.

Lastly, we shall add a point which in our opinion materially strengthens our case, and which will serve to place on it a firm, unbreakable seal of finality.

At the beginning of the argument under number 15 above, it was stated that there are two forms of monarchy, elective monarchy and hereditary monarchy; of which the latter is the subject of our present discussion.

There is a debate among political theorists as to which monarchy, elective or hereditary, is the better and more advantageous. We here set out in brief the arguments concerning both monarchies.

Some make the following points in favour of elective as against hereditary monarchy:

1.   That in an elective monarchy, the children of the nobility are encouraged to engage in all the liberal arts, each vying with the other, so that by impressing the people with his merits, he may some day prove worthy of election to the throne; whereas in an hereditary monarchy, the monarch's son who can calmly and confidently await the sceptre, will not apply himself to the liberal arts necessary for government; while the children of the subjects, being deprived of the hope of that high office, see no reason why they should trouble to acquire learning and merit.

2. В избирательной, глаголют, монархии, избранный государь, благодарен народу толь высоко себе вознесшему, не презорно державствует над ним, и с кротостию владеет.

3. В монархии избирательной, по смерти монарха, взыскуется на место его кто может лучший прочиих усмотрен быти: чего в монархии наследной делати не возможно, но нужда есть принимати за государя сына государева, не смотря, каков ни есть он, добрый или злонравный, мудрый или безумный.

Сия доводы представляют, которые за монархию избранием получаемую поборствуют.

Но как оные доводы, крепкие или не крепкие суть, не трудно показуют наследуемой монархии поборницы, и множайшими и крепчайшими доводами, наследное паче избираемого самодержавство утверждающии, а именно сими следующими:

1. Что дети благородные паче в наследной, нежели в избирательной монархии честным учениям прилежат. Монарх бо наследный, не опасаяся дому своему [63] и крови своей унижения, и беспечален пребывая в том, что сына его чуждый, каков бы ни был, предварити к постижению короны не может (разве бы самого монарха определением), желая же самому себе доброй от подданных службы, и нуждою детей своего подданства приводит к обучению воинскому и гражданскому. Во преки же, монарх избранный, издалече промышляя сыну своему по себе наследити корону, опасно наблюдает, да бы никто же от чуждых детей не был лучший; и есть ли видит сына своего не весьма к исправлению угодного, хотел бы да бы чуждые дети ни какового учения не коснулися; о самих же благородных детях (есть ли от родителей понуждени не будут, что мало в свете деется) да бы своею охотою, надеяся иногда корону получити, подвизалися в учениях и добродетелях, так мало надежды, как мало

2.   In an elective monarchy, it is said, the elected monarch is grateful to the people which has raised him so high, does not tyrannize over it, and rules with mildness.

3.   In an elective monarchy, on the monarch's death, the best man available is sought to take his place: which cannot be done in an hereditary monarchy, where the monarch's son must be accepted as monarch, regardless of his character, good or bad, wise or foolish.

These are the arguments advanced by the supporters of elective monarchy.

But how sound or unsound these arguments are is easily demonstrated by the supporters of hereditary monarchy, who confirm the superiority of hereditary monarchy over elective with many most powerful arguments, namely the following:

1.   The children of the nobility are more attentive to the liberal arts in an hereditary than in an elective monarchy. For an hereditary monarch, having no fear that his house or family will be displaced, secure in the knowledge that no stranger, whatever his merits, can prevent his son from acquiring the crown (unless the monarch himself so decides) and being himself desirous of good service from his subjects, compels their children to undergo military and civil instruction. An elective monarch, on the other hand, seeking long in advance to secure his son's succession, carefully watches out to see that no-one else's child surpasses his own; and if he sees that his son is little susceptible of improvement, he would prefer other men's children not to engage in education of any kind: as for the notion that the children of the nobility (unless compelled by their parents, which rarely happens) would of their own accord apply themselves to learning and merit in the hope of some day acquiring the crown, there is as little

прикладов того: есть ли бо от младых ногтей чего навыкати не начнут, не много случается, да бы к тому в большем возрасте преклонилися; а в самых отроческих летах помышляти о детях, будто они надеждою державной высоты к учениям поощряются, едино мечтание есть. Вина тому сия есть, что в избирательной монархии, каков бы кто ни был, ради множества короны желающих и ищущих, не известно ему и не близко получение короны.

И тако первый за избирательную монархию довод не токмо оной не служит, но и весьма служит наследной монархии.

2. Но и другий за избирательную монархию довод положенный [64] не так оной, яко наследной пособствует: кто бо не ведает, что не многии и редкии в человецех толикого любомудрия и великодушия обретаются, котории с низкого места, и яко Псаломник глаголет, *от гноища высоковозведеннии*, не забывают прежней низости своей? Повседневные примеры усмотревати можем, что таковии на высоту возлетевшии, не токмо первого своего состояния, но и самых себе не рассуждают, и того самого, что они человецы суть, не помнят; раждается же у них таковое забвение от непрестанного в них, о высоте своей яко необыклой, удивления; еще же и того ради, не ино что, только славу свою в мысли держат, да бы яко гладнии, донележе господствуют, помыслами величия своего насытилися. И понеже на время в дом свой приняли корону, того ради, поне память короны в роде своем утвердити желая, жестоко с подданными поступают, гордыню и свирепство вменяя властительское велелепие, и народ не забывать господствования их яростию убеждая. И не о самих зде от крайней нищеты на верх власти восшедших глаголем, но и о прочиих чинах не низких: всякий бо чин и сан подвластный, в соравнении верховной власти низкий есть, яко подданный, служащий и

hope of this as there are few examples: for unless they start to learn in childhood, it seldom happens that they turn to it as adults; and to think that children of tender years are encouraged to study by the hope of gaining the crown, is mere illusion. For in an elective monarchy, no matter what a man's merits, there are so many aspiring candidates for the crown, that his chance of acquiring it is doubtful and remote.

And so the first argument in favour of elective monarchy not only fails to support it, but rather supports hereditary monarchy.

2. But the second argument in favour of elective monarchy also supports it less than it does hereditary monarchy: for who does not know that there are few men so wise and magnanimous that, coming from a lowly station, and, as the Psalmist says, *raised up on high from the clay,*[37] do not forget their humble origins? We can see daily examples of such men who have risen to eminence, and give no thought not only to their origins, but even to their very selves, and forget the fact that they are human-beings; such forgetfulness arises from their constant amazement at their unexpected eminence; and therefore they think of nothing but their own glory, and, in their greed, for as long as they hold power, they sate themselves with thoughts of their own greatness. And having acquired the crown in their family only temporarily, they seek at least to make people remember that the crown was in their family, and so they treat their subjects harshly, equating pride and cruelty with regal pomp, and ensuring by their severity that the people do not forget their rule. We do not here mean only those who have risen from extreme poverty to supreme power, but also those whose origins are not so lowly; for every rank and office belonging to a subject is lowly in comparison

суду повинный. Наследный же монарх, яко не восшедший на высоту, но на оной родившийся, или и определением первого монарха поставленный, не имеет вины такового о себе высокоумия: аще бо рождением наследствовал державу, то ему она не вельми дивна; аще же усыновлением восприятый от монарха, получил наследие, [65] то смотря на образ его и ему подражая, сам себе не удивляется; еще же как рожденный, так и усыновленный, и того ради не свирепствует, что о вечном державствии своем беспечален есть. И сей честный характир на наследных государях очима мощно видети, и весьма дивно, когда некий и наследный не таков является.

3. О третием монархии избирательной доводе, что разумети подобает, нижае покажем. Наследной же монархии собственнии суть доводы, яко и собственные ее суть доброты и пользы. На монарха наследного, яко не имеют подданнии зависти, так и восставати на его не имеют страсти; и ведая не отъемлемое державство, еще же и отмщения бояся от наследника, не могут без крайнего отчаяния дерзати. Ведаем, что и таковое бывает дерзновение, но от крайне злобою ослепленных и отчаянных, и то не много, и не так часто, яко в монархии избирательной. Посмотрим в историю царей римских, и во всех совокупно наследных монархиах: не увидиши толь многих и толь жестоких, страшных и плачевных позорищ, колuкие и коль многие показалися в единой оной монархии избирательной.

4. Во избирательных монархиах не токмо могут сильнии помышляти, но и явственно говорят: *ныне сей, а я утро господствую*: из чего мотчание к послушанию указов монарших, и послушание студеное, и в преслушании

with the supreme power, being subordinate, subservient and subject to the law. An hereditary monarch, however, having not been raised to eminence, but born to it or appointed to it by his predecessor, has no reason to think so highly of himself: for if he has succeeded to power by right of birth, it comes to him as no great surprise; and if he has acquired the succession through adoption by the monarch, then, observing the latter's example and copying him, he is not amazed at his own position; and whether a true-born or adopted son, he does not tyrannize, being secure in the knowledge that his rule is permanent. This worthy characteristic can be clearly seen in hereditary monarchs, and it is quite exceptional for an hereditary monarch to prove other.

3. As for the third argument in favour of elective monarchy, we shall give our conclusion below. However, there are special arguments in favour of hereditary monarchy, just as there are special merits and advantages. Just as his subjects do not envy an hereditary monarch, so they have no desire to rebel against him; and because they know that his power is inalienable, and also because they fear retribution from his successor, they dare not do so unless reduced to extreme desperation. We know that such attempts do occur, but on the part of men utterly blinded and rendered desperate by malice, and even then they are fewer and less frequent than in an elective monarchy. Let us look at the history of the Roman emperors and at all the hereditary monarchies combined: you will not see as many cruel, terrible and pitiful sights as were seen in that elective monarchy alone.

4. In elective monarchies, the powerful may not only think, but indeed they openly say: *This man rules today, but tomorrow I shall rule:* hence arise delay and indifference in obeying the

не великий страх; еще же и на повеления государева, хотя бы и весьма нуждная, только не без труда исполняемая роптание, и добрых намерений злии и развратнии толки. А монарх бедный, аки связанный, [66] не так указует, яко просит воли у народа, и не так скоро и не так благопоспешно, как государственные нужды требуют, получает: понеже сильный, помня его прежднее с собою равенство, не вельми благоговейно, инии же и негодовательно, и аки бы стыдящеся, повинуются ему. Несть такого зла в наследной монархии: природный некий страх в народе, и говение к государю своему, и он не яко человек, но акибы изъятый от числа смертных почитаем есть. И в самых наследных монархиах делом является, что монархи бози суть, аще и прочиим титлу сию дает писание; и заповедь оная апостольская, повиноватися властем повелевающая *не токмо за гнев, но и за совесть,* аще и о всех властях глаголет, однакоже нигде таковаго своего исполнения, яко в наследных монархиах не обретает: наследием приемшему скипетр монарху не повинутися зазирает совесть простосердечному человеку, хотя и заповеди оной не знающему.

5. Наследный государь, известный о неотъемлемой державе своей, так о целости и добром состоянии государства прилежно печется, яко о домашнем добре своем, желая наследникам крепкую власть и славу оставити. Вопреки же, государь избранный о собственном дому своего, а не о общем всего общества благополучии промышляет; и донежеле может надеятися преклонити сенаторов и сильнейших в народе лиц к избранию по нем на государство сына своего, дотоль им всяким снисхождением угождает, и принужден бывает страстию своею болезновати лицеприятием, терпети сильных беззакония, попускати обиды

monarch's decrees, and little fear in disobeying them; complaints against the monarch's commands however essential, if they require hard work, and malicious misrepresentations of his good intentions. The poor monarch, as if fettered, does not so much command his people as beg their permission, and does not obtain it as fast and effectively as the interests of state demand; for the strong man, recalling that they were once both equals, does not obey him with very good grace, while others obey reluctantly, as if ashamed. There is no such evil in an hereditary monarchy: the people have a certain innate fear and reverence for their sovereign, and he is respected, not as a man, but as one distinct from mortal men. In hereditary monarchies, it is clear that monarchs are indeed gods,[38] although Scripture also gives this title to others monarchs; and the Apostle's command to submit to the powers that be, *not only for wrath, but also for conscience sake,* though it refers to all authorities, is nowhere so effective as in hereditary monarchies: not to submit to a monarch who has acquired the sceptre by right of succession would sting the conscience of an honest man, even though he did not know this commandment.

5.   An hereditary monarch, knowing that his power is inalienable, takes as much pains for the maintenance and welfare of the state as for his own domestic welfare, wishing to leave to his successors a well-established authority and glory. An elected monarch, on the other hand, concerns himself with the welfare of his own house and not with the general welfare of society as a whole; and as long as he can hope to induce the senators and the most powerful men in the nation to elect his son to rule the State after him, he humours them with every kind of indulgence, and is compelled, by his passion, to grant personal favours, to endure the

деемые немощным, [67] и прочие нестроения аки бы не видети, и не так повелителю, яко ласкательному рабу подобен есть. А когда не видит надежды сыновня наследия, то инамо мысли своя обратив, всячески тщится, дом свой от общих имений обогащая, сильный к удержанию скипетра сотворити; и тогожде ради свирепствует люте на подданных, сильнейшие от них истребити или привести в бессилие, умышляя, да бы по смерти его, не возмогли противостати сыну его скипетр удержати хотящему, к чему и всяких употребляет хитростей. Образ сего знатный есть в единой от европских монархий, аки бы избирательной: в которой некий монарх, промышляя дому своему неотъемлемое державство, двое нечто к промыслу своему угодное сделал: первое, многие и великие провинции, общим всего государства оружием завоеванные, приписал вечно дому своему, чим дом свой сотворил сильнейший от всего прочего государства: другое, сочинил вечный устав, что естьли бы когда вышел из дому его скипетр, тогда домашных его областей, с приписными провинциями наследник егож сын, внук, правнук, и прочии, не был бы подчинен монарху из иной фамилии избранному, но отделенное от монархии государство имел бы.

6. Бывают в государстве таковые нужды, которые исполнити кратким временем не возможно: что же в избирательной монархии деется. Государь настоящий трудов подымать не хощет, понеже не ведает, докончит ли оные кто по нем державу приимлет; и часто бывает, что новый избранный монарх, [68] завистию движим, зачатая от антецессора своего дела в несовершении оставляет, иногда же и совершенная разрушает. А

236

illegalities of the powerful, to tolerate wrongs done to the weak, and to connive at other irregularities, and resembles not so much a ruler as an obsequious slave. Moreover, if he sees no hope of securing the succession for his son, then, turning his thoughts elsewhere, he strives in every way to make his house strong enough to retain the sceptre, by enriching it out of public funds; and for the same reason he brutally tyrannizes over his subjects, plotting to eliminate the most powerful among them or to render them powerless, so that on his death they will be unable to resist his son in his desire to retain the sceptre; to which end he employs every kind of stratagem. There is a well-known instance of this in one of the European monarchies, ostensibly elective, in which a certain monarch, in order to secure inalienable supreme power for his house, did two things to further his purpose: first, he assigned to his house in perpetuity many great provinces, won by the armed forces of the whole State, whereby he made his house the most powerful in the State; second, he drew up a permanent statute, whereby if the sceptre should ever pass from his house, then his son, grandson, great-grandson, and so on, as heir to his private domains, together with the provinces which he had assigned to them, should not be subject to a monarch elected from another family, but should have a state separate from the monarchy.[39]

6.　　There are tasks in a State which cannot be accomplished in a short time: and that is their fate in an elective monarchy. The reigning monarch does not wish to exert himself, since he does not know whether it will be his successor who completes them; and it often happens that a newly elected monarch, out of envy, leaves unfinished the tasks begun by his predecessor, and sometimes even undoes what the latter has completed. It is different

в наследной монархии инако: наследник бо дела антецессора своего, яко своей славы здание, аще не совершенна видит, совершити тщится; аще же совершенна, то паче утверждает; и аще бы что погрешено было от антецессора, тое аки бы свой собственный вред врачует и исправляет.

7. Но что всего как в избирательной монархии вреднейшее, так в наследной здравейшее, сие есть, что в наследной, по преставлении государя, отдав народ, аки естественный долг, погребальные слезы умершему отцу своему, в тишине и безмятежии пребывает, и с великою радостию объемлет государя нового, беспрекословно престол наследствующего, так, аки бы и не умирал в государстве монарх. В избирательной же монархии, изрещи трудно, какие мятежи и смущения творит смерть государева, колики нестроения бывают донележе начнется избрание, какие факции в самом избрании. А когда два явятся равносильные конкурренты, то есть ищущии короны соперники, и народа часть за сим, а часть за другим станет, и аки бы на два народа государство разделится: колик междоусобие, колик внутренние брани, взаимные нападения, кровопролития, грабежи и разорения! Воистину таковая монархиа смертию своего государя и сама к смерти приближается. Какового бедства многие образы покажет нам и едина, сосед наш, республика польская. [69]

8. Но всегда ли надеятися, что избран будет добродетельный, мужественный, правдолюбивый, и весьма к царствованию угодный муж? Не токмо надеятися сего не всегда мощно, но мало когда таковой надежды не отпадаем. Посмотрим на обе стороны, на избирающих и на избираемых, и все увидим благонадежию противное. Избирающии мало когда на общую пользу смотрят: но инии того производят, которому

in an hereditary monarchy: for the successor strives to complete his predecessor's work if he sees that it is incomplete, for it is the foundation of his own glory; and if he sees that it is complete, he further consolidates it; and if there was any error on the part of his predecessor, he amends and corrects it as if the fault were his own.

7.   But what is most harmful of all in an elective monarchy, and most salutary in an hereditary one, is this: in an hereditary monarchy, on the monarch's demise, the people, having mourned its late father as a natural duty, remains peaceful and orderly, and with great joy welcomes the new monarch, who succeeds to the throne unopposed, as though no monarch had died. But in an elective monarchy it is painful to mention to what uprisings and upheavals a monarch's death gives rise: how many disorders ensue until the election begins, what factions arise at the election itself. And when there emerge two competitors of equal strength, that is, two rivals for the crown, and part of the people is for one, and part for the other, and the state is, as it were, split into two nations: what dissension ensues, what civil feuds, internecine attacks, bloodshed, rapine and destruction! Truly, on the death of its monarch, such a monarchy itself comes close to death. Of such misfortune, our neighbour, the Republic of Poland, will alone give us many examples.

8.   But is it always to be expected that the elected candidate will be a man of virtue and courage, a lover of justice and eminently fit to rule? Not only can this rarely be expected, but rather we are nearly always disappointed in the hope. Let us consider both sides, the electors and the candidates, and we shall see that everything is contrary to our high hopes. The electors seldom consider the common good; but some elect a candidate to whom

волю свою за данное или обещанное злато продали; инии того хотят, при котором сами бы могли всеми владети, и акибы царствовати, то есть, нарочно усмотревают немощного и скудоумного; инии паки, завистию на добрых и короны достойных жегами, представляют негодных но сильных, да бы лучших отрешити могли: и многие прочие страсти в избирании живут и действуют.

Из стороны же избираемых, честный и благоразумный муж, и властолюбием не болезнующий, добре ведая, как суетрудное, непокойное и малодействительное державство в таковом народе, не токмо оного не ищет, но и весьма опрятается от его, и разве насилием народным понужден, с воздыханием на престол взыдет. А которые доброхотно таковой державы ищут, тии ищут (обычне) не правильным способом, но подлогами, куплею, лестию, и аще могут, силою: и не поучаются, как бы добре государство управити, только бы себе возвеличити; и не рассуждают, каковую на высоте той получат славу, только бы великую. Кратко рещи: кто в таковой монархии намерен к пользе общей, [70] тот должен на вся бедствия и печали посвятити себе; а кто сих уклонитися хощет, тому нельзя мыслити о пользе общей. Так то благонадежное избрание есть. Наследная же монархиа, естьли бы иных угодий, которые имеет многие, не имела, то в едином сем блаженна была бы и благословенна, что таковым от избирания происходящим бедствам не подлежит.

Сия же вся как избирательной монархии вреды, так пользы наследной предлагаем того ради, что естьли покажем некий недостаток и в наследной монархии, а той исправитися инако не может, токмо избираемыми от государей наследниками, то не останется сумнение,

they have sold their vote for a gift or promise of gold; others favour a candidate under whom they will be able to control everything, and, as it were, reign themselves; that is, they deliberately seek out a candidate who is weak and of low intelligence. Others still, incensed by envy of good and worthy candidates for the crown, put forward unworthy but powerful candidates, in order to exclude the former; and many other passions also play an active role at an election.

As for the candidates, an honourable and right-thinking man, not smitten with ambition, knows full well how vain, troublesome and ineffectual it is to rule such a people, and not only does he not seek to do so, but he positively shrinks from it, and only if compelled by the people will he reluctantly ascend the throne. As for those who willingly seek such power, they usually do so not by proper means, but by fraud, bribery, flattery, and, if they can, by force; and they do not learn to rule well, as long as they can exalt themselves; nor do they consider what kind of glory they will gain at the summit, as long as they enjoy a reputation. In short: whoever aims at the common good in a monarchy of this kind must resign himself to every misfortune and sorrow; but whoever wishes to avoid these can have no thought for the common good. Such are the hopes that can be placed in an election. An hereditary monarchy, however, even without its many other advantages, would be sufficiently blessed in not being subject to such disasters as result from an election.

Our reason for setting out all these disadvantages of elective monarchy and advantages of hereditary monarchy is this: that if we point out some defect in hereditary monarchy, and this defect can only be put right by successors chosen by the monarchs, then no doubt will remain

что государи наследники и вольнии и должнии суть наследников по себе определяти: понеже таковое определение монархию изрядную но един некий недостаток имущую, совершенно исправляет. Исповести бо подобает, что и наследная монархиа вреду некоему подлежит, а именно тому, о котором помянулося выше, в третием доводе, от поборников государства избирательного положенном: то есть, что не всегда и от доброго государя сын ему подобный раждается, но иногда является аки весьма отличен от родителя, злонравный, нерадетельный, яростию побеждаемый, правды не ищущий, навыкати искусства или не хотящий или не могущий; таковый когда по родителе на место его взыдет, бедно деется с государством: а народ и такового наследника от короны родительской отрешить отнюдь не может, яко выше ясно показано. И сей един есть вред в наследной монархии, [71] прочая во всем благополучна.

Смотри же всяк благоразумный и непристрастный: не добре ли и от сего вреда предохраняется монархиа, когда монарх, не смотря на первородство между сынами своими, но кто от них лучший; или и на сыновство не смотря, но и чуждее достоинство, паче домашнего непотребства предпочитая, определяет при животе своем такового по себе наследника, который общему добру не попустит пресещися смертию антецессора своего, но начатая от него совершит, совершенная утвердит, намеренная произведет в дело, и весьма потщится всему миру показать, что не обманулся антецессор, нарекл себе его наследником. И ктож может усумневатися, что не только могут свободно но и должни суть наследнии государи которого лучшего усмотрят, определяти в наследники себе? Един вред остался в наследной монархии, что иногда страдати понуждена от худого наследника, а и той вред таковым наследных монархов определением отлагается: то кто не речет, что таковое

that hereditary monarchs both can and must appoint their successors: for by such an appointment, a monarchy which is excellent apart from one single defect, is set wholly to rights. For it should be confessed that even hereditary monarchy is subject to one fault, which was mentioned above in the third argument advanced by the supporters of elective monarchy: namely, that even a worthy monarch does not always beget a son like himself, but the son often proves very different from the father, of bad character, negligent, quick to anger, indifferent to justice, unwilling or unable to apply himself to learning: when such a son succeeds his father, woe betide the state: nevertheless the people can by no means bar such a successor from his father's crown, as was clearly shown above. This is the only fault in hereditary monarchy, which is blessed in all other respects.

So let every right-minded and impartial man consider whether a monarchy is not well protected from this fault too, when the monarch considers, not which of his sons is the first-born, but which is the best; or if, disregarding his sons altogether, and preferring merit in a stranger to unfitness in his own family, he appoints in his lifetime a successor such as will not let the common good be curtailed by the death of his predecessor, but will complete what the latter has begun, consolidate what he has completed, put his plans into action and strive hard to show the whole world that his predecessor was not deceived in naming him as his successor. Who now can doubt that hereditary monarchs are not only free to appoint but indeed must appoint as their successor the best man whom they can find? There remains one fault in an hereditary monarchy: that it must sometime suffer from a bad successor; but even this fault is avoided if hereditary monarchs make an appointment of the

определение не токмо не зазорно, но и преблагословенно есть, и разве крайне безумным, или врагам отечества своего не желаемо?

ЕКСЕМПЛИ ИЛИ ПРИМЕРЫ

По так ясных и многих доводах, время уже представить ексемпли или примеры, котории свободу и власть родительскую в определении наследников утверждают. Имеем же многие сего примеры в языческих и в христианских историах, некоторые же и в самом священном писании. [72] Первее предложим примеры от историй человеческих, а по том от писания священного, яко известнейшие и твердейшие, и котории аки печать быти могут сему рассуждению, и никоему прекословию места не оставят. Примеры же от историй человеческих взятые распологаем зде по чину времен, в которые сделаннии обретаются.

Примеры от историй человеческих

1. Кир, персидский царь, старшему сыну наследие державы своей оставляя, известил о изволении своем, что не ради старейшенства сыновня, но надеяся лучшего в нем искусства, определяет его наследником по себе. *из Ксенофонта, Гроциус о правде мира и войны, книга 2, глава 7, число 18.*
2. Дарий Истаспис, персидский царь, минув большого сына Артабана, или, якоже инии пишут, Артабазана, поставил короны своей наследником сына меньшего Ксеркса.
3. Артаксеркс, прозываемый Мнимон, персидский царь, имел кроме прочиих сынов два сына: Оха от жены, и Арсама от подложницы. Ох гордый и свирепый был, а Арсам благоразумный; и того ради Артаксеркс не Оху от жены законной, но Арсаму, хотя от подложницы рожденному, отдати царства наследие был намерен; но властолюбивый Ох разрушил

kind just mentioned: who, then, can deny that such an appointment is not merely no disgrace, but is indeed the greatest blessing, which only utter fools or enemies of their country can fail to desire?

Examples or Instances

After so many clear arguments, it is now time to give examples or instances which confirm the right and power of parents to appoint their heirs. We find many examples in pagan and Christian history and several in Holy Writ itself. We shall first give examples from secular history and then from Holy Writ, the latter being the best known and most cogent, and which can, as it were, set the seal on this treatise and will leave no room for contradiction. The examples from secular history we present here in chronological order.

Examples from secular history

1.　　Cyrus, king of Persia, in leaving the succession to his eldest son, made it known that he did so not because he was the eldest son, but because he hoped that he would be the best qualified to succeed him. (From Xenophon; Grotius, *On the Law of Peace and War,*[40] Book 2, Chapter 7, No. 8).

2.　　Darius Hystaspes, king of Persia, passing over his elder son, Artabanus (or, according to some, Artabazanus), made his younger son, Xerxes heir to the throne.

3.　　Artaxerxes, surnamed Mnemon, king of Persia, had, among others, two sons: Ochus, by his wife, and Arsamus, by his concubine. Ochus was proud and cruel, but Arsamus was wise; and therefore Artaxerxes intended to give the succession not to Ochus, born of his lawful wife, but to Arsamus, though born of a concubine; but the

родительское намерение братоубийством. *Плутарх в житии Артаксеркса при конце.*

4. Фемистоклес, славный афинейский богатырь, в юности своей, бесчестным житием раздражив родителей, лишен был от них всего наследия; но то ему произошло в пользу: ибо помыслив, что без труда и промысла не возможно от оного своего порока очиститися, всего себе вдал на службу [73] отечества своего, и толико успел, что и верховного в Афинех правительства достигл. *Звингер в Феатре грань 630.*

5. Манлий Торкват, славный вельможа римский, когда на сына его Иуниа Силлана, который Македонию властию преторскою управлял, подали послы македонстии доношение в сенат о его в оной провинции похищениях, просил у сената, да бы на его суд опустили сына, опущенного судил, и следованием винного быти увидев, изгнал из дому своего, и лишил его имене и достояния сыновня: которое осуждение и извержение понудило Силлана к саморучной смерти; однакож Манлий отец и погребения его присутствием своим почести не хотел. *Пишется сие с похвалою Манлиа в ексемплях Валериа Максима, книга 5, глава 8, и в сокращении Тита Ливиа, книга 54.*

6. Емилий Скавр, славный от вельмож римских, когда римское воинство, не стерпя на бою силы цимбров, неприятелей своих, и оставя своего проконсула, бегством с поля возвратилося, между которыми был и сын его, трепета и бегства их участник, отверг его от сыновства яко отродка, послав к нему такий выговор: *лучше бы,* рече, *принял я труп твой убиенного, нежели живого тебе видети так студным побегом порочного: того ради, естьли осталося в тебе мало нечто стыдения, иди куды хощеши, яко отродок, от очес родительских.* Не стерпел и сей сын

ambitious Ochus frustrated his father's plan by murdering his brother. (Plutarch at the end of his *Life of Artaxerxes*).

4.   Themistocles, the renowned Athenian hero, having in his youth angered his parents by his dishonourable mode of life, was disinherited by them; but this turned out to his advantage: for reflecting that without toil and industry he could not expunge his disgrace, he devoted himself entirely to his country's service, and with such success, that he attained supreme power in Athens. (Zwinger in his *Theatre*, paragraph 630).

5.   Manlius Torquatus, the renowned Roman dignitary, had a son, Junius Sillanus, who ruled Macedonia as praetor; when the Macedonian envoys complained to the Senate of his depredations in that province. Torquatus asked the Senate to commit his son to his court, where he tried him; and seeing after investigation that he was guilty, he banished him from his house, and deprived him of his name and honour as a son; condemned and disowned Sillanus was driven to suicide; but his father Manlius, would not even honour his funeral by his presence. (This appears together with a eulogy of Manlius in the *Examples* of Valerius Maximus. Book 5, Chapter 8, and in an abridged version in Livy, Book 54).

6.   When a Roman army failed to withstand the might of their enemy, the Cimbri, in battle, and fled from the field, abandoning its proconsul, among the fugitives was the son of Aemilius Scaurus, the renowned Roman dignitary, who fled with them in panic; Scaurus disowned him as a degenerate, sending him the following rebuke: *I would rather,* he said, *have received your dead body than have seen you alive, disgraced by so shameful a flight; if, therefore, there remains in you any vestige of shame, go where you will, degenerate that you are,*

такового отвержения, и сам себе смерти предал. *Валерий Максим, книга 5, глава 8.* [74]

7. От патрикийского рода римлянин, именем Цинциннат, сына своего Цезона, злонравного без надежды исправления, весьма отлучил от себе, отняв ему и нарицание сыновне. *Феодор Звингер в Феатре своем на грани 866.*

8. Аристипп философ неподобонравных себе и весьма негодных сынов так презирал, и отвергал от себе, акибы они не родилися от него, и не сыны ему были. И когда некто от другов порицал его за тое, вменяя ему в великое свирепство и жестосердие, отвещал Аристипп: *не чистые, рече, мокроты и пакостные животные из тела нашего раждаются, обаче оные от нас отвергаем. Диоген Лаертий в житии его.*

9. Метелл, римский патрикий, сынов своих всего наследия лишил; и сыны его по смерти не дерзали родительского завета толь себе вредного разрушати, изволяя лишатися имения, нежели воли родительской не исполнити. *Звингер в Феатре, грань 1034.*

10. Птоломей, египетский царь, прозываемый Лаги, определил по себе наследника самого малейшего сына, Птоломеа Филадельфа, от второй жены рожденного, миновав сынов и больших, и рожденных от первой жены. *Тит Ливий, книга 44 и 45; Иосиф иудей, книга 22, глава 2 древностей; Епифаний в книзе о весах и мерах.*

11. Птоломей Фискон жену свою Клеопатру определил по себе царствия наследницею с таковым договором, дабы она из сынов своих которого похощет, приняла к себе в державы участие. *Иустин, книга 39, глава 3.* [75]

12. Филипп, того имене вторый македонский царь, имел советы и намерение изринути из наследия сына Персеа за некое злодеяние, хотя

out of your father's sight. This son too could not bear to be thus disowned, and he took his own life. (Valerius Maximus, Book 5, chapter 8).

7.	The Roman patrician, Cincinnatus, disowned outright his incorrigibly wicked son, Caeso, even depriving him of the name of son. (Theodore Zwinger in his *Theatre*, paragraph 866).

8.	The sons of the philosopher Aristippus, who were unlike him in character and were indeed most unworthy, he despised and disowned, as if he had not begotten them and they were not his sons at all. And when one of his friends rebuked him for this, charging him with great cruelty and harshness, Aristippus replied as follows: *Foul liquids and foreign bodies,* he said, *are generated by our body, but we cast them out from us.* (Diogenes Laertius in his Life of Aristippus).

9.	The Roman patrician, Metellus, disinherited his sons; and on his death, his sons did not presume to overturn their father's will, prejudicial though it was to them, consenting to forfeit their patrimony rather than disobey their father's wish. (Zwinger in his *Theatre*, paragraph 1034).

10.	Ptolemy, king of Egypt, surnamed Lagus, appointed as successor his youngest son, Ptolomy Philadelphus, who was born of his second wife, passing over his elder sons born of his first wife. (Livy, Book 44, and 45; Josephus the Jew, Book 22, Chapter 2 of his *Antiquities*; Epiphanius in his book on weights and measures).

11.	Ptolomey Physcon appointed his wife Cleopatra as successor to his kingdom, on condition that she took one of his sons, whichever she chose, to rule jointly with her. (Justin, Book 39, Chapter 3).

12.	Philip II, king of Macedon, planned to bar his son Perseus from the succession for some

того совершить и не возмогл, понеже Персей великую себе силу прибрал. *Ливий, книга 40.*

13. Пишет Иустин историк в книзе 42, что Ород, парфийский царь, долго рассуждал, которому из сынов своих царство по себе оставити.

14. Август Агриппу, племянника своего, первее усыновил себе, потом же видя его злонравие, усыновления лишил и во изгнание на остров послал; и пожитки его в казну воинскую забрати повелел, и самого в воинской кустодии держати до смерти; и на то приговор сенатский сочинити указал. *Светоний в житии Августа, глава 65.*

15. Август, кесарь римский, когда требовал у народа, дабы сынов его имели в призрении, то есть, дабы не лишил их чести и власти, никогда о том не предлагал просто, но с таковым договором, аще будут достоини. *Светоний в житии Августа, глава 65.*

16. Тот же император дщерь свою Иулию, и от нее рожденную внучку Иулию за бесстудное житие в изгнание послал, и непреклонен народным молением, возвратити их не похотел. *Светоний в житии Августа, глава 65.*

17. Валентиниан император когда рассуждал, кого бы себе в товарищи и в участие власти приняти, конного воинства начальник такий ему (хотя и дерзкий) совет подавал: *естьли твоих,* [76] рече, *о император, любишь, имеешь брата: естьли же любишь государство, ищи кого можешь усмотрети.* Валентиниан брата своего Валента нарекл Августом, хотя и имел сынов Гратиана и Валентиниана, которых також в участие державы своей скоро восприял. *Пишут о сем Сократ, Созомен, Никифор, и проч.*

И сия едина историа сугубо показует, что на воле государей лежит, определяти себе кого хотят в соцарствование и наследие. Видим бо что

wrongdoing, though he was unable to do so, because Perseus raised a great force. (Livy, Book 40).

13. The historian Justin writes in Book 42 that Orodes, King of Parthia, long considered to which of his sons to leave his kingdom.

14. Augustus first adopted his nephew Agrippa, but later, seeing his bad character, revoked the adoption and banished him to an island; he ordered his goods to be confiscated and Agrippa himself to be kept in military custody for life; and he ordered the Senate to pass sentence to that effect. (Suetonius, in his Life of Augustus, Chapter 65).

15. When the Roman emperor Augustus asked the people to keep his sons under its supervision, that is, that it should not deprive them of their honour and authority, he did not propose this unconditionally, but on condition that they proved worthy. (Suetonius, in his Life of Augustus, Chapter 65).

16. The same emperor exiled his daughter, Julia, and her daughter, his granddaughter, Julia, for their shameless way of life; and unmoved by popular entreaty, refused to recall them. (Suetonius, Life of Augustus, Chapter 65).

17. When the emperor Valentinian was considering whom to adopt as his colleague and co-ruler, his commander of cavalry gave him the following somewhat bold advice: *If, o emperor,* he said, *you love your kinsmen, you have a brother; but if you love the state, seek whomever you can find.* Valentinian named his brother Valens as Augustus, although he had two sons, Gratian and Valentinian, whom he also soon made co-rulers with himself. (This is described by Socrates, Sozomen, Nicephorus and others).

This episode alone shows that monarchs are free to appoint whom they please both as co-ruler and as

Валентиниану полководец советовал, и что Валентиниан сделал.

18. Гратиан император, царствуя с братом своим Валентинианом, принял в участие державы и Феодосиа. *Сократ, книга 5, глава 2; Никифор, книга 12*

19. Лев, первый того имене император, первее молением Аспара патрикиа преклонен, сына его Ардабуриа поставил кесарем; а потом узнав аспаровы на себе наветы, Аспара и сына его кесаря убити повелел; и внука своего Леона, дщери Ариадны сына, императором поставил, а отца его, своего же зятя, Зинона, презрел. *Из хронологии Кассиодора.*

20. Зинон, умершу в младенчестве сыну его Леону, императорский престол получив, великое терпел гонение от Василиска, брата Верины императрицы, тещи своей. Когда же полководец василисков, Армат именем, передался к нему с воинством, и оного помощию победил Зинон Василиска, тогда Зинон сына арматова поставил кесарем, а Армата самого убил, сказуя, что который Василиску, господину [77] своему не был верен, не будет верен и ему, Зинону; по том же и сына его лишив власти цесарской, в причетники церковные поставити велел. *Из Евагриа, книга 3, глава 24.*

21. Тиверий вторый, император римский, Маврикиа, военного и добродетелного мужа, первее кесарем, потом же и Августом, то есть полным императором, поставил, и дщерь свою за него выдал. *Евагрий, книга 5.*

22. Фока император дщерь свою Домитию отдал в жену Комиту Приску. Когда же при брачном пиршестве было и некое по обычаю славное позорище, на том позорищи некотории человецы (зло или добро о императоре мыслящии) поставили образы Приска и Домитии новобрачных;

successor. For we see what the commander advised Valentinian, and what Valentinian did.

18. The emperor Gratian, ruling together with his brother Valentinian, also made Theodosius a co-ruler, (Socrates, Book 5, Chapter 2; Nicephorus, Book 12).

19. The emperor Leo I, at the entreaty of the patrician, Aspar, first named the latter's son, Ardaburius, as Caesar; but later, learning of Aspar's slanders against him, he had Aspar and his son, the Caesar, put to death; and appointed as emperor his grandson Leo, son of his daughter Ariadne, and passed over his father, Zeno, Leo's son-in-law. (From the *Chronology* of Cassicdorus).

20. Acceding to the imperial throne on the death in childhood of his son, Leo, Zeno suffered great oppression from Basiliscus, brother of the empress Verina, his mother-in-law. But when a general of Basiliscus, Armatus by name, defected to him together with his army, and with his help Zeno defeated Basiliscus, then Zeno appointed the son of Armatus as Caesar, but Armatus himself he put to death, saying that he who was disloyal to his master, Basiliscus, would also be disloyal to him, Zeno; later he also deprived Armatus' son of his authority as Caesar, and made him become a church sexton. (Evagrius, Book 3, Chapter 24).

21. The Roman emperor Tiberius II appointed Mauricius, a good soldier and a virtuous man, first as Caesar, and then as Augustus, that is as absolute emperor, and gave him his daughter in marriage (Evagrius, Book 5).

22. The emperor Phocus gave his daughter Domitia in marriage to Count Priscus. At the wedding-feast there was, as was customary, a grand spectacle, in the course of which several persons (whether well or ill disposed to the emperor) set up images of the newly-weds Priscus and Domitia; and

а народ воскликнул, Августами новобрачных нарицая; сие вельми неприятно стало императору, и многих смертию казнил, и зятя Приска возненавидел. *Сет Кальвизий, на лето господне 607.*

23. Лев четвертый, римский император, умоляем от народа, дабы сына своего Константина сотворил себе державы общником, не соизволял просто, но разве бы сенат и народ с клятвою обещалися, не иному кому, кроме сына его повиноватися. И тако первее нарекл императором сына своего; но потом в завете написал, да бы Константин и матерь его Ирина вместе царствовали. *Зонар и Кедрин.*

24. Михаил император, видя сам себе не довольна искусством к царствованию, отдал скипетр Леону Арменину, хотя ему в том и жена и дети его противилися. *Сет Кальвизий на лето 813.* [78]

25. Корол, французский король, Кароломанна сына своего, ков на отца умыслившего, лишил данных ему областей, и за арест послал; по том же простив и освободив, когда возобновленную от сына вражду и бунт увидел, первее судом епископов отлучил от церкви, потом же паки отдал за арест; но и еще за арестом бунтовских умышлений не отставал Кароломанн, и того ради очей избодение пострадал. *Кальвизий на лето 870, 871, 873.*

26. Конрад, западный император, видя себе к смерти близка, не брата своего Евергарда, но Генрика (который от противной ему факции избран был императором) избрал по себе на престол; а брата увещавал, да бы без всякого прекословия уступил оное достоинство Генрику, яко искусному и государство управити могущему. *Кальвизий на лето 918.*

27. Лудовик, император западный, сына своего Лудовика, военною на его отца наступати дерзнувшего, когда при смерти своей двоим прочиим

the people acclaimed them, calling them Augustus and Augusta; this was highly displeasing to the emperor, and he had many put to death, and conceived a hatred for his son-in-law, Priscus. (Sethus Calvisius, A.D. 607).

23.   The Roman emperor Leo IV, implored by the people to make his son Constantine co-ruler with him, would not consent outright, but only on condition that the Senate and people swore an oath to obey no-one but his son. Thereupon he first named his son as emperor; but later he laid it down in his will that Constantine and his mother Irene should reign together (Zonaras and Cedrenus).

24.   The emperor Michael, seeing himself insufficiently well qualified to rule, gave the sceptre to Leo the Armenian, despite the opposition both of his wife and his children. (Sethus Calvisius, year 813).

25.   The Frankish king Charles deprived his son Carolomannus of the domains he had given him, and put him under arrest for plotting rebellion against him; but later pardoned him and set him free; however, when he saw his son again hostile and rebellious, he first had him excommunicated by an episcopal court and then had him arrested again; but even under arrest Carolomannus still did not desist from his rebellious designs, and hence had his eyes gouged out. (Calvisius, year 870, 871, 873).

26.   The western emperor Conrad, seeing himself close to death, chose as his successor, not his brother Eberhard, but Henry (who had been elected as emperor by a hostile faction); and he enjoined his brother to yield that rank without objection to Henry, as a man well qualified and able to rule. (Calvisius, year 918).

27.   The western emperor Ludwig had a son, Ludwig, who had dared to take up arms against his father; on his deathbed, he divided the succession

сынам разделял наследие заветом, в завете том не именовал, и ничего ему наследствовати по себе не благоговил. *Бароний на лето 840.*

28. Оттон, западный император, в тяжкой болезни и в отчаянии жития быв, принял в участие державы своей сына Лудольфа, и наследником по себе нарекл его. Но по том сие определение отменил, видя его леность к военным делам, и надеяся рождения другого сына. Сын Лудольф войну на отца воздвигл, [79] на которой знатно побежден, и от всех сковников своих оставлен, великим покаяния и покорения образом умыслил родителя государя на милость к себе обратити: босоног, и в нищетном рубищи повергл себе пред ногами родительскима. И простил ему отец, однакоже не только отъятого наследия не возвратил ему, но и княжение даное ему отнял, и отдал зятю Генрикову. *Кальвизий на лето 946, 951, 952, 953, 954.* Сей Оттон преславный есть мужеством, благоразумием и добронравием между западными императорами, и Оттон Великий нарицается.

29. Исаакий Комнин, восточный император, когда гром его едва не ко смерти опалил, совлеклся порфиры, и в монастырь студийский отходя, избрал себе сукцессора или преемника короны не от крове своей, но от чуждей, мужа к царствованию угодного и достойного, Константина Дуку, который по нем царствовал седмь лет и месяцей шесть. *Зонар.*

30. Калоиоанн, восточный император, сам себе не волею, но случаем стрелами своими уязвив так, что ни каковое врачевство помощи житию его могло, видя близкую смерть свою, определил короны наследника меньшего возрастом сына своего Емманнуила, минув Исаакиа большего. *Кальвизий на лето 1143.*

31. Конрад, того имене третий, западный император, приближився болезнию к смерти, когда советовал с старейшинами о наследнике,

between his two other sons in his will, without mentioning him, and did not leave him anything after his death. (Baronius, year 840).

28. The western emperor Otto, being gravely ill and in despair of his life, appointed his son Ludolph as co-ruler and named him as his successor. But later he revoked this decision, seeing Ludolph's neglect of military affairs, and hoping for the birth of a second son. His son Ludolph, having started a war against his father, in which he was soundly defeated, and deserted by all his fellow rebels, sought to win mercy from his father by a great show of repentance and submission: barefoot and in a threadbare gown, he prostrated himself at his father's feet. His father did forgive him; however, not only did he not restore to him the succession of which he had deprived him, but he took back a principality which he had given to him, and gave it to his son-in-law Henry. (Calvisius, Year 946, 951, 952, 953, 954). This Otto is renowned among the western emperors for his courage, intelligence and virtue, and is known as Otto the Great.

29. Isaac Comnenus, the eastern emperor, having been almost killed by a thunderbolt, renounced the purple, and retiring to the monastery of Studion, chose his successor or heir to the throne not from his own family but from another, namely Constantine Dukas, a man fit and worthy to rule, who ruled after him for seven years and six months. (Zonaras).

30. The eastern emperor Caloioannes, having accidentally wounded himself with his own arrows. so that no medicine could save his life, seeing that death was near, appointed as successor his younger son, Emmanuel, passing over Isaac, the elder (Calvisius, year 1143).

31. The western emperor, Conrad III, being mortally ill, after consulting his elders about a

миновал сына своего Фридерика, но другого Фридерика, прозванием Барбароссу, [80] сына брата своего, подал вместо себе на императорский престол. *Кальвизий на лето 1152, и Бароний на тожде лето.*

32. Фридерик, того имене вторый, император западный, Генрика сына своего короновал на императорство в лето 1222; но тот сын его войною востал на отца в лето 1234, а по том в лето 1235, силы родительской убоявся, просил у отца прощения, и оное получил за молением вельмож; но понеже некие крепости удержати при себе намерен был, противо родительской воли, того ради повелением родителя государя, послан в Сикилию за арест, где и умер. *Кальвизий на лета помянутые.*

33. Ферквард, Евгениа четвертого, шотского короля сын, понеже добронравию и правдолюбию родительскому не подражал, еще же и между вельможами мятежные факции сочинял, не токмо наследия родительского не удостоился, но и во узы взят, и до смерти не испущен. *Звингер в феатре грань 1075.*

34. Гумберт, князь дельфинатский, да бы род свой, который не любим ему был, отрешил от наследия Дельфината (Дельфинат княжение нарицается) продал свое княжение французскому королю; но понеже оное княжение было подвластное римскому государству, того ради требовал Гумберт соизволения императорского, Карола четвертого, тогда владеющего. Соизволил император с таковым договором, чтоб Дельфинатом впредь не ин кто владел, только первородные сыны французских королей, [81] как то и доселе деется, чего ради первенцы французстии и дельфини нарицаются. *Иоанн Клуверий в Кароле четвертом; Гофман, в лексиконе; Кальвизий с летописца фландрийского на лето 1348.*

35. Маргарита цесарева, Лудовика императора жена, отняла сыну своему Вильгельму графство голландское, и отдала Лудовику, а Вильгельму

successor, passed over his son Frederick and gave the imperial throne to another Frederick, surnamed Barbarossa, the son of his brother. (Calvisius, year 1152, and Baronius, the same year).

32.   The western emperor Frederick II crowned his son Henry as emperor in the year 1222; but the son rose up in arms against him in 1234; but then in 1235, fearful of his father's strength, he begged his forgiveness, and received it at the entreaty of the grandees; but because he sought to keep certain fortresses against his father's will, he was sent under arrest, at his father's command, to Sicily, where he died. (Calvisius, years stated).

33.   Farquhart, son of Eugene IV, king of Scotland, because he did not emulate his father's virtue and love of justice, and indeed stirred up rebellious factions among the grandees, was not only not granted the succession, but was put in fetters for life. (Zwinger in *Theatre*, paragraph 1075).

34.   Humbert, duke of Dauphiné, in order to bar his family, whom he disliked, from succeeding to the Dauphiné (the Dauphiné is the name of the duchy), sold the duchy to the king of France; however, since the duchy was subject to the Roman empire, Humbert asked permission of the reigning emperor, Charles IV. The emperor consented, on condition that henceforth none should rule the Dauphiné except the firstborn sons of the kings of France, as happens to this day, for which reason the firstborn sons of the kings of France are called the dauphins. (Johannes Cluverius in *Charles IV*, Hofman in his *Lexicon*, Calvisius, from the *Flanders Chronicle* for the year 1348).

35.   The empress Margaretha, wife of the emperor Ludwig, took the county of Holland from her son Wilhelm and gave it to Ludwig, and gave

даровала Ганнонию провинцию. *Кальвизий на лето 1350.*

36. Альберт, князь баварийский, Вильгельма сына своего за то, что он его подложницу убил, не токмо из дому своего изгнал, но и бандитом сделал, то есть, извергл из чила человек государства своего публикованым в народ указом; и хотя Вильгельм ходатайством короля французского, которого дщерь понял в жену себе, получил у Альберта родителя прощение, однакож сим не помрачается власть родительская, но и паче утверждается. *Кальвизий на лето 1392.*

37. Лудовик брадатый, князь баварский, сына своего Лудовика лишил наследия. *Кальвизий на лето 1444.*

38. Арнольда, князя Гельдрии, сын его Адольф, яко пленника поимав, в заключении держал, властолюбием сам пленен, и не терпя дожидатися смерти родительской; но Карол, бургунский князь, пришед на помощь Арнольду, победил и пленил бессовестного сына его; а отец тако от бесчеловечия сыновня освобожден, извергл из наследия сына Адольфа, и Гельдрию княжение свое продал заступнику своему, Каролу бургунскому: изволилося бедному родителю толикую [82] область уронити из дому своего, нежели толь беззаконному отродку оную оставити. *Из хроники бельгийской, Кальвизий на лето 1465.*

39. Филипп, Карола пятого императора сын, король гишпанский, сына своего Карола в измене подозренного, лишив всего имения, предал в неисходное заключение, в котором он и умер скоро. *Иоанн Клуверий, Фамиан Страда, и прочии.*

40. Зде же воспоминаем и нашего российского государя, Великого Князя Иоанна Васильевича (которого помянул в объявлении своем о свободной в избрании наследника воли самодержцев, Император и Самодержец Всероссийский, Петр Великий). Тот Великий Князь перво мимо сыновей отдал внуку, а по том отставил внука уже венчанного, и отдал сыну свое

Wilhelm the province of Hainaut. (Calvisius, year 1350).

36.   Albert, duke of Bavaria, not only banished his son Wilhelm from his house for murdering his mistress, but also outlawed him, that is excluded him from the number of his subjects by public decree; and although Wilhelm, through the intercession of the king of France, whose daughter he married, won his father's pardon, yet this does not cast any doubt on parental authority, but rather confirms it still more. (Calvisius, year 1392).

37.   Ludwig the Bearded, duke of Bavaria, barred his son Ludwig from the succession. (Calvisius, year 1444).

38.   Arnold, duke of Guelders, was captured and held in confinement by his son, Adolph, who was himself consumed by ambition and impatient for his father's death; but Charles, duke of Burgundy coming to Arnold's aid, defeated and captured his unscrupulous son; and Arnold, thus freed from his son's inhuman treatment, barred him from the succession and sold the duchy of Guelders to his protector, Charles of Burgundy: the poor father preferred to let his family lose this great province rather than leave it to such a wicked degenerate. (From the *Belgian Chronicle*. Calvisius, year 1465).

39.   Philip, king of Spain, son of the emperor Charles V, suspecting his son, Charles, of treason, disinherited him and condemned him to life imprisonment, where he soon died. (Johannes Cluverius, Famianus Strada, and others).

40.   Here we may also recall our own Russian monarch, Grand Duke Ivan Vasil'evich, (who was also mentioned by Peter the Great, Emperor and Sovereign of All the Russias, in his declaration concerning the absolute right of sovereigns to choose a successor). The Grand Duke first passed over his sons and gave the succession to his

наследство.

41. Еще же и сие явственный образ и пример к нашему слову подает, что государи самодержцы могут разделяти, и мнози разделяли на части государство свое, и по части сынам своим во владение отдавали: якоже Константин Великий разделил государство сынам своим Консте, Константию и Константину, Феодосий Великий Аркадию и Онорию, Владимир Великий Ярославу, Борису, Глебу и прочиим. И зде уже не един, но многие примеры являются; и мощно бы многая показати, как в великих так и в средних государствах таковая разделения; но при таковом иных, как вышепомянутых, так и нижше поминаемых примеров довольствии, не исчисляем примеров разделения, но и вся за един воспоминаем. [83]

Воспоминая же примеры, такового государств разделения не хвалим, и хвалити не можем дела оного: вельми бо государствам вредное есть, и не токмо оные к нестроению и междоусобным браням, но иногда и к разорению крайнему приводит; чего домашный нам образ показала Россиа наша, разделена бывши по частям детям владимировым. Всяк бо из российских летописцев (о чем и мнози иностраннии пишут) видети может, каковые настали между частными оными владимировыми наследниками несогласия, раздоры, междоусобные войны, которыми в толикое бессилие пришла Россиа, что под власть варварства татарского с великим своим студом и бедством подпала; и дивное есть божие о ней смотрение, что не в конец порабощена стала, и имене своего между народами не погубила. До толеже приити в силу первую, и от варварского ига освободити себе не могла, дондеже рассыпанные ее части в едино паки тело не собраны, и монаршескою короною не связаны явилися, что премудро и благополучно сделал вышепомянутый Великий Князь Иоанн Васильевич; того ради не можем хвалити оного в государствах разделения; однакоже разделение

grandson, but later deposed the grandson, who had already been crowned, and gave it to his son.

41.   Another clear example and instance of our argument is that sovereign monarchs can partition their realm; and many have done so, and have given a part to each of their sons to rule: for example, Constantine the Great divided his realm between his sons Constans, Constantius and Constantine; Theodosius the Great between Arcadius and Honorius; Vladimir the Great between Iaroslav, Boris, Gleb and his other sons. There are many such examples; and we could give many such both from large states and states of average size; but with so many other examples given above and below, we shall not enumerate them, but shall reckon them as one.

In giving examples, however, we do not approve of such partitioning of states, nor can we approve it: for it is thoroughly bad for states, and leads not only to disorder and internal feuds but sometimes even to utter ruin; of which Russia herself gave us a familiar example, when she was divided among the children of Vladimir. For everyone can see from the Russian chroniclers (as many foreigners also report) what dissensions, factions and civil wars ensued among Vladimir's divided successors, whereby Russia was reduced to such impotence, that, to her great shame and misery, she succumbed to the sway of the barbarian Tartars; and it is thanks to God's miraculous care that she was not totally subdued, and that her name did not perish among the nations. She could not regain her former strength and free herself from the barbarian yoke until her scattered parts were reincorporated and reunited under the crown, which was most wisely and happily brought about by the abovementioned Grand Duke Ivan Vasil'evich; for this reason we cannot approve of

оное подает нам довольный довод и пример, что самодержец, наипаче же наследный, имеет полную, не зазорную и прекословию не подлежащую власть определяти наследство свое, которому похощет сыну своему, или и иному мимо сыновей, усмотревая достойного. Аще бо не имел бы от Бога таковой власти, и аки долг некий отдавати сыну большему [84] наследство свое был бы должен, то како мог бы государь вышепомянутым образом разделяти государство свое, и по частям раздавати сынам своим, как то мнози, хотя неполезно, делали, и никто о том и спорил и не прекословил им?

Но уже на конец, как выше мы обещали, предложим сего примеры из священного писания; сии бо паче всех предложенных крепкии суть, к вероятию несумненнии и прекословия отнюд не терпящии.

Примеры от историй священного писания

42. Первый из писания образ или пример есть Сиф, третий сын адамов: той, по мнению Святого Златоустого на главу 4 Бытия, в беседе 20, первенство Каину отъятое и себе данное, получил; и утверждает мнение свое Златоустый тем, что писание мало нечто о наследии каиновом помянувше, всю прочую историю ведет о сифовом наследии, род каинов, аки не сущий, молчанием предая.
43. Вторый из писания пример имеем (который и в объявлении монаршем предложен есть) Исаака патриарха, который на меньшего сына своего, Иакова, перенесл власть первенства, отняв оную большему сыну, Исаву, но его и род его Иакову и иаковлю наследию поработив, якоже пишет в книзе Бытия, 27.

И да не речет кто, что оное наследство хитростию матери Ревекки, и

the partition of states; however, such partition gives us ample proof and evidence that a sovereign, and especially an hereditary sovereign, has an absolute, unimpeachable and incontrovertible right to grant the succession to whichever son he wishes, or, passing over his sons, to some other whom he considers worthy. For if he did not have such a right from God, but was, as it were, duty bound to grant the succession to his eldest son, how could a monarch partition his state in the manner stated above, and apportion it among his sons, as many have done, albeit disadvantageously, without anyone's disputing this or gainsaying them?

Finally, as promised above, we shall give examples from Holy Writ; for these are sounder than all the previous examples, are of undoubted veracity and are incontrovertible.

Examples from sacred history

42.   The first example or instance from Scripture is that of Seth, the third son of Adam: in the opinion of Saint Chrysostom, in his 20th homily, on Chapter 4 of Genesis, Seth received the birthright that was taken from Cain;[41] and Chrysostom supports his opinion with the fact that Scripture says very little of Cain's successors, but relates all further history from Seth's successors, passing over in silence the family of Cain as if non-existent.

43.   Our second example from Scripture (which also appears in the Monarch's declaration) is that of the Patriarch Isaac, who transferred the birthright to his younger son, Jacob, after taking it from his elder son, Esau, and placing him and his family in subjection to Jacob and Jacob's successors, as is written in the Book of Genesis, 27.

Let no-one say that because the inheritance was transferred to Jacob through the cunning of his

265

не без печали Исаака перенеслося на Иакова, и по тому аки бы нам в пример неугодное. Подобает рассудити нам вся оной истории обстоятельства: (1) что оная Ревекки хитрость была по смотрению божию, [85] якоже известно есть из пророка Малахии, от слова божия *Иакова возлюбих, Исава же возненавидех (Малахии, гла. 1),* которое слово и Апостол приводит в послании к римлянам (*рим., 9)*. Златоустый же Святый все преносимого первенства оного действие восписует изволению божию, в беседах своих на Бытия 51 и 53; (2) что Исаак определения своего не отменил, но настоящему и пременения просящему Исаву ответствовал, что быть ему и его наследию рабами у Иакова; (3) что Исаак, когда обещался Исаву дати свое прежде своей смерти благословение, тем самим обещанием изъявил власть воли своей к подаянию наследства: ибо всуе кто обещает дати, чего дати не может по воле своей; (4) что Исав весьма безумный и бездельный был, который и жены себе поял противо воли родительской, и прежде еще первенство свое продал Иакову за едино яствие; и тако весьма первенства недостоин явился; (5) что таковому из Исава на Иакова преложению первенства следовало и благословение божие, как то известно от следующих в писании историй (что премудро помянулося и в объявлении Императорского Величества). И тако повесть сия изрядный пример есть к предложению нашему.

44. Третий пример из писания Иаков патриарх. Между сынами его первородный был Рувим; но за вину первенства лишен, якоже сам Иаков свидетельствует в Бытии, глава 49 *(Бытия, глава 49, стих 3, 4)*.

Сугубо же первенство Иаков Рувиму отнял. Первое персональное его, или самоличное: ибо сие [86] перенесл Иаков на Иуду, и потому сам Рувим стал подчинен Иуде, как и прочии братия *(Бытия, глава 49, стих 8)*.

mother, Rebecca, and not without distress to Isaac, it is therefore not a valid example for us. We should consider all the following circumstances of that episode: (1) the fact that Rebecca's cunning came about under God's providence, as is clear from the Prophet Malachi, where God says: *I loved Jacob, and I hated Esau* (*Malachi*, 1), which words the Apostle also cites in his Epistle to the Romans (*Romans*, 9). Saint Chrysostom also attributes the whole matter of the transfer of the birthright to the will of God, in his Homilies on Genesis, 51 and 53; (2) the fact that Isaac did not alter his decision, but when Esau insisted and begged him to alter it, replied that he and his successors should be slaves to Jacob; (3) the fact that Isaac, when he promised Esau to give him his blessing before he died, showed by that very promise his absolute right to assign the inheritance: for he promises in vain, who promises what is not in his power to give; (4) the fact that Esau was a most foolish and idle man, who married against his parents' wish, and before that had sold his birthright to Jacob for a mess of potage; and so had proved quite unworthy of the birthright; (5) the fact that this transfer of the birthright from Esau to Jacob was followed by God's blessing, as is clear from the accounts in Scripture that follow (which is also most aptly mentioned in his Imperial Majesty's declaration). And so this episode serves as an excellent example for our argument.

44. The third example from Scripture is the Patriarch Jacob. The first-born of his sons was Reuben; but he forfeited his birthright for his wrongdoing, as Jacob himself attests in Genesis chapter 49, 3, 4.

Indeed Jacob deprived Reuben of his birthright in a twofold way. First, he deprived him of his personal or individual birthright: for he transferred this to Judah, and so Reuben, like his other brothers.

Другое же первенство наследия рувимля: ибо сие перенесл Иаков на внучат своих Ефрема и Манассию, сынов иосифовых, якоже известно от словес Иакова, в 48 главе Бытия *(Бытия глава 48, стих 5,6)*; и потому наследный род рувимов в нижшем степени стал от рода ефремова и манассиина, что извествуется и от первых книг паралипоменон глава 5 *(паралипом., гла. 5. стих 2)*.

45. Четвертый пример: когда тот же Иаков патриарх усыновлял себе внучата своя, Ефрема и Манассию, сынов иосифовых, и повелел Иосифу, дабы подвел их к благословению его, понеже сам за старость очима не видел; Иосиф по чину естественному поставил Манассию яко первородного под руку десную Иакова, а Ефрема яко меньшего под руку левую. Но Иаков переложив руки своя, положил десную на главу меньшего внука Ефрема, а левую на Манассию старейшего. Напомянул же Иосиф отцу дабы инако возложил руки, десную на Манассию, а левую на Ефрема, по чину естества, помышляя, что Иаков неведением погрешил; но Иаков отвещал, что ведая их, кто где стоит, делал то; и прорекл о Ефреме юнейшем, что больший будет от старейшего Манассии. Повесть сия пишется Бытия в главе 48.

46. Пятый пример, книги вторые паралипоменон, глава 11. Царь иудейский, Ровоам, имел многие жены, и из них дети многие: но за любовь жены не первой, которую любил над всеми женами своими, сына из нее рожденного, Авиа, *постави начальника* [87] *и князя над всею братиею своею: того бо и царем сотворити помышляше* (слова суть писания, на месте помянутом); как то его намерение и совершилося: по нем бо царствовал Авиа в Иуде. Ведати же подобает, что Ровоам был царь

became subject to Judah (*Genesis,* Chapter 49, 8). Second, he deprived Reuben's successors of their birthright: for Jacob transferred this to his grandsons, Ephraim and Manasseh, the sons of Joseph, as we know from Jacob's words in Genesis, Chapter 48, 5, 6; and hence the tribe of Reuben was subordinated to the tribes of Ephraim and Manasseh, as we also know from the first book of Chronicles, chapter 5, 2.

45.   The fourth example is as follows: when that same Patriarch, Jacob, adopted his grandsons, Ephraim and Manasseh, the sons of Joseph, he told Joseph to bring them to him for his blessing, for he himself could not see because of old age; Joseph, following the natural order, placed Manasseh, the firstborn, under Jacob's right hand, and Ephraim, the younger son, under his left hand; but Jacob, changing hands, placed his right hand on the head of his younger grandson, Ephraim, and his left hand on that of Manasseh, the elder. Whereupon Joseph reminded his father to place his hands the other way round, the right hand on Manasseh, and the left on Ephraim, in the natural order, supposing that Jacob had erred out of ignorance; but Jacob answered that he knew where each stood when he acted as he did; and he prophesied that Ephraim, the younger, would be greater than Manasseh, the elder. (This account is in *Genesis*, Chapter 48).

46.   The fifth example is from the second book of Chronicles, chapter 11. Rehoboam, king of Judah, had many wives, and many children by them; but for the love of one of his wives (though not his first), whom he loved above all the others, he made Abijah, his son by her, *to be ruler among his brethren: for he thought to make him king* (these are the words of Scripture, in the place cited); and it fell out as he intended: for Abijah ruled after him in Judah. It should be noted, moreover, that Rehoboam

православный, и определения его писание не порочит.

47. Шестый пример есть дивный и славный, и которым единым довольно рассуждаемое от нас предложение утверждается. Есть же сей пример и образ на царе израильском Давиде, который мимо большего сына своего Адонии, нарекл по себе царствия наследником, и еще в животе своем возвел на престол царский сына юнейшего Соломона; в котором деле давидовом не едино обстоятельство усмотреваем, которое ясно показует, как свободная и полная власть родителя государя во определении наследника своего: (1) что Адониа больший был сын Давиду от Соломона; (2) что Давид Вирсавии, матери соломоновой, обещал от ее рожденного сына, то есть Соломона, израильским по себе монархом поставити; а как бы тое обещати возмогл муж по сердцу божию, святый и праведный, естьли бы грех был меньшего сына мимо большего ставити наследником? (3) что Вирсавиа в просительном своем к Давиду слове о определении наследства его сыну своему Соломону, глаголет тако: *очи всего Израиля на тебе взирают, да возвестиши им, кто сядет на престоле господина моего царя.*

А естьли бы наследство старейшему сыну было весьма должное, [88] и естьли бы Давид не мог в том по воле своей действовати, то для чего бы народ ожидал, кого наследником скипетра своего определит Давид? Знал народ, что у Давида старейший сын есть Адониа, а Соломон юнейший; того ради и не было бы сумнительство в народе, кто по Давиде имать царствовати; всяк бы несумненно ведал, что Адониа царем будет, естьли бы не сильнейшая в том была воля давидова, нежели первенство адониево. Но не так деялося: обращал очи свои народ израильский на Давида, смотря и ожидая определения его, кого по себе подаст им самодержца. (4) Был же тогда и пророк божий Нафан, не льстец и не ласкатель, который

was an orthodox king and Scripture does not censure his decision.

47. The sixth example is a remarkable and celebrated one, and is alone sufficient to confirm our proposition. It is the example and instance of David, king of Israel, who, passing over his eldest son, Adonijah, named his youngest son, Solomon, as heir to his kingdom, and during his own lifetime raised him to the throne; in which act of David we see more than one circumstance which clearly shows a monarch's full and absolute right to appoint his successor: (1) the fact that David's son Adonijah was older than Solomon; (2) the fact that David promised Bath-Shebah, Solomon's mother, to make their son, Solomon, his successor as king of Israel; for how could a man after God's own heart, a holy and righteous man, have made this promise, if it had been a sin to pass over the eldest son and make his youngest son the successor? (3) the fact that Bath-Shebah, in her request to David to appoint her son Solomon as his successor, speaks as follows: *The eyes of all Israel are upon thee, that thou shouldest tell them who shall sit on the throne of my lord the king after him.*

Now if the eldest son had had an absolute right to the succession, and if David had not been free to follow his own wish in the matter, why would the people have waited to see whom David would appoint as heir to his throne? The people knew that Adonijah was David's eldest son, and Solomon his youngest; so the people would have been in no doubt who would rule after David; everyone would have known without a doubt that Adonijah would be king, unless David's authority was of greater force than Adonijah's birthright. But this did not happen: the people of Israel turned their eyes upon David, to wait and see whom he would decide to appoint as their sovereign after him. (4) Moreover, there was

прежде Давиду сугубый грех его обличил, и его на покаяние обратил; той муж святый, видя, что Давид, презирая адониево первенство, вручает скипетр Соломону, естьли бы ведал или мыслил, что таковое его определение незаконно, неправедно и грешно есть, отнюд бы не умолчал, яко посол божий и закона его ревнитель; но сказал бы Давиду: *что се твориши, о царю; меньшего сына на престол возводиши, а старейшего презираеши; не в твоей се воле есть, и воле божией противно есть.* Но не только Нафан не говорил того, и давидову определению не противился, но еще и всячески возведению соломонову пособствовал. (5) Еще же и весь народ, слышав поставленного Давидом царя Соломона, не токмо никакова прекословия или пререкания не явил, [89] но и паче пребезмерно веселился; глаголет бо писание: *и взят Садок иерей рог с елеем от скинии, и помаза Соломона, и вострубиша рогом, и реша вси людие: живет Царь Соломон. и взыдоша вси людие в след его, и ликоваху в лицех, и веселяхуся веселием великим, и расседеся земля от гласа их.* Так тогда всем известно было, что совершенную и полную власть имеют государи поставляти по воле своей по себе наследника. (О сей же истории, и ее обстоятельствах, зри в книгах третиих Царств, в главе первой).

also living at that time a prophet of God, Nathan who was no fawning flatterer, and who had previously charged David with his twofold sin[42] and had turned him to repentance; if that holy man, when he saw David overlock Adonijah's birthright and entrust the sceptre to Solomon, had known or believed his decision to be unlawful, unjust or sinful, he would, as God's envoy and a zealot for His law, by no means have kept silent, but would have said to David: *What doest thou, o King? Dost thou raise thy youngest son to the throne, and overlookest the eldest? This lies not in thy power, and is contrary to the will of God.* But not only did Nathan say no such thing, and did not oppose David's decision, but rather he assisted Solomon's elevation in every way. (5) Moreover, the whole people, on hearing that Solomon had been made king by David, not only raised no protest or objection, but rather rejoiced exceedingly; for Scripture says: *And Zadok the priest took an horn of oil out of the tabernacle, and annointed Solomon. And they blew the trumpet; and all the people said, God save King Solomon. And all the people came up after him, and the people piped with pipes, and rejoiced with great joy, so that the earth rent with the sound of them.* So clear was it to all in those days that monarchs have the full and absolute right to appoint a successor at their will. (For this event, and its circumstances, see the third book of Kings, Chapter 1).

Се уже видиши всяк благосовестный читателю, как довольное число (по предреченному из начала обещанию нашему) показали мы помощию божию, и доводов и примеров. Доводы были сугубии: едини от рассуждения власти просто родительской, а другии от рассуждения власти монаршей; и кийждо из предложенных доводов сам един собою доволен есть; кольми же паче вся совокупно приятии, суть сильнии к утверждению слова нашего: и яснее полуденного света показуют, как свободни и полномощни монархи определяти по себе державы наследников, кого из сынов, внуков, племянников, сродников, или и отвне фамилии своея усмотрят угоднейшего к тому. Примеры же мнози и от историй человеческих, и от священных писаний, так сильно тожде утверждают, что хотя бы самый от жестосердых жесточайший хотел нам прекословити, не изобрящет вины прекословию своему. [90]

Что же прочее остается тому, кто по непременной своей злобе, и не усладимой, да тако речем, сердца своего горести, не сломит и истине не поработит прекословного ума своего, и на сей толь полезный отечеству нашему монарший устав, который есть не новый, но всех государств и всех веков устав, роптать в помыслах своих не престанет? Тому и таковому враждебнику не что ино зде остается, токмо непрестанное совести страдати угрызение, и пред самим собою стыдитися, еще же и ожидати вечного в будущий век студа и мучения. Узрев бо толикую доводов силу, и толикий свидетелей облак, от естественного разума, от законов народных, от примеров исторических, еще же и от неложного

274

[AFTERWORD]

You see now, honest reader, what an ample number of both arguments and examples we have given, with God's help,[43] in accordance with our promise at the beginning. The arguments were twofold: some derive from a consideration of parental power in general, others from a consideration of monarchical power; and each of the arguments advanced is sufficient in itself; how much more powerful, therefore, are all of them, taken together, to confirm our proposition: they show more clearly than the light of noon, what full and absolute power monarchs possess to appoint as their successor, from among their sons, grandsons, nephews, kinsmen, or even from outside their family, whomever they deem fittest. Moreover, the many examples, both from secular history and from Holy Writ, so strongly confirm this, that if our harshest critic sought to contradict us, he would find no grounds on which to do so.

What else, then, remains for that man, who, in his incessant malice and, so to speak, unassuageable bitterness of heart, will not subdue his contentious mind and make it submit to the truth, and will not cease complaining in his thoughts against the Monarch's statute, which is so advantageous to our country, and which is not new, but has existed in all states and in all ages? For him and similar adversaries nothing else remains but to suffer continual pangs of conscience and shame in this world, and to await eternal shame and torment in the world to come. For after seeing such a wealth of arguments and such a host of witnesses, drawn from natural reason, from the laws of nations, from historical examples, and also from the infallible

слова божия, не токмо видит, что трудно ему аки против рожна прати, но и устами зенути отнюд не может.

Что бо зде вопреки нам речет? Не оный ли безумный упрямым и безответным обычный ответ: *дело новое.* О студного и окаянного суесловия! Аще бы и новое се дело, что же самая новость вредит? Вещи новые, якоже и ветхие, ни от доброты, ниже от худости своея, но токмо от времене нарищаются: зло и старое - зло есть, добро и новое - добро есть. Еще же и сие внуши и рассуди всяк: что некие вещи за самую ветхость похвалы своея лишаются; новость же сама собою ничего отнюд не порочит. И есть ли бы за самую новость охуждати подобало, то ничтоже останется, чего бы уничтожити и бесчестити [91] не подобало: все бо, что ни есть старое, было иногда новое; поищи коея либо вещи старыя и предревния начала, в начале своем была она новая.

Но как же не бесстудный будет, кто бы устав сей и новым назвал? Обычаи бо многих народов, еще прежде пришествия христова в историах означеннии, новии ли суть? Законы иустиниановы и древнейших монархов от Иустиниана собраннии, новии ли суть? Писание священное в книгах царских, и прочиих, и еще в моисейских книгах написанное, новое ли? Писанию же тому, яко самого Бога слову, и тогда, когда было новое, прекословити мощно ли было? Что же рещи о примерах, от двоих тысящ назад лет, и вящше, долгим веков течением, дела многих народов следуя? Помянутые примеры собрали мы многое число, и еще можно бы и десять крат собрати множайшее: не все же и в историах написано; от всех же тех и доводов и примеров монарший устав сей беспрекословно утверждается: как же новый есть он? Не токмо не новый, но и не престающий, от всех народов, во вся времена употребление свое имевший, и доселе употребляемый.

word of God, not only does he see that it is difficult for him, as it were, to kick against the pricks,[44] but indeed he finds himself bereft of speech.

For what has he to say against us? Is it not that foolish answer which stubborn men are wont to make who have no other, namely: *it is an innovation.* What shameful and wretched nonsense! Even if it were an innovation, what harm is there in novelty? Things are called new or old, not from their goodness or badness, but simply from their age: an old evil remains an evil, and a good thing is good, even if it is new. Let everyone also hear and consider this: that certain things lose their worth through their very age; but novelty in itself is no reproach. And if mere novelty were a reason for censure, then there would be nothing that should not be done away with and rejected; for whatever is old, was once new; seek the origin of anything old and of great antiquity: it was new originally.

But whoever were to call this statute new must surely be utterly shameless. Are those customs of many nations new, which are recorded in history before the coming of Christ? Are the laws of Justinian new, and the laws of the earlier monarchs, collated by Justinian? Is Holy Writ in the Books of Kings, and elsewhere, and in the Books of Moses, new? And even when Scripture was new, could it really be criticized, being the word of God himself? What, too, shall we say of the examples from two thousand years ago and more, ages old, tracing the deeds of many nations? We have collected a large number of those examples, and we could have collected ten times more, although not everything is recorded in history; the Monarch's statute is irrefutably confirmed by all those arguments and examples: how, then, can it be new? Not only is it not new, but it has been in continual use among all peoples in all ages to this day.

Разве бы еще сказал кто, что дело сие у нас не бывало; хотя бы и не бывало, что противно? Бывало у персидов, у египтян, у греков, у римлян, у парфян, у испанов, германов, и прочиих, и что больше всего, у израильтян и христиан, в восточной и западной империи. [92] Что же, хотя бы у нас и не бывало, естьли доброе и полезное есть, якоже есть, бедни мы были, есьли не было у нас, а благополучни, что и у нас настало. Первее явилося огненное оружие у прочиих народов, нежели у нас; но естьли бы и к нам оное доселе не пришло, что бы была, и где бы уже была Россиа? Тожде разумей и о книжной типографии, о архитектуре, о прочиих честных учениях. Разумный есть и человек и народ, который не стыдится перенимати доброе от других и чуждых: безумный же и смеха достойный, который своего и худого отстати, чуждого же и доброго приняти не хощет. Достоин таковый сего суждения, что, хотя бы и за премногие и великие службы своя искал себе повышения чести, то отогнати его таковым ответом: *у тебе таковая честь не бывала.* Но что не бывало, и настало, то разве новостию опорочитися может; да как праведно, уже выше мы показали.

Солжет же явно, кто дело сие и у нас не бывалое наречет: понеже противное показуется от Великого Князя Иоанна Васильевича, от Великого Владимира, детям своим государство разделившего, и прочиих. Но кто сказати посмеет, что и многочастно сие дело у российских монархов не бывало? Многим истории неведущим мнится, что и женитьбы государей наших с иностранными не бывали: есть же известно противое. Се едино истинно, что у нас, за скудостию учений, совершенная [93] историа не бывала: и по тому скудоумнии человецы, чего не знают, было

Someone might still say that it was never customary among us. Even if that were so, what is the objection? It was customary among the Persians, the Egyptians, the Greeks, the Romans, the Parthians, the Spaniards, the Germans and others, and, above all, among the Israelites, and the Christians of the Eastern and Western Empire. So that even if indeed it were not customary among us, if it is good and useful, which it is, we were the poorer without it, and we are lucky to have it now. Firearms were in use among other nations before us; but if they had not reached us to this day, what would have become of Russia and where would she be now? The same is true of printing, architecture and the other liberal arts. Wise is the man and the nation which is not ashamed to adopt what is good from strangers and foreigners; foolish and ridiculous is he who will not leave off his bad ways and accept what is good from others. Such a man, should he seek promotion for his many great services, deserves to be dismissed with this reply: *You never had such an honour before.* Whatever was not customary and has been introduced later may certainly be condemned as an innovation; with what justice, however, we have already shown above.

He clearly lies, however, who says that this was not customary among us: for the opposite is clear from the Grand Duke Ivan Vasil'evich, from Vladimir the Great, who divided the realm among his children, and from others. But who will dare to say that this was not often practised by Russia's monarchs? Many who are ignorant of history also suppose that marriages with foreigners were not customary among our monarchs: but we know that the opposite is true.[45] This alone is true, that for lack of learning, we have had no complete written history;[46] and hence people of scant intelligence,

ли, помышляют, но безумно, что оное никогда не бывало.

И от сих известно, что упрямому прекословцу ничтоже ино зде остается, только нестерпимый студ и жегомой совести страдание.

Всем же прочиим истинным российского отечества сынам, яко прямым добра общего любителям, что им творити надлежит, сказовати пространно, нет нам нужды: сами бо они, ясно видяще превеликую в сем монаршем уставе всероссийскую пользу, ведают, что должни суть от всего сердца благодарити цареви небесному, толь дивно самодержца нашего прославившему, и на сие преполезнейшее уставление умудрившему; самому же отцу отечества нашего, его императорскому величеству Петру Великому, желати многолетного, победительного и в сем благопоспешного царствования, и добрых, то есть, ему подобных, наследников.

when they do not know whether something was customary, foolishly suppose that it was not.

It is therefore clear that for a stubborn critic nothing else remains in this world but intolerable shame and burning pangs of conscience.

As for all other true sons of the Russian fatherland, as staunch supporters of the common good, we need not expatiate on where their duty lies: for they themselves, clearly seeing the great advantage to the whole of Russia from the Monarch's statute, know that they must thank the Heavenly King with all their heart, who has so wonderfully glorified our Sovereign, and has inspired him to introduce this most useful enactment; and as for the Father of our Fatherland himself, His Imperial Majesty, Peter the Great, they must wish him a long and victorious reign, crowned with success in this regard, and worthy successors, that is, successors like himself.

1. i.e. Saint Paul (II *Timothy,* 11).

2. Peter's order for the publication of a commentary on the *Statute on the succession* was formally conveyed to the Synod by Archbishop Feodosii of Novgorod, representing the Synod, and Count P. A. Tolstoi, representing the Senate. Peter authorized publication of *Pravda voli monarshei* at a meeting of the Synod on 24 December 1722. His order was implemented by a decree of the Synod, dated 28 December. (Voskresenskii, pp. 113-114; *Polnoe sobranie postanovlenii i rasporiazhenii po vedomstvu pravoslavnogo ispovedaniia rossiiskoi imperii,* vol. II, (St Petersburg: 1874), No. 950).

3. Absalom rebelled against his father, David (II, *Samuel,* 15-18).

4. *Ob'iavlenie rozysknogo dela i suda, po ukazu ego Tsarskogo Velichestva Alekseia Petrovicha, v Sank-piterburkh otpravlennogo, i po ukazu ego Velichestva v pechat', dlia izvestiia vsenarodnogo,* June 25. Cf. 'Manifesto of the criminal process of the Czarewitz Alexei Petrowitz, judged at St Petersburg by order of his Czarish Majesty, the 25 day of June, 1718', in F. C. Weber, *The Present State of Russia,* volume II, (London: 1723), pp. 95-206, and Peter's rescript to his ministers at foreign courts, 27 June, 1718 (Solov'ev, Book IX, pp. 188-189).

5. Ivan III, Grand Duke of Muscovy, ruled 1462-1505.

6. The 12 sons of Vladimir the Great, ruled 978-1015.

7. The *Stepennaia kniga* was a genealogical chronology of the tsars from Vladimir the Great to Ivan IV, compiled 1560-63.

8. i.e. in 1498. The Muscovite calendar, following that of Byzantium, purported to date from the creation of the world in 5508 B.C. At the end of 1699 (7208), Peter announced the adoption of the Julian calendar, and the next year was classified as 1700.

9. i.e. in 1502.

10.   The Decree on Unigeniture in Succession (*Ukaz o edinonasledii*), 23 March, 1714 (P.S.Z., vol. V, No. 2789). The decree was repealed in 1731.

11.   The oath of allegiance was first sworn in the Cathedral of the Assumption (*Uspenskii Sobor*) at Moscow by 2 senior ecclesiastics (including Feofan Prokopovich) and 10 senators. (Voskresenskii, pp. 176-177). Such oaths were taken by all members of the civil service and clergy.

12.   See footnote 2.

13.   Isaiah (*Isaia*) should almost certainly read Hosea (*Osia*). *Hosea,* I, describes the children of Israel as "the sons of the living God."

14.   Cf. Pufendorf, *De Officio Hominis et Civis iuxta legem naturalem* (1673) (which was translated at Peter's order in 1726), chapter iii: "Sed si tamen citra spem emendationis omnem disciplinam pertinaciter adspernetur puer, poterit domo patria eici atque abdicari."

15.   By "civil laws" are meant actual, existing laws (as opposed to divine law or natural law).

16.   For the Latin text of Justinian, see Appendix 2.

17.   Under Russian law, anyone was free to adopt, except a noble, who could do so only under certain conditions and with the tsar's permission. (Latkin, p. 527).

18.   Under the *Military Statute* (1716), the killing of a child was, like all murder, a capital offence, unless the death was unintentionally occasioned in the course of parental chastisement, when a lesser penalty was substituted.(Latkin, p. 477).

19.   Or Denis Godefroy (1549-1621).

20.   For the Latin text of Cicero, see Appendix 3. In the Manifesto of June 25, 1718, the Tsarevich Aleksei was declared to be guilty of a "heinous intent to commit a double parricide" (*bogomerzkoe, dvoinoe roditele' ubistvennoe namerenie*) against Peter as his father and sovereign. (Ustrialov, p. 532). The penalty for parricide under the *Military Statute* was death by quartering (Latkin, pp. 476-477).

21. In his manifesto of 3 February, 1718, on the exclusion of the Tsarevich Aleksei from the succession, Peter referred to the "divine and civil laws whereby even ordinary fathers, let alone a sovereign monarch, such as we, have complete and unimpeachable authority over their children," (p. 307). The abbé Jubé, a jansenist priest in Russia between 1729 and 1732, noted that "les parens à l'égard de leurs enfans, même mariés,... conservent toujours la même autorité que s'ils étoient encore dans leur maison, et qu'ils sont maîtres de déshériter, et donner leur bien à qui bon leur semble," (Jacques Jubé, *La Religion, les moeurs et les usages des Moscovites,* (ed.) M. Mervaud, (Oxford: The Voltaire Foundation, 1992), p. 157).

22. "Summa potestas civilis illa dicitur, cuius actus alterius juri non subsunt, ita ut alterius voluntatis humanae arbitrio irriti possint reddi; alterius cum dico, ipsum excludo, qui summa potestate utitur; cui voluntatem mutare licet."

23. *Psalms,* 63,7.

24. *Psalms,* 44, 21.

25. David committed adultery with Bath-sheba, the wife of Uriah the Hittite, and had Uriah sent "in the forefront of the hottest battle," to be slain. (II, *Samuel,* 11).

26. *The Children's Catechism* (or *Primer*) (*Pervoe uchenie otrokam. V nemzhe bukvy i slogi. Tozhe: kratkoe tolkovanie zakonnogo desiatosloviia, molitvy gospodni, simvola very, i deviati blazhenstv),* St Petersburg, tipografiia Aleksandro-Nevskogo monastyria, 1720, was written by Propokovich at Peter's order and frequently reprinted. An English version, entitled *The Russian Catechism,* translated by J. T. Philipps, was published at London in 1723, a second edition in 1725. In the section on the fifth commandment, "the duty of kings" is defined as "to defend their subjects, and seek what is best for them, both in temporals and spirituals, and therefore [they] must have a watchful eye to all ecclesiastical, military and civil affairs, that men do conscientiously execute their

respective employments." (Philipps' translation, 1723, p. 10).

27.   2 *Samuel,* 17.

28.   In his address on the occasion of Aleksei's exclusion from the succession, 3 February, 1718, Peter declared, according to the report of the Danish ambassador, Tyrholm: "en mourant, je lui [Aleksei] aurais assurément remis [le sceptre] à lui, et à point d'autre, si par ses faits et par ses inclinations, il m'eut laissé entrevoir seulement la moindre apparence qu'il deviendrait un jour un prince vertueux, habile et capable à conserver mes acquisitions et mes établissements pour la mélioration des affaires intérieures de mes états, et d'éxécuter le reste de mes desseins après ma mort. Mais hélas! Ce mon indigne fils n'a de son berceau donné que de marques d'un coeur abject, des inclinations basses et malicieuses, enfin d'une disposition tout à fait impropre pour regner." After swearing allegiance to Piotr Petrovich, Aleksei also bound himself, should Peter die without surviving issue, "se soumettre... à celui que le Czaar aujourd'hui regnant aura institué par testament à lui succéder... fût ce que Sa Majesté aurait nommé pour son successeur quelque personne privé." (10/21 February, 1718, Copenhagen, Rigsarkivet, TKUA Speciel Del. B49. Relationes aus Rusland).

29.   By 'democracy' is meant what was also called republican government. (Prokopovich wrote of "*narodnoe vladetel'stvo, koe obychno vol'noiu respublikoiu nazyvaiut.*" (D. A. Korsakov, *Votsarenie Imperatritsy Anny Ioannovny,* (Kazan: tipografiia imperatorskogo universiteta, 1880), p. 78).

30.   By 'aristocracy' is meant what was also called oligarchy. (Prokopovich complained of the plans of the *verkhovniki* in 1730 "*kotoryi vladeniia obraz, v tol' malom chisle vladeiushchikh, ne mozhet nareshchis' vladetel'stvo izbrannykh, grecheska aristokratiia.*" A. D. Korsakov, *loc. cit.*) The Decemviri ruled from 444 to 442 B.C.

31.   i.e. from 48 B.C. to A.D. 1453,

32.   i.e. the Holy Roman Empire.

33.   Nimrod, king of Assyria, is said to have conquered Babylonia in the second millennium B.C. (*Genesis,* 10 and *Micah,* 6).

34.   This refers to the trial of Charles I and his execution on 30 January, 1649. During his visit to England in 1698, Peter is said to have recommended abolishing the day of mourning, since it could prove divisive and might some day inspire a repetition. ("Petr I v Anglii v 1698g." [Peter I in England in 1698], in *Petr Velikii. Sbornik statei* [Peter the Great. A Collection of Articles], (ed.) A. I. Andreev, (Moscow/Leningrad: Akademiia Nauk SSSR, 1947), p. 82).

35.   i.e. by the Salic law.

36.   The changes in social and cultural mores referred to were brought about by legislation introducing western dress (P.S.Z. vol. IV, No. 1887); the requirement for houses in St Petersburg to be built of stone (P.S.Z., vol. V, No. 2848), the Decree on the Assemblies (P.S.Z. vol. V, No. 3246) and regulations affecting weddings and funerals.

37.   This probably refers to *Psalms,* 40,2.

38.   "I have said, Ye are Gods," *Psalm* 82, 6. Cf. Bossuet, "A divine element attaches to the prince and inspires fear in the peoples," ("La politique tirée des propres paroles de l'Ecriture sainte" 1709), in J. B. Bossuet, *Textes choisis et commentés,* (ed.) H. Bremond, (Paris: Plon, 1913), vol. II, p. 201).

39.   This refers to the "Pragmatic Sanction" laid down by the emperor Charles VI in 1713, which asserted that the German, Bohemian and Hungarian dominions of the Habsburgs constituted a single indivisible and inalienable state, hereditary in the house of Habsburg.

40.   This should read *On the Law of War and Peace.*

41.   Cain was punished for the murder of his brother, Abel. (*Genesis,*4).

42.   2, *Samuel,* 12. See Footnote 25.

43.   'With God's help' was Peter's personal motto. Cf. p. 131 and manifesto of 3 February 1718, p. 303.

44.   *Acts,* 9,5.

45.　　This alludes to resentment at Peter's marriage to Catherine, born Marta Skavronskaia, the daughter of a Lithuanian peasant, who after living with him as his mistress, became his wife in 1712. Peter arranged foreign marriages for his son, Aleksei, who married Sophia-Christina of Brunswick-Wolfenbüttel, sister-in-law to the Habsburg emperor Charles VI, in 1711 (cf. manifesto of 3 February, 1718, p. 299); for his nieces Anna and Catherine, who married the Duke of Courland and the Duke of Mecklenburg in 1710 and 1716 respectively; and for his daughter Anna, who married the Duke of Holstein in 1725. In his tract on intermarriage between Russians and non-Orthodox (*O brakakh pravovernykh lits s inovernymy*, (St Petersburg: 1721), reprinted in P.S.Z., vol. VI, No. 3814), Prokopovich gives historical examples of the marriage of Russian Grand Dukes and members of their family with Polish, Lithuanian, Swedish, French and other foreign royalty.

46.　　Peter was concerned at the dearth of historical studies in Russia. He ordered historical sources to be collected, and planned for the writing of history books. According to A. K. Nartov, Peter once asked Prokopovich: "When shall we see a complete history of Russia?" (T. S. Maikov, 'Petr I i 'Gistoriia Sveiskoi voiny'" [Peter I and the "History of the Swedish War"], in *Rossiia v period reform Petra I* [Russia in the age of the reforms of Peter I], (ed.) N. I. Pavlenko, (Moscow: Akademiia Nauk SSSR, 1973, pp. 107-109).

APPENDIX 1

SOURCES CITED IN *PRAVDA VOLI MONARSHEI*

BIBLICAL

Old Testament

Genesis
Exodus
Leviticus
Deuteronomy
Judges
Kings
Chronicles
Esther
Job
Psalms
Proverbs
Ecclesiastes
Isaiah [probably in error for Hosea]
Lamentations
Daniel
Malachi
Wisdom of Solomon

New Testament

Romans
Corinthians
Galatians
Timothy
Peter

Appendices

PATRISTIC AND ECCLESIASTICAL

Church Fathers

Ambrose
Arnobius
Theodor Balsamon
Ecumenius
Epiphanius
Evagrius
Jerome
John Chrysostom
Theophylact

Church Historians

Cassiodorus
Cedrenus
Nicephorus
Socrates Scholasticus
Sozomen
Zonaras

CLASSICAL AND BYZANTINE

Latin

Cicero
Diogenes Laertius
Justin
Justinian
Livy
Suetonius
Valerius Maximus

Greek

Josephus
Leo I
Plutarch
Procopius
Xenophon

Appendices

MODERN (references are to first edition)

Baronius [Cesare Baronio] (1538-1607), *Annales ecclesiastici,* (12 volumes), (Rome: ex typographia Vaticana, 1588-1607).

Sethus Calvisius [Seth Kalwitz] (1556-1615), *Chronologia, ex autoritate potissimum Sacrae Scripturae, et historicorum fide dignissimorum, ad motum luminarium coelestium, tempora & annos distinguentium, secundum characteres chronologicos contexta & deducta,* (Leipzig: Jacob Apelius, 1605).

Johannes Cluverius [Johann Cluvier] (1583-1633), *Historiarum totius mundi epitome, a prima rerum origine usque ad annum Christi MDCXXX,* (Leiden: apud Jacobum Marci, 1631).

Dionysius Gothofredus [Denis Godefroy] (1549-1621), *Corpus iuris civilis,* (Geneva: Jacobus Stoer, 1583).

Hugo Grotius [de Groot] (1583-1645), *De lege belli et pacis libri tres,* (Paris: apud Nicolaum Buon, 1625).

Johann Jacob Hofmann (1635-1706), *Lexicon universale historico-geographico-chronologico-poetico-philologicum. Continens historiam omnis aevi, geographiam omnium locorum, genealogiam principum familiarum, addita ubique chronologia... mythologiam... discussionem philologicam... aliaque*

291

plurima scitu dignissima, (Basel: typis Jacobi Bertschii & Jon. Rodolphi Genathii, 1677).

Famianus [Famiano] Strada (1572-1649), *De bello belgico decades duo,* (Antwerp: typis I. Cnobbari, 1635).

Theodorus [Theodor] Zwinger (1533-1588), *Theatrum vitae humanae... in XIX libros digestae,* (Basel: per Frobenios fratres, 1565).

APPENDIX 2

Justinian, *Novellae,* 115, iii

1. Si quis parentibus suis manus intulerit.

2. Si gravem et inhonestam iniuriam eis ingesserit.

3. Si eos in criminalibus causis accusaverit, quae non sunt adversus principem sive rempublicam.

4. Si cum maleficis hominibus ut maleficus conversatur.

5. Vel vitae parentum suorum per venenum, aut alio modo insidiari tentaverit.

6. Si novercae suae, aut concubinae patris, filius sese immiscuerit.

7. Si delator contra parentes filius extiterit, et per suam delationem gravia eos dispendia fecerit sustinere.

8. Si quemlibet de praedictis parentibus inclusum esse contigerit, et liberi qui possunt ab intestato ad eius successionem venire, petiti ab eo vel unus ex his in sua eum noluerit fideiussione suscipere vel pro persona, vel pro debito, in quantum esse qui petitur, probatur idoneus...

9. Si convictus fuerit aliquis liberorum ex eo, quia prohibuerit parentes suos condere testamentum...

10. Si praeter voluntatem parentum inter arenarios vel mimos sese filius sociaverit, et in hac professione

permanserit: nisi forsitan etiam parentes eiusdem professionis fuerint.

11. Si alicui ex praedictis parentibus volenti suae filiae vel nepti maritum dare.... ,illa non consenserit, sed luxuriosam degere vitam elegerit....

12. Si quis de praedictis parentibus furiosus fuerit, et eius liberi... obsequium ei et curam competentem non praebuerint...

13. Si unum de praedictis parentibus in captivitate detineri contigerit, et eius liberi, sive omnes, sive unus, non festinaverint eum redimere,... in eius sit potestate, utrum hanc causam ingratitudinis testamento suo velit adscribere. Si autem per liberorum negligentiam vel contemptum non fuerit liberatus, et in captivitate vita decesserit, illos ad successionem eius venire non patimur...

14. Si quis de praedictis parentibus orthodoxus constitutus senserit suum filium vel liberos non esse catholicae fidei, nec in sacrosancta ecclesia communicare,... licentiam habeant pro hac maxime causa ingratos eos et exheredes in suo scribere testamento.

(*Authenticae seu novellae constitutiones domini nostri Justiniani sacratissimi principis,* vol. II, (Metz: Lamort, 1810), pp. 121-124).

APPENDIX 3

Cicero, *Pro Roscio Amerino*, 2 6

O singularem sapientiam, iudices! Nonne videntur hunc hominem ex rerum naturae sustulisse et eripuisse, cui repente caelum, solem, aquam terramque ademerint, ut, qui eum necasset, unde ipse natus esset, careret iis rebus omnibus, ex quibus omnia nata esse dicuntur? Noluerunt feris corpus obicere, ne bestiis quoque, quae tantum scelus attigissent, immanioribus uteremur; non sic nudos in flumen deicere, ne cum delati essent in mare, ipsum polluerunt, quo cetera, quae violata sunt, expiari putantur; denique nihil tam vile neque tam vulgare est, cuius partem ullam reliquerint. Etenim quid tam est commune quam spiritus vivis, terra mortuis, mare fluctuantibus, litus eiectis? Ita vivunt, dum possunt, ut ducere animam de caelo non queant, ita moriuntur, ut eorum ossa terra non tangat, ita iactantur fluctibus, ut numquam abluantur, ita postremo eiciuntur, ut ne ad saxa quidem mortui conquiescant.

(Cicero, vol. VI, Loeb Classical Library, (Cambridge, Massachusetts: Harvard University Press, 1967), pp. 182, 184).

Божиею милостию мы, Петр Первый, царь и самодержец всероссийский и протчая и пр. и пр., объявляем духовного, военного и гражданского и всех протчих чинов людям всероссийского народа, нашим верным подданным:

1. Мы уповаем, что большой части из верных подданных наших, а особливо тем, которые и резиденциях наших и в службе обретаются, ведомо, с каким прилежанием и попечением мы сына своего первородженного Алексея воспитать тщились. И для того ему от детских его лет учителей не токмо русского, но и чужестранных языков придали и повелели его оным обучать, дабы не токмо в страхе божием и в православной нашей христианской вере греческого исповедания был возращен, но для лутчего знания воинских и политических (или гражданских) дел и иностранных государств состояния и обхождения, обучен был и иных языков, чтоб читанием на оных гисторий и всяких наук воинских и гражданских, достойному правителю государства принадлежащих, мог быть достойный наследник нашего всероссийского престола.

2. Но то наше все вышеписанное старание о воспитании и обучении помянутого сына нашего видели мы вотще быти, ибо он всегда вне прямого послушания нам был и ни о чем, что довлеет доброму наследнику, не внимал, ни обучался и учителей своих, от нас представленных, не слушал, и обхождение имел с такими непотребными

APPENDIX 4

Manifesto of 3 February 1718 on the exclusion from the succession of the Tsarevich Aleksei

By the grace of God, we, Peter I, tsar and sovereign of all the Russias, etc., etc., etc., declare to our faithful subjects of the ecclesiastical, military and civil and all other ranks of the people of all the Russias:

1.   We trust that most cf our faithful subjects especially those in our capital cities and in our service, are aware with what zeal and diligence we strove to bring up our first-born son, Aleksei. And to that end from his childhood we assigned to him teachers not only of Russian but also of foreign languages, and we ordered him to be taught them, so that not only should he be brought up in the fear of God and in our Greek Orthodox Christian faith, but that for a better understanding of military and political (or civil) affairs and of the condition and manners of foreign states, he should also be instructed in other languages, so that by reading in them about history and all the military and civil arts proper to a worthy ruler of a state, he might be a worthy heir to our throne of all the Russias.

2.   But we saw that all our aforementioned efforts for the upbringing and instruction of our aforesaid son were in vain, for he was always disobedient to us and paid no heed to anything befitting a worthy heir, nor did he learn from the teachers whom we had appointed to him, but

людьми, от которых всякого худа, а не к пользе своей научитися мог. И хотя мы его многократно ласкою и сердцем а иногда и наказанием отеческим к тому приводили, и для того и во многие компании воинские с собою брали, дабы обучить воинскому делу, яко первому из мирских дел, для обороны своего отечества, а от жестоких боев его всегда удаляли, проча наследства ради, хотя во оных и своей особы не щадили; також иногда и в Москве оставляли, вруча ему некоторые в государстве управления, для предбудущего обучения; а потом и в чужие краи посылали, чая, что он, видя так регулярные государства, поревнует и склонится к добру и трудолюбию.

Но все сие наше радение ничто пользовало, но сие семя учения на камени пало, понеже не точию оному следовал, но и ненавидел и ни к воинским, ни к гражданским делам никакой склонности не являл, но упражднялся непрестанно во обхождении с непотребными и подлыми людьми, которые грубые и замерзелы обыкности имели.

3.   И хотя мы, желая его от таких непотребств отвратить и ко обхождению с честными и знатными людьми склонить, увещевании своими возбудили, чтоб он избрал себе в супружество из знатных чужестранных государей свойственницу (как инде обыкновенно, також и у предков наших российских государей чинилось, что с другими государями своились), дав ему на волю, где он излюбит. И он, улюбя внуку тогда владеющего герцога вольфенбительского, а своячину родную его величества ныне государствующего цесаря римского, а племянницу короля аглинского, просил нас, дабы ему оную в жену исходатайствовали и позволили на ней жениться, что мы и учинили, не пожалея на сие

associated with dissolute persons of a kind from whom he could learn all manner of evil, and nothing to his advantage. And time and again we treated him with gentleness and kindliness, albeit sometimes with fatherly chastisement, and took him with us on many military campaigns in order to teach him the art of war, this being the most important branch of secular knowledge, for the sake of the defence of our country, yet always kept him away from fierce battles, for the sake of the future succession, though we did not spare our own person in them; and sometimes we left him in Moscow, entrusting him with responsibility for several branches of government, for his future instruction; and later we also sent him abroad, thinking that the sight of regular states would inspire him and incline him to virtue and industry. But all this solicitude on our part was of no avail, and this seed of learning fell on stony ground, for not only did he not pursue it, but rather he hated it and showed no inclination either for military or for civil affairs, but consorted constantly with dissolute and base persons, of crude and corrupt habits.

3.   And wishing to turn him from such dissolute ways and to direct him towards association with people of honour and note, we encouraged and exhorted him to choose in marriage a kinswoman of the notable foreign monarchs (such intermarriage being customary elsewhere, and having also taken place among our forbears, the sovereigns of Russia), giving him freedom to choose a bride wherever he wished. And he, falling in love with the granddaughter of the then duke of Wolfenbüttel, sister-in-law of his Majesty, the present Holy Roman Emperor, and niece of the king of England, asked us to request her hand in marriage on his behalf and to permit him to wed

супружество многих иждивений.

4.   Но, по совершении того супружества (от которого мы чаяли особливого плода и премены худых обычаев и поступков его, сына нашего), усмотрели мы весьма противное той надежды нашей, ибо, хотя оная супруга его, сколько мы устмотреть могли, была ума довольного и обхождения честного, и он ее по своему избранию взял, но однакож он с нею жил в крайнем несогласии и еще вяще умножил обхождения с непотребными людьми, на стыд дому нашему пред чужестранными государи, с тою супругою его свойственными, в чем нам великие жалобы и нарекания были. И хотя мы его частыми напоминании и увещании к поправлению приводить трудились, но все то не успевало.

5. Нопоследи он, еще при оной жене своей, взял некакую бездельную и работную девку и со оною жил явно беззаконно, оставя свою законную жену, которая потом вскоре и жизнь свою скончала, хотя и от болезни, однакож, не без мнения, что и сокрушение от непорядочного его жития с нею много к тому вспомогло.

6. И видя мы его упорность в тех его непотребных поступках, объявили ему на погребении помянутой жены его, что ежели он впредь следовать нашей воле и обучаться тому, что наследнику государства пристойно, не будет, то его лишим наследства, несмотря на то, что он у меня один (ибо тогда еще другого сына не имел); и дабы он на то не надеялся, понеже мы лутче чужого достойного учиним наследником, нежели своего непотребного, ибо не могу такова наследника оставить, который бы

her; which we did, without sparing large expenses
for this marriage.

4.　　But after the celebration of that marriage,
(from which we hoped for special benefit to our son
and the abandonment of his evil ways and conduct),
we saw the very opposite of that hope: for although
his wife, as far as we could see, was intelligent
enough and honourable in her conduct, and he had
chosen her of his own freewill, yet he lived with
her in great disharmony and continued to associate
still more with dissolute people, to the shame of our
house before the foreign monarchs who were
kinsfolk of his wife, as to which many complaints
and reproaches reached us. And although we tried
to bring him to mend his ways with frequent
reminders and exhortations, yet all this was of no
avail.

5.　　But finally, even during his wife's lifetime,
he took a certain idle working-girl as his mistress
and lived openly with her in sin, abandoning his
lawful wife, who soon after died, and although her
death was the result of sickness, yet it was also
believed that distress at his disgraceful treatment of
her had much to do with it.

6.　　And seeing him persist in his dissolute
behaviour, we informed him, at the funeral of his
aforesaid wife, that unless henceforth he followed
our will and applied himself to the studies
appropriate to the heir to the throne, we would
deprive him of the succession, notwithstanding that
he was my only son (for at that time I did not have a
second son); and that he should not count on the
succession, since we would rather make another's
worthy son our successor than a worthless son of
our own; for I could not leave a successor who would

растерял то, что чрез помощь божию отец получил, и испроверг бы славу и честь народа российского, для которого я здоровье свое истратил, не жалея в некоторых случаях и живота своего; к тому ж, и боясь суда божия, вручить такое правление, знав непотребного к тому, увещевая его со многими обстоятельствы, как ему поступать в пути добродетели надлежит, и дал ему время на исправление.

7. И хотя он на то ко мне ответствовал, признавая себя во всем том винна и представляя, что будто он, за слабостию своего здравия и ума, труда понести во обучениях потребных не может, и для того себя сам за нестодойна наследства признавает и оттого отреченна себя иметь просит, но мы, увещевая его родительски и угрожая, и прещением трудились его на путь добродетели обратить. И по отъезде своем для воинских действ в датскую землю, оставили его в Санкт Петербурге, дав ему время на размышление и поправление. Но потом, слыша о прежних его непотребных тамо без нас поступках, писали к нему, чтоб он был к нам в Копенгаген для присутствия в компании военной и лутчего обучения.

8. Но он, забыв страх и заповеди божия, которые повелевают послушну быть и простым родителям, а не то что властелинам, заплатил нам толь многие вышеобъявленные наши родительские о нем попечении и радении неслыханным неблагодарением: ибо вместо того, что к нам ехать, забрав с собою денег и помянутую жонку, с которою беззаконно свалялся, уехал и отдался под протекцию цесарскую, объявляя многие на нас, яко родителя своего и государя, неправдивые клеветы, будто мы его гоним и без причины наследства лишить хотим, и якобы он от нас и в животе своем

undo that which, through God's help, his father received, and who would subvert the glory and honour of the Russian people, for whom I have exhausted my health, on some occasions risking my life; nor, from fear of God's judgment, could I entrust the government to him, knowing him to be unfit for it, exhorting him in great detail as to how to proceed in the path of virtue; and I gave him time to amend.

7.   And although he replied to me, acknowledging his guilt in all that and alleging that because of weakness of body and mind he could not bear the toil of acquiring the necessary instruction, and that therefore he acknowledged himself unworthy of the succession and asked to be excluded from it; but we, exhorting him in fatherly fashion and threatening him, strove by our very threats to turn him to the path of virtue. And on our departure for military action in Denmark, we left him at St Petersburg, giving him time for reflection and amendment. But later, hearing that he had reverted there to his bad old ways in our absence, we wrote to him to join us in Copenhagen to attend the military campaign and for his better instruction.

8.   But he, forgetting the fear of God and His commandments, which enjoin submission to ordinary parents, let alone to potentates, repaid our many aforementioned fatherly cares and solicitude for him with unheard-of ingratitude: for instead of joining us, taking with him money and the aforesaid wench with whom he was unlawfully consorting, he went off and placed himself under the protection of the Emperor, making many unjust slanders against us, his father and sovereign, to the effect that we were persecuting him and sought to

не безопасен. И просил оного, дабы его не токмо от нас скрыл, но и оборону свою против нас и вооруженною рукою дал. И какой тем_своим поступком стыд и бесчестие пред всем светом нам и всему государству нашему учинил, то всяк может рассудить, ибо такого прикладу и в гисториях сыскать трудно. И хотя его цесарское величество о его непотребных поступках и как он с своячиною его, а с своею женою, жил, известен был, однакож, по его многому домогательству, дал ему место к пребыванию, где он просил себя так тайно держать, дабы мы о нем ни малого известия получить могли.

9. И когда мы, по долгом его в пути медлении, признали, что то не просто, родительски о нем соболезнуя и опасаясь, не прилучилось ли ему в пути несчастие, послали его искать в разные пути; и по долгом труде осведомились о нем чрез посланного нашего, капитана от гвардии Александра Румянцова, что он в некоторой цесарской крепости в Тироле тайно содержится. И потому писали мы собственноручно к цесарю, прося оного о присылке его, сына нашего, к нам. И хотя цесарь к нему посылал, представляя ему то наше желание и увещевая, дабы ехал к нам, повинуясь воле нашей, яко родителя и государя, но он многими неправдивыми на нас клеветами цесарю представлял, чтоб он его в руки наши, аки некакова ему неприятеля и мучителя, не отдавал, от которого будто он чает пострадать смерть, и к тому склонил, что тогда его он к нам не послал, но наипаче, по прошению его, отослал в дальние места владения своего, а имянно в Италии лежащий город Неаполь. И содержал его тамо в замке под иным именем, секретно.

deprive him of the succession without cause, and that his very life was in danger from us. And he asked him not merely to hide him from us but even to afford him protection against us by force of arms. And what shame and dishonour before the whole world he brought upon us and our whole state by this conduct, everyone may judge, for it is hard to find a parallel in history. And although His Imperial Majesty knew of his dissolute behaviour and how he had treated his wife, the Emperor's sister-in-law, nevertheless, at his many importunities, he gave him a place of abode, where he asked to be held in such secrecy that we could not receive the slightest information about him.

9.   And when, after the long delay in his arrival, we realised that something was amiss, out of our fatherly compassion for him and fearing that some accident had befallen him on the way, we sent out various search-parties to find him; and after long toil we learned from our envoy, captain of the guard Alexander Rumiantsev, that he was being held in secret in a fortress of the Emperor in the Tyrol. And therefore we wrote personally to the Emperor, asking him to send our son to us. And although the Emperor sent to him, informing him of our wish and exhorting him to join us and to submit to our will as his father and sovereign, yet he, with many unjust slanders against us, besought the Emperor not to deliver him into our hands, as though we were some enemy and oppressor, from whom he expected to suffer death; and he convinced him, so that he did not send him to us at that time, but rather, at his request, he sent him on to remote parts of his possessions, namely to the town of Naples in Italy. And he kept him there in a castle under another name and in secret.

10. Однакож, мы, чрез помянутого ж нашего капитана от гвардии уведав о его тамо пребывании, послали к цесарю тайного нашего советника Петра Толстого да помянутого ж капитана от гвардии Румянцова с грамотою, в крепких изображениях писанною, представляя, коль неправо б то было, ежели б он нашего сына, против божественных и гражданских прав, удержать похотел, по которым и простые родители, а не то что самодержавный государь, яко мы, полную власть без всякого суда над детьми своими имеют, и представляя правые и добродетельные наши к нему, сыну нашему, поступки и, против того, его противности; и напоследок объявляя, какие злые следования из того удержания и ссоры между нами произойтить могут, ибо мы того так оставить не можем, наказав вышеупомянутым нашим посланным еще и жесточае того говорить на словах, и что мы всякими способы и образы принужденны будем то удержание сына нашего мстить.

11. И при том писали собственноручно и к нему, сыну нашему, представляя ему тот его богомерзкий поступок и преступление пред нами, яко родителем, за которое Бог в заповедях своих непокоривых чад угрожает вечною смертию казнити, и угрожая при том его родительскою нашею клятвою, також и представляя, яко его государь, объявить его, ежели не послушает и не возвратится, за изменника отечествию, и при том обнадеживая, ежели воле нашей повинуется и возвратится, прощением того его преступления.

12. И те наши посланные получили от цесаря позволение, по многим домогательствам и по тому письменному нашему и изустному их представлению к нему, сыну нашему, ехать и его склонять к возвращению. И при том им объявлено от цесарских министров, какие будто от нас ему гонения и опасности живота его были, о которых он цесарю доносил, и

10.   However, having learned of his presence there through our aforesaid captain of the guard, we sent our privy councillor Piotr Tolstoi and the aforesaid captain of the guard, Rumiantsev, to the Emperor with a strongly worded letter, pointing out how wrong it would be if he sought to detain our son, contrary to divine and civil laws, whereby even ordinary fathers, let alone a sovereign monarch, such as we, have complete and unimpeachable authority over their children, and pointing out our just and virtuous course of conduct towards our son, and, conversely, his recalcitrance; and finally, indicating what evil consequences and quarrels between us might result from his detention: for we could not leave the matter there, having instructed our aforesaid envoys to reiterate our words still more forcefully, and to say that we would be compelled to use every means to avenge our son's detention.

11.   And at the same time we also wrote personally to our son, pointing out his heinous conduct and transgression against us as a father, for which God in His commandments threatens to punish disobedient children with eternal death; and also threatening him with our parental curse, also pointing out, as his sovereign, that unless he obeyed and returned, we would declare him a traitor to his country, and at the same time assuring him of forgiveness for his transgression, if he submitted to our will and returned.

12.   And after many solicitations and our written and their oral representations, our envoys received permission from the Emperor to visit our son and to induce him to return. And at the same time they were informed by the Emperor's ministers of his allegations of persecution by us and the dangers to

для того к сожалению привел, что оный его в свою протекцию принял, и что, увидя наши в том подлинные и истинные представления, повелит цесарь его всяким образом и с своей стороны к возвращению к нам склонять со объявлением, что он его против всякой правости от нас, яко от отца, удерживать и за то с нами в ссору приттить не может.

13. Но хотя те наши посланные наше собственноручное писание, приехав, вручить ему желали, но оные к нам писали, что он их к себе сначала и допустить не хотел, но от вицероа цесарского к тому уже таким образом приведен, что он его позвал к себе в гости. Потом, противно воле его, их ему представил. Но он, и приняв от них ту нашу грамоту и отеческое увещевание, с угрожением клятвы, нималой склонности к возвращению не явил, но отговаривался, представляя на нас многие неправдивые клеветы, как будто он за многими от нас опасностьми не может и не хочет возвратиться, хвалясь, что цесарь его обещал против нас не токмо охранять и оборонять, но и противно воле нашей престола российского и вооруженною рукою доставить; что видя, те наши посланные употребляли всякие способы его к тому возвращению наговорить, как добродетельными от нас обнадеживаниями, так и прещением и угрозами, и что мы его и вооруженною рукою отыскивать будем, и что цесарь за него с нами войны иметь не похочет, и протчая. Но он на все то не посмотрел и не склонился к нам ехать, пока, уже видя сию его упорность, цесарский вицерой ему именем цесарским представлял, чтоб он к нам ехал, объявляя, что цесарь ни по какому праву его от нас удержать не может и, при нынешней с турки, также и в Италии с гишпанским королем войне, с нами за него в ссору вступить не может, и протчая. Что он увидя и

his life of which he had told the Emperor, and because of which he had moved him to pity, so that he had taken him under his protection; and that, having seen our genuine and truthful representations in the matter, the Emperor, for his part, also ordered every means to be used to induce him to return to us, stating that he could not keep him from us, his father, contrary to all justice, and enter into a quarrel with us in consequence.

13.   But although on their arrival our envoys sought to deliver to him our personal letter, they wrote to us that at first he refused even to receive them, but was finally brought to do so by the Emperor's viceroy, who invited him to his quarters. Then, against his will, he presented them to him. But even after receiving from them our letter and fatherly exhortation, together with the threat of our curse, he showed not the slightest inclination to return, but found excuses not to do so, making many unjust slanders against us, and alleging that, for fear of many dangers at our hands, he could not and would not return, boasting that the Emperor had promised not only to keep him and protect him from us, but even to secure the throne of Russia by force of arms against our will; seeing this, our envoys used all means to persuade him to return, pointing out both our virtuous assurances and our warnings and threats, and saying that we would seek him out by force of arms and that the Emperor would not go to war with us for his sake, and so forth. But he took no notice of any of this and declined to come to us until, seeing his obstinacy, the Emperor's viceroy told him in the Emperor's name to come to us, saying that the Emperor could not rightly keep him from us, and that, with the present war with the Turks, and also in Italy with the King of Spain, he could not enter into a quarrel

опасаясь, чтоб противно воли его нам не выдали, уже склонился к нам ехать и объявил о том тем нашим посланным, також и цесарскому вицерою; и к нам о том, признавая преступление свое, оттуды писал повинную, с которой при сем список приобщается.

И тако сюда ныне приехал.

14. И хотя он, сын наш, за такие свои противные от давных лет против нас, яко отца и государя своего, поступки, особливо ж за сие на весь свет приключенное нам бесчестие чрез побег свой и клеветы, на нас рассеянные, от нас, яко злоречивый отца своего и сопротивляяйся государю своему, достоин был лишения живота, однакож, мы, отеческим сердцем о нем соболезнуя, в том преступлении его прощаем и от всякого наказания освобождаем.

15. Однакож, в рассуждении его недостоинства и всех вышеписанных и непотребных обхождений, не можем по совести своей его наследником по нас престола российского оставить, ведая, что он, по своим непорядочным поступкам, всю полученную по божией милости и нашими неусыпными трудами славу народа нашего и пользу государственную утратить, которую с каким трудом мы получили; и не токмо отторгнутые от государства нашего от неприятелей провинции паки присовокупили, но и вновь многие знатные городы и земли ко оному получили; також и народ свой во многих воинских и гражданских науках к пользе государственной и славе обучили, то всем известно.

16. И тако мы, сожалея о государстве своем и верных подданных, дабы от такого властителя наипаче прежнего в худое состояние не были приведены, властию отеческою, по которой, по правам государства

with us for his sake, and so forth. On seeing this and fearing to be handed over to us against his will, he now agreed to join us and told our envoys so and also the Emperor's viceroy; and he wrote a confession to us from there, admitting his transgression, a copy of which is appended herewith.

And so now he has arrived here.

14. And although for such hostile acts over many years against us, his father and sovereign, and especially for this disgrace which has befallen us before the whole world through his flight and by the slanders broadcast against us, he, our son, has deserved to lose his life for speaking ill of his father and for resisting his sovereign, yet showing compassion on him with a fatherly heart, we forgive him his transgression and we free him from all punishment.

15. However, in consideration of his unworthiness and all the instances of his dissolute conduct described above, we cannot in our conscience leave him as successor to the throne of Russia after us, knowing that by his disgraceful conduct, he will squander all the glory of our people and the advantage to the state, which by the grace of God and our incessant efforts, we have acquired with such toil; and not only have we recovered provinces torn from our state by enemies, but have acquired many great towns and lands in addition, and have also instructed our people in many military and civil arts, to the benefit and glory of the state, as is well known.

16. And so, taking pity on our state and our faithful subjects, lest they be brought by such a ruler to a condition worse than before - by our

нашего, и каждый подданный наш сына своего наследства лишить и другому сыну, которому хочет, оное определить волен, и, яко самодержавный государь, для пользы государственной, лишаем его, сына своего Адексея, за те вины и преступления наследства по нас престола нашего всероссийского, хотя б ни единой персоны нашей фамилии по нас не осталось.

17. И определяем и объявляем по нас помянутого престола наследником другого сына нашего, Петра, хотя еще и малолетна суща, ибо иного возрастного наследника не имеем.

18. И заклинаем преждепомянутого сына нашего Алексея родительскою нашею клятвою, дабы того наследства ни в которое время себе не претендовал и не ислал.

19. Желаем же от всех верных наших подданных духовного и мирского чина и всего народа всероссийского, дабы, по сему нашему изволению и определению, сего, от нас назначенного в наследство, сына нашего Петра, за законного наследника признавали и почитали; и во утверждение сего нашего постановления на сем обещанием пред святым олтарем, над святым Евангелием и целованием креста утвердили.

20. Всех же тех, кто сему нашему изволению в которое ни будь время противны будут, и сына нашего Алексея отныне за наследника почитать и ему в том вспомогать станут и дерзнут, изменниками нам и отечеству объявляем.

paternal authority, by virtue of which, in accordance with the laws of our state, every subject is free to disinherit his son and to bequeathe his estate to whichever other son he chooses, so we, as an absolute monarch, for the good of the state, do deprive our son Aleksei, for those offences and transgressions, of the succession to our throne of all the Russias after our death, even if there should not remain a single person in our family after us.

17. And we ordain and declare as successor to the aforesaid throne after us our second son, Piotr, even though he is still of tender years: for we have no other adult heir.

18. And we pronounce on our aforementioned son Aleksei our paternal curse, lest he should at any time lay claim to and seek the succession for himself.

19. And we desire all our faithful subjects, spiritual and secular, and all the people of all the Russias, in accordance with this our will and ordinance, to acknowledge and accept our son Piotr, whom we have designated to the succession, as lawful successor; and in confirmation of this our ordinance, to confirm this by a promise before the holy altar, on the holy Gospels and by kissing the cross.

20. And all those who at any time oppose this our will and henceforth regard our son Aleksei as successor and help him or venture to do so in this regard, we declare to be traitors to us and to the country.

21.   И сие для всенародного известия повсюду объявить и разослать повелели.

Петр.

Дан в Москве, 1718 году, февраля в 3 день, за подписанием нашея руки и печатию.

[Печать]

21.   And for the information of all the people, we have ordered this to be declared and distributed everywhere.

Peter

Issued in Moscow, on the 3rd day of February in the year 1713, under our hand and seal.

[Seal]

(Russian text edited from Ustrialov, pp. 438-44 and Voskresenskii, pp. 164-9).

SELECTED BIBLIOGRAPHY

Absolutism in Seventeenth-Century Europe, (ed.)J. Miller, (London: Macmillan, 1990).

Acta eruditorum, Leipzig, August 1723.

M. S. Anderson, *Europe in the Eighteenth Century 1713-1783,* 3rd edition,(London: Longman, 1987).

T. Anderson, *Russian Political Thought. An Introduction,* (Ithaca, New York: Cornell University Press, 1967).

E. Anisimov, *Vremia petrovskikh reform* [The age of the petrine reforms], (St Petersburg: Lenizdat, 1989).

Sumner Benson, "The role of western political thought in Petrine Russia," *Canadian-American Slavic Studies,* vol. 8, No. 2, (summer 1974), pp. 254-273.

"F. C. von Bergholz, Großfürstlichen Oberkammerherrns Tagebuch, welches er in Russland von 1721 bis 1725 als holsteinischer Kammerjunker geführet hat," in *Magazin für die neue Historie und Geographie,* (ed.) A. F. Büsching, vols. 19-20, (Halle, 1785).

P. N. Berkov, "Tomas Konsett, kapellan angliiskoi faktorii v Rossii" [Thomas Consett, chaplain to the English factory in Russia] in *Problemy mezhdunarodnykh literaturnykh sviazei v 1720e gody* [Problems of international literary contacts in the 1720s], (ed.) B. G. Reizov, (Leningrad: Leningradskii Gosudarstvennyi Universitet, 1962), pp. 3-26.

Bibliography

J. Black, "Russia and the British Press in the early eighteenth century," *Study Group on Eighteenth-Century Russia Newsletter,* No. 11, 1983, pp. 16-33.

M. M. Bogoslovskii, *Oblastnaia Reforma Petra Velikogo* [Peter the Great's provincial reform], (Moscow: Imperatorskoe Obshchestvo Istorii i Drevnostei Rossiiskikh pri Moskovskom Universitete, 1902).

Bossuet, *Textes Choisis et Commentés,* vol. 2 (ed.) H. Bremond, (Paris: Plon, 1913).

W. E. Butler, "Grotius' Influence in Russia," in *Hugo Grotius and International Relations,* (eds.) H. Bull, B. Kingsbury, A. Roberts, (Oxford: Oxford University Press, 1990).

T. A. Bykova and M. M. Gurevich, *Opisanie izdanii napechatannykh pri Petre I. Svodnyi katalog. Opisanie izdanii grazhdanskoi pechati (1708-ianvar' 1725g.)* [Inventory of editions published under Peter I. Union catalogue. Inventory of editions of the civil press (1708-January 1725)], (Moscow/Leningrad: Akademiia Nauk SSSR, 1955).

T. A. Bykova and M. M. Gurevich, *Opisanie izdanii napechatannykh pri Petre I. Svodnyi katalog. Opisanie izdanii napechatannykh kirillitsei 1689-1725* [Inventory of editions published under Peter I. Union catalogue. Inventory of editions published in church script 1689-1725], (Moscow: Akademiia Nauk SSSR, 1958).

T. A. Bykova and R. I. Kozintseva, *Opisanie izdanii napechatannykh pri Petre I. Svodnyi katalog. Dopolneniia i prilozheniia* [Inventory of editions published under Peter I. Union catalogue. Supplements and additions], (Leningrad: Akademiia Nauk SSSR, 1972).

Bibliography

I. Chistovich, *Feofan Prokopovich i ego vremia* [Feofan Prokopovich and his Times], (St Petersburg: Imperatorskaia Akademiia Nauk, 1868).

James Cracraft, *The Church Reform of Peter the Great,* (London: Macmillan, 1971).

James Cracraft, "Feofan Prokopovich," in *The Eighteenth Century in Russia,* (ed.) J. G. Garrard, (Oxford: Clarendon Press, 1973), pp. 75-105.

James Cracraft, "Feofan Prokopovich: a Bibliography of his Works," *Oxford Slavonic Papers,* new series, vol. viii, 1975, pp. 1-36.

James Cracraft, "The Succession Crisis of 1730: a view from the inside," *Canadian-American Slavic Studies,* vol. 12, No. 1, spring 1978, pp. 61-85.

James Cracraft, "Feofan Prokopovich and the Kiev Academy," in *Russian Orthodoxy under the Old Regime,* (ed.) R. L. Nichols and T. G. Stavrou, (Minneapolis: University of Minnesota Press, 1978), pp. 44-64.

James Cracraft, "Did Feofan Prokopovich really write *Pravda Voli Monarshei?*," *Slavic Review,* vol. 40, No. 2, (summer 1981), pp. 173-193.

James Cracraft, (ed.), *For God and Peter the Great. The Works of Thomas Consett, 1723-1729,* East European Monographs, No. XCVI, (New York: Columbia University Press, 1982).

James Cracraft, "Empire versus Nation: Russian Political Theory under Peter I," *Harvard Ukrainian Studies,* 10, No. 3-4, 1986, pp. 524-541.

318

James Cracraft, "Opposition to Peter the Great," in *Imperial Russia 1700-1917. State. Society. Opposition. Essays in honour of Marc Raeff,* (ed.) E. Mendelsohn and M. S. Schatz, (DeKalb, Illinois: Northern Illinois University Press, 1988), pp. 22-36.

James Cracraft, *The Petrine revolution in Russian architecture,* (Chicago: Chicago University Press, 1988).

Robert C. Crummey, *The Old Believers and the World of Antichrist. The Vyg Community and the Russian State, 1694-1855,* (Madison, Wisconsin: University of Wisconsin Press, 1970).

Isabel de Madariaga, "Autocracy and Sovereignty" *Canadian-American Slavic Studies,* vol. 16, Nos. 3-4, 1982, pp. 369-387.

Isabel de Madariaga, "Portrait of an Eighteenth-Century Russian Statesman: Prince Dmitry Mikhaylovich Golitsyn" *The Slavonic and East European Review,* vol. 62, No. 1, January 1984, pp. 36-60.

Diplomatische Beiträge zur russischen Geschichte aus dem königlichen Sächsichen Hauptstaatsarchiv zu Dresden, (ed.) E. Herrmann, vol. l, (St Petersburg: Akademiia Nauk, 1868).

I. I. Ditiatin, "Verkhovnaiia vlast' v Rossii XVIII stoletiia" [Supreme power in 18th-century Russia], *Stat'i po istorii russkogo prava* [Articles on the history of Russian law] , (St Petersburg: izd. O. N. Popovoi, 1895).

Dnevnik A. V. Khrapovitskogo [The Diary of A. V. Khrapovitskii], (ed.) N. Barsukov, (St Petersburg: izd. A. F. Bazunova, 1874).

319

Bibliography

Paul Dukes, *Russia under Catherine the Great*, vol. 1, *Select Documents on Government and Society*, (Newtonville, Massachusetts: Oriental Research Partners, 1978).

Paul Dukes and Brenda Meehan-Waters, "A neglected account of the succession crisis of 1730: James Keith's Memoir," *Canadian-American Slavic Studies*, vol. 12, No. 1, Spring 1978, pp. 00

200-letie Kabineta ego imperatorskogo Velichestva 1704-1904. Istoricheskoe Issledovanie [The bicentenary of His Imperial Majesty's Cabinet. An historical investigation], (St Petersburg: 1911).

P. P. Epifanova, "'Rassuzhdenie' P. P. Shafirova o voine so Shvetsiei" [P. P. Shafirov's "Considerations" on the war with Sweden], in *Problemy obshchestvennoi-politicheskoi istorii Rossii i slavianskikh stran. Sbornik statei k 70-letiiu akademika M. N. Tikhonravova* [Problems in the socio-political history of Russia and the Slav countries. A collection of articles on the 70th birthday of academic M. N. Tikhonravov], (Moscow: izd. vostochnoi literatury, 1963), pp. 296-303).

N. B. Golikova, *Politicheskie protsessy pri Petre I. Po materialam Preobrazhenskogo Prikaza* [Political trials under Peter the Great. From the records of the Preobrazhenskii Prikaz], (Moscow: izd. Moskovskogo Universiteta, 1957).

N. V. Golitsyn, "Novye dannye o biblioteke kn. D. M. Golitsyna (verkhovnika)" [New data about the library of Prince D. M. Golitsyn (verkhovnik)', *Chteniia v obshchestve istorii i drevnostei rossiiskikh pri moskovskom universitete* [Lectures in the society of Russian history and antiquities at Moscow University], 1900, vol. 4, section 4, pp. 1-16.

Bibliography

A.D. Gradovskii, "Nachala russkogo gosudarstvennogo prava" [Principles of Russian Constitutional Law], *Sobranie Sochinenii* [Collected Works], 2nd edition, vol. 7, (St Petersburg: tipografiia M. M. Stasiulevicha, 1907).

Conrad Grau, *Der Wirtschaftsorganisator, Staatsman und Wissenschaftler Vasilij N. Tatiscev (1686-1750)*, (Berlin: Quellen und Studien zur Geschichte Osteuropas, 1963).

G. Gurvich, *"Pravda Voli Monarshei" Feofana Prokopovicha i ee zapadnoevropeiskie istochniki* [Feofan Prokopovich's "Pravda Voli Monarshei" and its western European sources], (Iur'ev: Uchenye zapiski imperatorskogo iur'evskogo universiteta, 1915).

H. Hjärne, "Ryske Konstitutionsprojekt år 1730 efter Svenske förebilder," *Historisk Tidskrift*, No. 4 (1884), pp. 189-272.

Lindsey Hughes, "A note on the children of Peter the Great," *Study Group on Eighteenth-Century Russia Newsletter*, No. 21, 1993, pp. 10-16.

J. Jubé, *La Religion, les moeurs et les usages des Moscovites*, (ed.) M. Mervaud, (Oxford: The Voltaire Foundation, 1992).

V. O. Kliuchevskii, *Sochineniia* [Works], vols. 4, 8, (Moscow: izd. sotsial'no-ekonomicheskoi literatury, 1958-1959).

D. A. Korsakov, *Votsarenie Imperatritsy Anny Ioannovny. Istoricheskii Etiud* [The Accession of the Empress Anna Ioannovna. A Historical Study], (Kazan: tipografiia imperatorskogo universiteta, 1880).

A. Lappo-Danilevskij, "L'idée de l'état et son évolution en Russie depuis les troubles du XVIIe siècle jusqu'au réformes du XVIIIe," in *Essays in Legal History*, (ed.) P.

Vinogradoff, (Oxford: Oxford University Press, 1913), pp. 356-83.

V. N. Latkin, *Uchebnik Istorii Russkogo Prava perioda Imperii* [A Manual of the history of Russian law in the period of the Empire], (St Petersburg: tipografiia Montvida, 1909).

A. Liutsh, "Russkii absoliutizm XVIII veka" [18th-century Russian absolutism], in *Itogi XVIII veka v Rossii* [Results of the 18th century in Russia], (ed.) A. Liutsh, V. Zommer and A. Lipovskii, (Moscow: tipografiia t-va I. D. Sytina, 1910).

Philip Longworth, *The Making of Eastern Europe,* (London: Macmillan, 1994).

G. Maker, *Publishing, Printing, and the Origins of Intellectual Life in Russia 1700-1800,* (Princeton, New Jersey: Princeton University Press, 1985).

"Manifesto of the Criminal Process of the Czarevich Alexei Petrowitz, judged at St Petersbourg by order of his Czarish Majesty, the 25th day of June, 1718," in F. C. Weber, *The Present State of Russia,* volume II, (London: W. and J. Innys, 1723), pp. 95-206.

Memoirs of Peter Henry Bruce, Esq. A Military Officer in the services of Prussia, Russia and Great Britain, (Dublin: J. and R. Byrn, 1783),

P. N. Miliukov, *Verkhovniki i Shliakhetsvo* [Verkhovniki and Gentry], (Rostov: 1905).

K. R. Minzloff, *Pierre le Grand dans la littérature étrangère,* (St Petersburg: I.I. Glasounow, 1872).

Modernization of Russia under Peter I and Catherine II,(ed.) Basil Dmytryshyn, (New York: John Wiley, 1974).

Bibliography

Sidney Monas, "Anton Divier and the Police of St Petersburg," in *For Roman Jakobson. Essays on the occasion of his sixtieth birthday,* (The Hague: Mouton, 1956), pp. 361-66.

P. Morozov, *Feofan Prokopovich kak pisatel'* [Feofan Prokopovich as a writer], (St Petersburg: tipografiia V. I. Balasheva, 1880).

John Motley, *The History of the Life of Peter the First, Emperor of Russia,* (London: J. Read,1739).

G. A. Nekrasov, *Russko-shvedskie otnosheniia i politika velikikh derzhav v 1721-1726gg.* [Russo-Swedish relations and the politics of the Great Powers 1721-1726], (Moscow: Nauka, 1964).

Ob'iavlenie rozysknogo dela i suda, po ukazu ego Tsarskogo Velichestva, na tsarevicha Alekseia Petrovicha, v Sankpiterburkh otpravlennogo, i po ukazu ego Velichestva v pechat', dlia izvestiia vsenarodnogo [A declaration concerning the investigation and trial of the Tsarevich Aleksei Petrovich, held by order of His Czarish Majesty at St Petersburg, and published by His Majesty's order for general information], (St Petersburg: 1718). (see 'Manifesto of the Criminal Process of the Czarevich Alexei Petrowitz').

Ocherki istorii SSSR. Period Feodalizma. Rossiia v pervoi chetverti XVIIIv. Preobrazovaniia Petra I, [Outlines of the history of the USSR. The Period of Feudalism. Russia in the first quarter of the 18th century. The Reforms of Peter I] (ed.) B. B. Kafengauz and N. I. Pavlenko, (Moscow: Akademiia Nauk SSSR, 1954).

Oprechte Haerlemse Dingsdaegse Courant, 1718, Nos. 15, 21, 31.

Bibliography

Osmnadtsatyi Vek. Istoricheski Sbornik [The Eighteenth Century. A Historical Collection], (ed.) P. Bartenev, book 3, (Moscow: 1869).

K. A. Papmehl, *Freedom of Expression in Eighteenth Century Russia,* (The Hague: Martinus Nijhoff, 1971).

J. Paaskoski, "Om priviligierna för Viborgs provins vid freden i Nystad 1721," *Historisk Tidskrift för Finland,* No. 3, 1993, pp. 361-388.

N. I. Pavlenko, "Idei absoliutizma v zakonodatel'stve XVIIIv" [Ideas of absolutism in 18th-century legislation] in *Absoliutizm v Rossii (XVII-XVIIIvv). Sbornik statei* [Absolutism in Russia (17th-18th centuries) A Collection of articles], (Moscow: Nauka, 1964).

N. I. Pavlenko, "Petr I (k izucheniiu sotsial'no-politicheskikh vzgliadov" [Peter I (towards the study of his socio-political views)], in *Rossiia v period reform Petra I* [Russia in the period of the reforms of Peter I], (ed.) N. I. Pavlenko, (Moscow: Akademiia Nauk SSSR, 1973), pp. 40-102.

P. P. Pekarskii, *Nauka i Literatura pri Petre Velikom* [Science and Literature under Peter the Great], vol. II, (St Petersburg: tipografiia t-va 'Obshchestvennaia Pol'za', 1862).

R. Pipes, *Karamzin's Memoir on Ancient and Modern Russia. A Translation and Analysis,* (New York: Atheneum, 1966).

Plans for Political Reform in Imperial Russia, (ed.) Marc Raeff, (Englewood Cliffs, New Jersey: Prentice-Hall, 1966).

Polnoe sobranie postanovlenii i rasporiazhenii po vedomstvu pravoslavnogo ispovedaniia rossiiskoi imperii [Complete collection of decrees and orders relating to the

Orthodox confession in the Russian Empire], (St Petersburg: 1874).

N. A. Popov, *Tatishchev i ego Vremia* [Tatishchev and his Times], (Moscow: tipografiia V. Gracheva, 1861).

V. Iu. Poresh, "Kniaz' D. M. Golitsyn (Verkhovnik) i frantsuszkie knigi ego biblioteki" [Prince D. M. Golitsyn (the Verkhovnik) and the French books in his library], in *Knigopechatanie i knizhnye sobraniia v Rossii do serediny XIXv.* [Book-publishing and book collections in Russia to the mid-19th century], (ed.) A. I. Kopanev *et al.*, (Leningrad: Akademiia Nauk SSSR, 1979), pp. 98-111.

Ivan Poseshkov, *The Book of Poverty and Wealth,* (ed.) A. P. Vlasto and L. R. Lewitter, (London: The Athlone Press, 1987).

Pravda Voli Monarshei vo opredelenii naslednika derzhavy svoei [The Justice of the Monarch's Right to appoint the heir to his throne], (Moscow: v moskovskoi tipografii, 1722). 2nd edition, 1726.

La Première Catherine. Seconde femme de Pierre le Grand. Notes et anecdotes sur Catherine Ire de Russie d'après un manuscrit inédit du 18e siècle, (ed.) C. Ziegler, (Paris: Institut des Sciences Historiques, 1958).

The Prerogative of Primogeniture, shewing that the Right of Succession to an Hereditary Empire depends not upon Grace, etc., but only upon Birthright...Written on occasion of the Czar of Muscovy's Reasons in his late Manifesto for the Disherison of his Eldest Son from the Succession to the Crown. To which is added the manifesto itself, (London: W. Boreham, 1718).

Feofan Prokopovich, *Sochineniia* [Works], (ed.) I. P. Eremin, (Moscow: Akademiia Nauk SSSR, 1961).

Bibliography

Feofan Prokopovich,*De arte rhetorica libri X,* (ed.) Renate Lachman, *Slavische Forschungen,* Band 27/11, 1982.

A. B. Prosina, "Apologiia absoliutizma v uchenii Feofana Prokopovicha" [The Apologia of absolutism in the teaching of Feofan Prokopovich], *Vestnik Moskovskogo Universiteta, seriia pravo,* 1969, No. 2, pp. 52-59.

G. A. Protasov, "Konditsii 1730g. i ikh prodolzhenie" [The Conditions of 1730 and their continuation], *Uchenye zapiski tambovskogo pedagogicheskogo instituta,* 1957, vol. 9.

Marc Raeff, "Les slaves, les allemands et les 'Lumières'," *Canadian Slavic Studies, 1, No. 4* (Winter, 1967). pp. 521-551.

Marc Raeff, "The Enlightenment in Russia and Russian Thought in the Enlightenment," in *The Eighteenth Century in Russia,* (ed.) J. D. Garrard, (Oxford: The Clarendon Press, 1973), pp. 25-47.

Marc Raeff, *The Well-Ordered Police State. Social and Institutional Changes through Law in the Germanies and Russia 1600-1800,* (London: Yale University Press, 1983).

Marc Raeff, *Understanding Imperial Russia. State and Society in the Old Regime,* (New York: Columbia University Press, 1984).

Marc Raeff, "La noblesse et le discours politique sous le règne de Pierre le Grand," *Cahiers du monde russe et soviétique,* vol. xxxiv (1-2), 1993, pp. 33-46.

Marc Raeff, "Transfiguration and Modernization. The Paradoxes of Social Disciplining, Paedogogical Leadership and the Enlightenment in 18th Century Russia," *Political*

Bibliography

Ideas and Institutions in Imperial Russia, (Boulder, Colorado: Westview Press, 1994), pp. 334-347.

David J. Ransel, "The Government Crisis of 1730," in *Reform in Russia and the USSR,* (ed.) Robert O. Crummey, (Chicago: University of Illinois Press, 1989), pp. 45-71.

Das Recht der Monarchen, in willkühriger Bestellung der Reichsfolge... aus der Rußischen Sprache getreulich ins Teutsche übersetzt, (Berlin, bei Ambrosius Haude, 1724).

W. Recke, "Die Verfassungspläne der russischen Oligarchen im Jahre 1730," *Zeitschrift für Geschichte Osteuropas,* 1911, vol. 2.

N. V. Riasanovsky, *The Image of Peter the Great in Russian History and Thought,* (Oxford: Oxford University Press, 1985).

The Russian Catechism, composed and published by order of the Czar, (transl.) J. T. Philips, (London: W. Meadows, 1723), from *Pervoe Uchenie Otrokam,* (St Petersburg: 1720).

Russian Intellectual History. An Anthology, (ed.) Marc Raeff, (New York: Harcourt, Brace & World, 1966).

Russland unter Peter dem Grossen. Nach den handschriftlichen Berichten J.G. Vockerodt's, (ed.) E. Herrmann, (Leipzig: Duncker & Humblot, 1872).

D. A. Schafly, jr., "The popular image of the west in Russia at the time of Peter the Great," in *Russia and the World of the Eighteenth Century,* (ed.) R. P. Bartlett, A. G. Cross, Karen Rasmussen, (Columbus Ohio: Slavica, 1988), pp. 2-21.

P. P. Shafirov, *A Discourse concerning the Just Causes of the War between Sweden and Russia 1700-1721,* (ed.) W. E.

Bibliography

Butler, (Dobbs Ferry, New York: Oceana Publications, 1973).

M. M. Shcherbatov, "Rassmotrenie o porokakh i samovlastii Petra Velikogo," [A Consideration of the vices and despotism of Peter the Great] *Sochineniia Kniazia M. M. Shcherbatova* [Works of Prince M. M. Shcherbatov], vol. 2, (ed.) I. P. Khrushchov and A. G. Voronov, (St Petersburg: izd. kniazia B. S. Shcherbatova, 1898), pp. 23-50.

Prince M. M. Shcherbatov, *On the Corruption of Morals in Russia,* (ed.) A. Lentin, (Cambridge: Cambridge University Press, 1969).

E. Shmurlo, *Vol'ter i ego kniga o Petre Velikom* [Voltaire and his book on Peter the Great], (Prague: Orbis, 1929).

K. Sivkov, "Petr-pisatel'" [Peter the writer], in *Tri Veka. Rossiia ot Smuty do nashego vremeni. Istoricheskii Sbornik* [Three Centuries. Russia from the Time of Troubles to Our Own Time. A Historical Collection], (ed.) V. V. Kallash, vol. 3, (Moscow: izd. t-va I. D. Sytina, 1912), pp. 42-68.

Sobranie raznykh zapisok i sochinenii, sluzhashchikh k dostavleniiu polnogo svedeniia o zhizni i deiianiiakh gosudaria imperatora Petra Velikogo, izdannoe trudami i izhdeveniem Fiodora Tumanskogo [A Collection of various writings and works serving to provide a complete information on the life and actions of the sovereign emperor Peter the Great, published by efforts and at the expense of Fiodor Tumanskii], part 10, (St Petersburg: Shnor, 1788).

S. M. Solov'ev, *Istoriia Rossii s drevneishikh vremen* [A History of Russia from the most ancient times], books 9-10, (Moscow: izdatel'stvo sotsial'no-ekonomicheskoi literatury, 1963).

Bibliography

The Spiritual Regulation of Peter the Great, translated and edited by A. V. Muller, (Seattle: University of Washington Press, 1972).

G. Stökl, "Das Problem der Thronfolgeordnung in Russland," in *Der dynastische Fürstenstaat. Zur Bedeutung von Sukzessionsordnungen für die Enstehung des frühmodernen Staates*, (ed.) H. Neumaus and J. Kunisch, (Berlin: Duncker & Humblot, 1982), pp. 273-289.

R. Stupperich, *Staatsgedanke und Religionspolitik Peters des großen*, (Berlin: Osteuropäische Forschungen, neue Folge 1, vol. 21, 1936).

Succession to the Imperial Throne of Russia, edited under the supervision of Antony, Archbishop of Los Angeles and South California, (Bridgeport, Connecticut: 1984).

B. I. Syromiatnikov, *"Reguliarnoe" gosudarstvo Petra Pervogo i ego ideologiia* [Peter the First's 'Regulated' state and its ideology], (Moscow: Akademiia Nauk SSSR), 1943.

V. N. Tatishchev, *Istoriia Rossiiskaia* [A History of Russia], vol. 1, (Moscow/Leningrad: Akademiia Nauk SSSR), 1962.

J. Tetzner, "Theofan Prokcpovic und die russische Frühaufklärung," *Zeitschrift für Slawistik*, iii, 1958, 351-363.

B. Titlinov, "Feofan Prokopovich," in *Russkii Biograficheskii Slovar'* [Russian Biographical Dictionary] (*Iablonskii-Fomin*), (St Petersburg: Imperatorskaia Akademiia Nauk, 1913), pp. 399-448.

A. Titov, "Episkop Afanasii Kondoidi" [Bishop Afanasii Kondoidi], *Russkii Arkhiv*, Book 3, pp. 5-24.

Bibliography

G. S. Treuer, *Untersuchung nach dem Recht der Natur wie weit ein Fürst Macht habe seinen erstgebohrnen Printzen von der Nachfolge in der Regierung auszuschliessen,* (Wolffenbüttel: 1718).

V. Ulanov, "Oppozitsiia Petru Velikomu" [Opposition to Peter the Great], in *Tri Veka. Rossiia ot Smuty do nashego vremeni. Istoricheskii Sbornik* [Three Centuries. Russia from the Time of Troubles to Our Own Time. A Historical Collection], (ed.) V. V. Kallash, vol. III, (Moscow: izd. t-va I. D. Sytina, 1912), pp. 69-100.

N. G. Ustrialov, *Istoriia tsarstvovaniia Petra Velikogo,* [The History of the Reign of Peter the Great] vol. VI, (St Petersburg: tipografiia II-go otdeleniia ego imperatorskogo velichestva kantseliarii, 1863).

M. Vasmer, *Russisches Etymologisches Wörterbuch,* vol. I, (Heidelberg: Universitätsverlag, 1953).

P. V. Verkhovskoi, *Uchrezhdenie dukhovnoi kollegii i dukhovnyi reglament* [The establishment of the Spiritual College and the Spiritual Regulation], vols. 1-2, (Rostov-on-Don: Imperatorskii Varshavskii Universitet, 1916).

G. V. Vernadskii, *Ocherk istorii prava russkogo gosudarstva XVIII-XIXvv. Period imperii* [An Outline History of the Law of the Russian State from the 18th to 19th centuries], (Prague: izd. Plamia, 1924).

N. A. Voskresenskii, *Zakonodatel'nye Akty Petra I* [Legislative Acts of Peter I], (ed.) B. I. Syromiatnikov, vol. I, (Moscow/Leningrad: Akademiia Nauk SSSR, 1945).

Martinus A. Wes, *Classics in Russia 1700-1855,* (Leiden: E. J. Brill, 1992).

Bibliography

Cynthia H. Whittaker, "The Reforming Tsar: the Redefinition of Autocratic Duty in Eighteenth-century Russia," *Slavic Review,* vol. 51, No. 1, (Spring 1992), pp. 77-98.

E. Winter, *Halle als Ausgangspunkt der deutschen Russlandkunde im 18 Jahrhundert,* (Berlin: Akademie-Verlag, 1953).

Richard S. Wortmann, *The Development of a Russian Legal Consciousness,* (Chicago: University of Chicago Press, 1976).

Richard S. Wortman, *Scenarios of Power. Myth and Ceremony in Russian Monarchy. Vol. 1. From Peter the Great to the death of Nicholas I,* (Princeton: Princeton University Press, 1995).

A. B. Zaichenko, "Teoriia prosveshchennogo absoliutizma v proizvedeniiakh F. Prokopovicha [The theory of enlightened absolutism in the works of F. Prokopovich], in *Iz istorii razvitiia politiko-pravovykh idei* [From the history of the development of politico-legal ideas], (Moscow: 1984), pp. 76-83.

D. Zharinov, "Petr Velikii kak zakonodatel' i 'Pravda Voli Monarshei'" [Peter the Great as legislator and "Pravda Voli Monarshei"] in *Tri Veka. Rossiia ot Smuty do nashego vremeni. Istorcheskii Sbornik* [Three Centuries. Russia from the Time of Troubles to Our Own Time], (ed.) V. V. Kallash, vol. 3, (Moscow: izd. t-va I. D. Sytina, 1912), pp. 182-199.

M. Zyzykin, *Tsarskaia vlast' i zakon o prestolonasledii v Rossii* [Royal power and the law of succession to the throne in Russia], (Sofia: izd. kn. A. A. Liven, 1924).

331

INDEX

Page references to the translation of *Pravda Voli Monarshei* are in bold

Index

Index

Natural law, natural reason, common sense, 2, 24, 33, 34, 35, 41, 42, 43, 44, 45, 48, 49, 52, 57, 60, 63, 79n, 91n, 92n, 95n, 100n, **135, 137, 139, 145, 167, 175, 181, 187, 275,** 283n
Naval Statute (Morskoi Ustav) (1720), 88n, 93n
Nekrasov, G. A., 98n, 113n
Nicephorus, **251, 253,** 290
Nimrod, **205,** 286n
Novgorod, 20, 282n
Novikov, N. I., 58
Nystad, treaty of (1721), 11, 94n, 115n

Ochus, **245, 247**
Old Believers, 18, 26, 54, 56, 101n
Opposition, criticism, dissent, 1, 14, 20, 22, 25, 26, 43, 52, 53, 54, 55, 56, 57, 62, 65, 66, 73n, 101n, 103n, **197, 209, 227**
Orodes, king of Parthia, **251**
Otto the Great, emperor, **257**

Parental authority; paternal, patriarchal authority; *patria potestas,* 24, 34, 35, 45, **139, 169, 177, 261,** 313
Paris, 75n, 86n
Parthians, 34, **279**
Paul, saint, 32, 40, 51, 282n
Paul I, emperor, 68, 69, 116n
Pekarskii, P. P., 58, 72n, 74n, 77n, 78n, 80n, 81n, 82n, 86n, 87n, 88n, 91n, 94n, 98n, 102n, 104n, 105n, 110n, 111n, 112n, 114n, 115n, 116n
Perseus, **249, 251**
Persia, 21, 65, **151, 245**
Persians, 34, **153, 279**
Peter, saint, 40, **195**
Peter, 40, **195, 199,** 289
Peter the Great, emperor, 1, 2, 3, 5n, 6n, 9n, and the succession issue, 11-17, and Feofan Prokopovich, 17-20, and *Pravda Voli Monarshei,* 21-27, ideology and *Pravda Voli Monarshei,* 28-43, theories of government and *Pravda Voli Monarshei,* 43-52, and dissent, 52-57, and authorship of *Pravda Voli Monarshei,* 61-62, and publication and subsequent history of *Pravda Voli Monarshei,* 65-68, throughout notes to Introduction, 72n-117n, as named monarch and patron in text of *Pravda Voli Monarshei,* **121-281,** throughout notes to text, 282n-287n, as nominal author of manifesto on exclusion from succession, 297-315
Peter II, Piotr Alekseevich, emperor, 16, 17, 22, 46, 47, 56, 66, 68, 76n, 77n, 82n, 84n, 99n, 115n
Peter III, emperor, 68, 69

340